BRAND VALUATION

BRAND VALUATION

Third Edition

Edited by Raymond Perrier
Interbrand

PREMIER
B O O K S

PUBLISHED IN 1997 BY PREMIER BOOKS

Haymarket House, 1 Oxendon Street, London SW1Y 4EE

Telephone: (0171) 925 2544

Facsimile: (0171) 839 4508

Internet: books@premiermags.co.uk

Premier Books is a division of Premier Magazines

First edition published 1989

Second edition published 1991

British Library Cataloguing in Publication Data

A catalogue entry for this book is available from the British Library

ISBN 1-900617-00-5

CONSULTING EDITOR: JANE SIMMS

PUBLISHER: FIONA HARDIE

INTERBRAND CO-ORDINATOR: VENETIA DAVIE

COVER DESIGN: SASHA KIDAKOVIC

BOOK DESIGN: HENRY REDMAN

DESIGN AND PRODUCTION DIRECTOR: CLARE BROADBENT

EDITORIAL SERVICES: KEYWORD PUBLISHING SERVICES LTD

REPRO AND PRINTING: BUTLER & TANNER

CONTENTS

INTERBRAND

Interbrand was formed in London in 1974 to provide clients with a specialist service in the area of brand and corporate name development.

As time passed, we opened new offices in major international markets and added depth and dimension to our services; we introduced marketing experts to our creative team, set up a separate legal practice specialising in international trade mark law and acquired computer capabilities to aid creativity and help us check brand name availability.

We then added full design capabilities realising that, though a name may be at the core of a brand or corporate personality, design can make a very significant contribution. We have been operating in Singapore in collaboration with Design Counsel (now Interbrand Design Counsel) and have become the first multi-disciplinary branding consultancy in South East Asia. In 1995 and 1996 we further strengthened our design offer through a merger with two major design companies in New York, Schechter Group and Gerstmann + Myers and with Zintzmeyer & Lux, the leading Swiss brand identity consultancy.

Finally, we have pioneered the development of new techniques and processes in the fields of brand evaluation, brand strategy, and new product development.

In short, we now offer all of the services needed for the creation and maintenance of their clients' most valuable assets - their corporate and product brands. Today, Interbrand is the only organisation able to offer a truly complete range of brand-related services on an international basis.

Interbrand has 16 offices worldwide with the principal offices being based in London, New York, Zurich and Tokyo. We employ around 400 people from a variety of backgrounds: accountants, strategic consultants, brand management experts, designers, copywriters, trade mark lawyers and market researchers.

INTERBRAND'S EXPERIENCE IN BRAND VALUATION

Interbrand first became involved in the largely unexplored world of brand valuation when we were asked to assist Ranks Hovis MacDougall to defend itself against an unwelcome takeover bid by Goodman Fielder Wattie, the Australian foods group. Our subsequent brand valuation exercise demonstrated the value of RHM's brand portfolio and helped them repel the GFW bid.

In the course of Interbrand's close relationship with RHM, we developed, in collaboration with the London Business School, a highly innovative model for brand valuation. In the intervening 7 years, Interbrand's valuation methodology has become the accepted standard for valuation for a wide range of applications. Having pioneered brand valuation techniques, we have now valued more than 1,200 of the world's leading brands with an aggregate value in excess of $50 billion.

Some of our previous clients in the area of brand valuation include B.A.T., Ford, Nestlé, Danone, United Biscuits, Nabisco, Grand Metropolitan, IBM, Gucci, Chanel, Pacific Dunlop, BP, British Airways, Burmah Castrol and MCI.

We believe very strongly that a proper brand valuation requires an understanding of the marketing performance of the brand as well as of its financial prospects. We therefore combine in our brand valuations the international experience of brand management and brand strategy acquired over 20 years with the brand accounting models that we have developed and tested with hundreds of brands.

Interbrand's valuations have been used for litigation support, as evidence in Fair Trading investigations, for expert witness submissions in complex tax cases, and for internal and external communications. In fact, our valuation methodology has now even been accepted by the UK Accounting Standards Board as the basis for balance sheet valuations of brands. Our method of cashflow analysis, brand strength scoring and discounted cashflow valuation is universally recognised as reliable, comparable and acceptable as evidence in a wide range of circumstances.

FOREWORD
TO THIRD EDITION

This is the third edition of *Brand Valuation*. Its predecessors set out the case for the valuation of brands, arguing vigorously that the shift in wealth creation from tangible to intangible assets necessitated a re-definition of 'capital'. They concluded that accountants were largely incapable of providing this.

However, since the publication of the second edition, in 1991, there have been significant developments in the 'brands on the balance sheet' debate, in which the accountancy profession has been to the fore.

The relevant UK authority, formerly the Accounting Standards Committee – the Accounting Standards Board (ASB) has changed its position on the inclusion of brand values in financial statements gradually in recent years. From being implacably opposed, it warmed to the general principle, though in a somewhat muddled way, accepting assets with a finite life and rejecting those with a potentially indefinite life.

The ASB has now declared, in its recent exposure draft, that where brands can be valued reliably, it should become standard practice to include them on the balance sheet. Also, that where it can be demonstrated that they have an expected life of more than 20 years, and subject to an annual review, they will not have to be written off.

The ASB has been pushed in this direction by several bodies, not least the 'Hundred Group' (the financial directors of the top 100 UK quoted companies). This august body has made its public endorsement of such balance-sheet treatment clear from the outset.

The International Accounting Standards Committee (IASC) – influenced not just by the profession in the UK and France but also in the USA and Germany – has been ambivalent on the subject. Its most recent exposure suggested the acceptance of the principle of the recognition of intangibles in theory although in practice members were not convinced that it could be done. However, informally the IASC has let it be known that it is not opposed to the likely UK position if it can be reconciled with its own.

Elsewhere, the Australian authority has been swinging between the UK ASB and the IASC but, similarly, has indicated to the press that the UK's new position and the IASC's softening may allow it to take a more positive stance.

Meanwhile, the UK ASB, at the forefront of this debate, has publicly recognised the inconsistencies that might arise from a situation in which acquired brands could be recognised but home-grown ones ignored: the balance sheet of a company which has grown through acquisition could not be compared directly with that of a company which has grown organically. It seems more likely than ever that a full resolution of the problem – with guidelines for both acquired and home-grown intangibles – will eventually emerge. Meanwhile, companies such as Lion Nathan in New Zealand and Pacific Dunlop in Australia, continue to recognise both acquired and home-grown brands in their balance sheets.

The debate now seems to be moving to a higher plane as the concept of a 'Statement of Value', separate from the Balance Sheet, continues to gain ground. Companies in the US, UK and Scandinavia have taken this initiative and the European Commission has instituted a working party to consider the validity of such an idea.

Though the debate has been long and at times fierce, there has been consensus on at least one matter. It has rarely been doubted that brands have value. The key issue has always been whether it is the sort of value which, when acquired, can be treated separately from 'goodwill'; and if it can whether it should be subject to a different rule for amortisation.

It is also worth noting that the deliberations of the accounting bodies have not stood in the way of other organisations recognising brand value. At a very early stage the RHM valuation – the first major portfolio valuation by a brand owner – was accepted by the London Stock Exchange for the purposes of class tests. Additionally brand valuations have been presented to and accepted by tax authorities in the UK, the USA and Australia and by anti-trust bodies in the UK and Australia. They have also been used as expert witness in the High Courts in England, Ireland and Hong Kong.

The most important measure of the recognition of brand value, however, is that it is now an accepted measure of management performance. More and more companies realise that the management of their intangible assets is as important as the management of their tangible assets and have been involved in implementing brand-valuation techniques to put in place mechanisms for optimising brand-asset management.

The debate about brand valuation has inevitably moved on. Much of the heat and the light that dramatised the early exchanges between company managements and accountants has died away. The spotlight now rests on accountability for brands and whether – and how – brand-valuation techniques can be used for measuring the incremental value that marketing executives and advertising agencies add to these indisputably vital assets. The latest edition of *Brand Valuation* concentrates more on these issues. Brands have now established themselves in their rightful place – at the heart of businesses. It is now incumbent upon their owners to manage them for profit, a process that must involve accountability. The evidence that such a concept has become part of the way that businesses are run will provide compelling material for our fourth edition!

Tom Blackett, Deputy Chairman, Interbrand, London
February 1997

Editor's Note
Being at the forefront of debate on the subject of brands and brand valuation, Interbrand is pleased to have been involved in initiating and co-ordinating this book. We are grateful to those people inside and outside Interbrand who have contributed to it and we hope you will find their views of interest. However, we stress that opinions expressed here are the opinions of the authors and are not necessarily endorsed by the Interbrand Group.

PART ONE

THEORY

CHAPTER

1

THE NATURE OF BRANDS

KEN RUNKEL AND CHARLES E. BRYMER,
INTERBRAND SCHECHTER

Despite what appears to be a kind of 'brand renaissance',
there is still a common misunderstanding as to what brands
actually are. This chapter examines the development and role of
branding, analyses the difference between 'products' and 'brands',
and outlines how moving to a more brand-oriented culture
can give a company a competitive edge.

There is no known shortage of textbooks or published articles on the subject of brands. Yet despite what appears to be a 'brand renaissance' in the past few years, it is disturbing to find the absolute level of misunderstanding that seems to remain on the subject of brands – particularly among those charged with their development, growth and long-term well-being in many corporations. This, perhaps, explains the proliferation of business books of late entitled 'Myths of' something-or-other connected to the topic of brands.

Without question, there is a host of successful brands in the world today. And not all of this success can be attributed to good fortune, accident, or the alignment of certain stars. While it is true that many of today's so-called 'power brands' are the fruits of our grandfathers' labours, many dating back over 100 years (eg Ivory, Kodak, Coca-Cola, Nabisco, Gillette), there are also more recent additions to this list that stand as testimony to the fact that this misunderstanding has not yet metastasised to a fatal level. These include names such as AT&T, Nike, Häagen-Dazs, Sega, Microsoft, Lexus, Compaq. Some of these did not exist in 1980.

More recent brand success stories seem to be the exception rather than the rule, and one could easily conclude that many companies have seemingly forgotten why they have or should have brands . . . or they do not completely understand what their brands mean or stand for. A recent research study entitled 'Brand Asset Management in the 1990s' (Kuczmarski & Associates, Chicago) substantiates this view.

According to this study, 'more than one-third of companies polled indicated that the most critical threat to the long-term success of their brands is *an internal lack of understanding of what the brand represents*'. One can imagine that short-term sales orientations and corporate-profit pressures do not give much help to the long-term brand prognosis either.

THE DEVELOPMENT OF BRANDING AND THE ROLE OF BRANDS

Brands, and the 'art' of branding, are anything but a new phenomenon. While this seems somewhat self-evident, it is interesting to note that a client commenting on the topic of his own corporate brand identity recently made the statement that branding was, in his judgement, 'faddish'. This view misses the point. Brands are indeed topical, and rightly so given the increasing percentage of total corporate worth represented by these important intangible assets. But not faddish. Indeed, branding is quite old despite the apparent renaissance, and dates back centuries. If it is a fad, it is an enduring one.

Brand derives from the old Norse word *brandr*, meaning literally 'to burn'. Branding was then, and remains today, the principal means by which owners of livestock marked their animals. It has, on occasions, also been used to mark thiefs and wrongdoers. In similar fashion, producers of whisky placed identifying marks on to wooden whisky casks – which handily display the maker's mark. Today, a brand is still the means by which a business differentiates its goods and services from those of its competitors.

At the simplest level, brands serve a functional purpose – they are (to paraphrase Kotler's definition) a means of identifying and distinguishing one item (or service) from the next. This functional benefit has relevance to both brand owner and brand purchaser alike.

For the brand owner, a brand (as communicated by the trade mark or symbol, the trade name, or a combination of these elements) identifies property and provides a certain level of legal protection. Most countries in the world today have trade mark laws on their statute books that allow the owners of brands to claim the title to their brand names and logos through trade mark registration. Legal systems now recognise that brands (along with other forms of intellectual and/or intangible property) are indeed protectable, similar to tangible property such as land, buildings and equipment.

For the consumer, brands also provide important functional benefits. Even in the earliest of times, brands served as a guarantee of homogeneity and as a signal of product quality. Potters in medieval trade guilds in Europe, for example, identified their products by putting a thumbprint, a fish, cross, star, or other differentiating 'mark', into the wet clay of their wares. The expectation was, presumably, that customers would seek out their particular 'brand' of goods if satisfied by the original purchase.

This particular benefit of branding became increasingly important over time as manufacturers and sellers of goods lost face-to-face contact with their customers – a development brought on most notably in the nineteenth century with the advent of railways, and later with the invention of the internal combustion engine, both providing a means of distributing products across wide trading areas. Good news for product sales volumes, bad news for maintaining close customer-relationships and ongoing seller–buyer dialogue!

In the absence of a direct, face-to-face supplier–customer relationship, a brand serves as a means of assuring product authenticity and consistency of quality – it is, in effect, a promise or 'pact' between manufacturer and buyer. The brand name assures us that the features, functions and characteristics of the brand will remain invariable from purchase to purchase. In this way, the brand provides its maker with the means to provide consistently the consumer with intrinsic value or the illusion of such value, or both.

Additionally, with the proliferation of consumer goods in virtually every product-category today, and increasingly in industrial and service sectors as well, brands help us find what it is we are looking for in a sea of apparent sameness. No small contribution in, and of, itself. Brands facilitate product or service specification, and allow customers and potential customers to simplify choice and, ultimately, their selection. This is particularly important where actual tangible product-differences are subtle, almost non-existent or invisible, such as in many areas of high technology, telecommunications, and in the very near future, utilities.

Brand management must now, out of necessity, be increasingly concerned with creating a *Gestalt* for the brand – defined as being 'the unified physical, psychological or symbolic configuration or mix of elements, that when combined, are greater than the sum of the parts'. This is no easy task, particularly in the identification and 'blending' of the relevant mix of psychological values that a brand needs to embrace and reflect. Even when properly done, successful brands require considerable time and significant financial investment, and of equal importance, the consistency of a well-managed brand-identity programme to effectively 'take root' in the minds of consumers.

It is this *Gestalt*, however, guided by a vision or philosophy for the brand – a reason for its being – that lies at the heart of brand differentiation, its brand identity and resulting image, the strength and (hopefully) ever-increasing economic value of the asset . . . in short, a brand's ultimate long-term success.

PRODUCTS VERSUS BRANDS

'Products are made in factories', a well-known English advertising man once said. Brands are not. 'Brands are made (and exist) solely in the consumer's head' (King, 1973).

Products are tangible. As such, the ability to develop and sustain distinct or superior competitive differentiation at the product level is, today, a short-lived proposition. Even where a patent or copyright would seem to hold promise for longer protection commercial reality may limit their power.

The painful truth is that most new and seemingly innovative products can, and often are, copied or cloned in a matter of months – sufficiently different from a technical point of view to evade copyright infringement, but virtually indistinguishable in form, function or benefit to most consumers. By themselves, features and functions of products or services are not the best foundation from which to build strong, enduring brands.

This is not to suggest that the generic product or service is unimportant to the totality of the brand concept. Clearly, a truly innovative product, or one of superior performance, exceptional quality or high value should be at the core of any brand. But these dimensions of a brand, while extremely important, are now 'table stakes' in many respects – they are the minimum requirements of virtually all product, service, or corporate brands, if any market place success is to be expected.

Unfortunately, many companies continue to believe that brands are no more than named entities or 'things' – the assumption being that 'if they name it, consumers will come!'. This is 'Field of Dreams' brand management. While all companies and their products and/or services must be called something, the mere creation, application and use of a name does not make a brand. A brand is much more than its name, or the object it identifies. Harley-Davidson is not just a corporate name of a motor cycle manufacturer – for hundreds of thousands of people, Harley-Davidson is a way of life rich in imagery, attitude, meaning and distinctive expressive and central values.

This phenomenon of 'name equals brand' seems to be most prevalent in companies that have, historically, operated as manufacturing-driven organisations, and where business success has come, simply from meeting market demand. The need to create a strong brand in markets where demand exceeds supply, or where customers have little or no choice of product/service provider (as in regulated, monopolistic environments such as telecommunications and utilities, or the very early days of the automotive industry) is certainly less than in highly competitive ones.

Competition and product/service parity sooner or later force companies to change to a more marketing-oriented and brand-centred culture. Companies in this type of market environment soon realise that one of the best means of standing apart, being perceived as unique, and increasing sales and revenues, lies in the creation and on-going management of brands.

Compaq Computers, for one, has done an excellent job of making this transition, and in the process, has made significant gains in strengthening and adding value to the Compaq brand. Only recently the company stood on the brink of financial collapse, despite having a reputation for offering some of the best engineered personal and portable computers available at the time. Not all of the company's problems were brand-related, nor was its turn-round solely a function of better brand management. Significant efforts were undertaken to understand what the brand stood for among relevant audiences, as well as countless hours of senior management soul-searching dedicated to considering what the brand could come to mean and represent.

Compaq recognised that indestructible hardware would not win the market battle. It was what consumers thought and, importantly, how they felt, about the brand. The Compaq brand needed a new meaning, a new identity and persona, and the commitment of both management and investment. Some four years ago it was given all these. The result? Compaq is now number one in world-wide PC sales – a category many have dubbed as near-commodity for a brand many viewed as 'cold, boring, over-engineered and over-priced'. Today, Compaq continues to be in favour on Wall Street as well as among shareholders, mainly as a result of this brand-conscious sea change.

TRENDS AND CHALLENGES

The past roads of brand success are no longer guarantees for future success, or even brand survival. Looking back is the death-wish for brand management. The world is not the same, so that doing things 'the way they've always been done' or 'the way "P&G" did it' in the heyday of mass marketing is no longer a valid rationale or sound logic. The successful practices and protocols of the 1960s, or even the 1980s, may feel comfortable but are unforgiving and may lead down expensive paths resulting in brand demise within ten years.

One of the recent key shifts in management is ownership and responsibility for the brand or brands. Brand management can no longer be viewed as the sole purpose or responsibility of the marketing department. It makes little sense to hand over responsibility for what are often the 'corporate jewels' to a junior brand manager. It is for this reason that chief executive officers (CEOs) are increasingly assuming the charge and challenge of being brand stewards – a development more true of monolithic corporate brand-dominant organisations than FMCG multi-brand companies (for pragmatic reasons), but a positive step nonetheless.

Only the CEO or chairman in these instances can effectively set course for the brand – articulating the reason it exists, its values and beliefs – and importantly, ensuring that all appropriate initiatives are put in place to realise the brand's long-term ambition. If brands are the most valuable assets of many corporate holdings, then who better to monitor and guide their well-being?

Brand development can also no longer be justified on short-lived product or service features, or on what appears at the moment to be new and relevant functionality. Nor should brand development be considered in markets where relatively low sales volumes seem likely or revenue potential appears weak. Although these sound like 'no brains' marketing concepts (and they truly are!), they are apparently ones easily forgotten in the ether of many new-product and service-development processes. The costs associated with launching a new brand and generating sufficient awareness to begin to 'move the needle' on purchase consideration are simply too prohibitive, and the risks of failure too great, to pursue such endeavours.

Brand-development cost is one reason why there is movement towards having fewer brands with greater 'stretch' potential in many company brand portfolios. Additionally, this explains the trend towards increasingly important and visible corporate brands in more monolithic brand structures.

The Japanese have followed this path exceedingly well, departing from conventional wisdom, by deploying, in the case of Yamaha, a single brand name (mainly corporate brands) across such diverse categories as motorcycles, musical instruments and canned tuna! These companies, and others following suit, are able to traverse broad industries, markets, categories and across both geographic and cultural borders with a single brand because they have successfully instilled it with higher order values and meaning that are universally relevant and appealing. The rationale is clear: fewer brands of greater range provide the opportunity to focus brand-building efforts – a more sensible and certainly more economically efficient strategy.

Increasing a brand's strength (and hence its value) is also no longer simply an issue of spending more on advertising or brand support. It is not just a matter of media tonnage or the cost of investment. Brands must clearly be supported at meaningful cost levels with a consistency of message, purpose and presence over time. A brand is very much like a bucket, and a leaky one at that. You can never take out more than you put in – and it is in constant need of refilling!

It is possible, however, to achieve high levels of brand awareness and recognition and remain either low-interest, irrelevant or unconvincing. The bucket is full, perhaps even overflowing . . . but no one cares. While this is not typical (more brands suffer from insufficient investment than over-investment), it does happen. As a case in point, witness the 'tune-out' of many consumers to the long-distance telecommunications brand battle that has taken place in the USA over the past few years. The main players raise the stakes higher and higher as they turn up the volume on their advertising but consumers respond, often, by blocking out all the messages. This situation is only likely to get worse as more players take to the field as a result of legislative reform. And continually chasing low prices as a basis of brand differentiation or sales generation is a slippery slope.

Maximising brand sales, which has been the focus of the past three decades, is no longer the most profitable objective. It is actually possible to increase sales without increasing profits where the cost of customer-acquisition offsets gains in achieved production or service provision! Unless you are the lowest cost producer in a respective category with price as the principal business driver, this is not a sustainable strategy. Low price may stimulate short-term sales, but it does little to foster long-term brand loyalty.

Brand loyalty (and therein, the implied concept of creating customer satisfaction) will be of ever-increasing importance. According to Larry Light, chairman of the Coalition for Brand Equity, the brand is not the asset, but rather brand loyalty. It is only through the creation, build-up and retention of a brand's loyal customer base that a corresponding increase results in brand revenues and, over time, in brand value. Numerous studies would seem to prove Light correct on the economics of his premise – most say that the cost-multiple of attracting new customers versus retaining current ones is at least four and possibly six times more.

While Mr Light is correct that loyalty to the brand provides the level of certainty for future revenue-generation, it seems certain that the brand is indeed the asset . . . the invisible net into which value (both financial and non-financial value, or brand equity) is accrued. This perspective reflects, in part, the accountancy rule that brands can be viewed (for purpose of valuation) as identifiable, separable pieces of legal property that can be sold independent of other assets of the brand owner's business. By contrast brand loyalty, it seems, cannot be bought and sold.

This does not diminish the importance of brand loyalty, and the author is a strong proponent of this critically important dimension of a brand's strength. The forward challenge to brand-owners is, thus, precisely one of cultivating and building customer loyalty – the development of a bonding relationship between brand and consumer, with the ultimate goal being the creation of lifetime customers. But, how is this to be done?

Building strong, differentiated brands and loyal brand franchises will increasingly come to rest on the brand-owner's ability to create a vision for the brand and a reality in which people can share. It will require that the brand's meaning rises above physical attributes, characteristics, functional benefits and an overall fact-based foundation, to a more socially aware, philosophical reason for being – a more humanistic entity with a particular view on the world and accompanying core values. Leadership brands will convey a sense of 'self', a spirit and consciousness – a brand 'life-force' – in addition to the expected dimensions of high quality, reliability, impeccable service, overall good value, and so forth.

Creating leadership brands requires that brand-meaning is understood throughout the internal organisation, and lived in day-to-day practice. Only then will the brand be able to communicate convincingly to the external world, attract and retain consumers who share in its vision, stand apart from others, and ultimately increase in its economic value as an asset.

2

THE BENEFITS
OF VALUING BRANDS

GERALD CORBETT, GRAND METROPOLITAN

In 1988, food and drink giant Grand Metropolitan became one of the
first companies to put the value of its acquired brands on the balance
sheet. Its decision precipitated the 'long hard look' at accounting for
intangibles that has culminated in the ASB exposure draft. This chapter
explains the logic behind GrandMet's move, tracks the company's history
since then, and examines how brand valuation has helped the group
manage its brands and its brand strategy development.

Grand Metropolitan is an international brand-owning company operating in two sectors, food
and drink. In terms of market capitalisation it ranks, at over £9bn, in the top 25 UK companies. Its portfolio of brands includes many of the world's leading names, including the
world's best-selling vodka, Smirnoff, the leading US vegetable brand, Green Giant, the
second-biggest hamburger chain in the world, Burger King, and what has to be the world's
most sensual ice-cream brand, Häagen-Dazs. Another claim to fame was its revolutionary
action in 1988 of being the first company to put the value of its acquired brands on its
balance sheet.

GRAND METROPOLITAN AND BRANDS

Formed as a hotel company in 1962 by Sir Maxwell Joseph, GrandMet expanded to
embrace pubs and breweries, dairies, dance and bingo halls and betting shops.

A review in the mid-1980s sought to identify the group's key strengths. It soon became
clear that many of its most successful businesses were within the branded products sector,
and that its ability to manage and develop brands was the group's principal competitive
advantage. Management perceived that the ownership of a successful brand meant an almost
guaranteed profit stream for the foreseeable future; brand ownership frequently ensured that
the profits earned per unit of sales were significantly higher than from a similar non-branded
or generic product. While other aspects of business management – such as cost control and

technological leadership – were important to success they were unlikely to influence the group's long-term profitability as could a leading brand.

The group therefore focused on a strategy of building and supporting its brands on an international basis. At the beginning of 1987, GrandMet had a portfolio of good businesses but relatively modest borrowings. The stage was set for the concentrated drive to become a leading international branded food and drinks group.

The acquisition of Heublein

The first major step along this route came in 1987 with the acquisition of Heublein, a major US drinks company, from RJR Nabisco. Heublein was started in 1875 by Andrew Heublein and his sons in Hartford, Connecticut. One of its earliest products was bottled cocktails, but the company soon expanded its range, adding its own products as well as imported wines and spirits. Innovative marketing helped the company to grow rapidly. Its greatest coup came in 1939 when it paid $14,000 together with a small ten-year royalty, for the Smirnoff vodka brand. This once-proud brand had, prior to the Russian Revolution, graced the tables of the Tsar and his court as the biggest-selling vodka in the country. Heublein's marketing skills were used to establish vodka, and Smirnoff in particular, as the favourite spirit drink of the American people. By 1987 Smirnoff was also the best-selling vodka in the world, selling approximately 14m cases per annum, and was second only to Bacardi in all spirit brands world-wide. Heublein also owned Popov vodka, the second-ranking vodka in terms of sales, Dreher brandy, Heublein cocktails, and, as a world-wide agency brand, José Cuervo tequila.

From a commercial point of view the logic of the acquisition of Heublein by GrandMet is clear; the addition of the Heublein brands and North American distribution network to those of GrandMet created significant synergy benefits and thus fully justified the price paid, a view which was not only held by the company. The day after the deal was announced the *Financial Times* reported that 'Analysts . . . warmly welcomed the Heublein acquisition' and that 'The Heublein acquisition was seen in the City yesterday as good for Grand Metropolitan'.

In conventional accounting terms, however, the Heublein brands acquired by GrandMet were worthless. While property, plant, and other tangible assets could be attributed a value, generally applied practice dictated that brands should not be valued.

In January 1988, GrandMet published its first set of accounts following the acquisition. Because the Heublein brands were not valued, £565m of the £800m paid for the company was written off as goodwill, and though this write-off was made against reserves rather than as a charge to profits, it meant that the balance sheet net assets fell substantially and hence gave the impression that £565m of the company's money had been wasted.

The problem facing the directors of GrandMet was whether the consolidated balance sheet truly and fairly presented the assets of the group. The balance sheet complied with generally accepted accounting principles in the UK (UK GAAP) but it failed to recognise the Group's most valuable assets, its brands. In the first set of accounts published after the Heublein acquisition, conformity won the day, but the board were left pondering a number of questions.

Was the money spent on Heublein lost or irrecoverable?

The answer here was clearly no. Not only were the brands already contributing significantly to the profitability of the group, they were also saleable. Unlike goodwill and certain other intangibles that are inextricably linked with the other assets and systems of the business, brands could be sold separately. This is most easily demonstrated in licensing agreements where brand rights to particular territories are sold for a specified period of time (or rather, lent), and there is no reason why a world-wide brand could not be sold in the same way. (In practice, the assets used in producing the brand are usually sold along with the brand. Normally this is to avoid the vendor being left with idle assets rather than because the assets are an integral part of the brand.)

Would the inclusion of Heublein at its cost be a radical departure from standard accounting practice?

Again the answer was no. Whereas on consolidation, goodwill was written off and only the value of the tangible assets was included in the group's balance sheet, within the individual accounts of the acquiring company this was not the case. Here the acquired company is included in the parent's balance sheet as an investment at its cost, unless its current value has permanently declined to a level below that cost. In the case of Heublein the changes wrought by GrandMet since acquisition had added to its value rather than detracted from it. It was therefore worth at least as much as was originally paid and no write-down would be necessary.

Although not normally valued by UK companies, was the valuation of brands specifically disallowed by UK accounting standards?

Once again, the answer was no. Indeed, careful reading revealed that the accounting standards appeared to require brands to be valued. SSAP 23 stated that following an acquisition a company should value 'all separable tangible and *intangible* assets acquired'. The italics are ours, but it appears indisputable that intangible assets should be valued.

Did the valuation of brands breach the historic cost convention under which accounts are drawn up?

Again, no. Following an acquisition, all assets acquired are valued at their market value and this is deemed to be the price the acquiring company has paid for them. The difference between the sum of these values and the price paid is goodwill. Valuing brands on acquisition in fact would be attributing a cost to them in the same way that a cost is attributed to manufacturing plant. They would then be carried at cost in the balance sheet.

The result of this period of consideration was a realisation by the board of GrandMet that their instinctive feeling that brands should be included in the balance sheet was correct. Not only did their obvious value make a persuasive argument for their inclusion in the balance sheet, but their capitalisation was consistent with UK accounting principles.

In August 1988, GrandMet announced its intention to value its brands and set out the key principles to be applied. It was decided to incorporate not only brands acquired with

Heublein, but other recently acquired major brands, principally Smirnoff. The 1988 balance sheet included brands with a cost of £608m. As with any innovative idea, the reaction from analysts was cautious. Most of them welcomed this step towards the provision of greater clarity in accounts and rightly forecast that others would follow suit.

The acquisition of Pillsbury

The next major step in GrandMet's metamorphosis from a property company to a branded products company was the acquisition in the USA of Pillsbury in January 1989. The price paid of $5.8bn (or £3.2bn) was large, but the brands acquired were a mouth-watering proposition for both consumers and GrandMet.

Pillsbury's origins date back to 1869 when Charles A. Pillsbury acquired a 50 per cent interest in a small Minneapolis flour mill. Within 13 years The Pillsbury Flour Company was the largest flour producer in the world. During the next decades a volatile wheat market gave the company financial problems, but despite this it continued to expand, adding a wide range of prepared dough and oven-ready products. The Pillsbury brand was extended to accommodate many of these new products and became a major, broadly-based brand. Other products like pizza and gravy powder were added later and major acquisitions continued with Burger King in 1967, Green Giant in 1978 and Häagen-Dazs in 1983.

Although one of the reasons for the takeover of Pillsbury by GrandMet was its belief that it could significantly improve the management and direction of Pillsbury, the brands were also a very strong part of the attraction. For example, the Pillsbury brand was the undisputed leader in the USA with 80 per cent of the market for prepared dough products. Green Giant was the leader in the processed vegetables sector of its home market and had a significant share of a number of overseas markets, particularly France, Canada and the UK, and was sold in over 50 countries. Häagen-Dazs is a super-premium ice-cream brand which had over 60 per cent of the UK super-premium market and, despite its concentration on superior quality (and price), was second in the total US ice-cream market. Burger King was the undisputed number two in the world-wide hamburger restaurant market.

Once the acquisition was completed the major brands were valued using the same criteria as those applied to the Heublein brands, and a value of £1.9bn was attributed to them. This valuation did not, however, include all the Pillsbury brands; a number of strong but less important brands were not included due to their smaller size.

Following this acquisition GrandMet's balance sheet at 30 September, 1989 demonstrated the importance of brands to the group:

	£bn
Brands	2.7
Other assets	6.9
Liabilities (mainly debt)	(6.7)
Net assets	2.9

Without brand capitalisation the balance sheet would have shown net assets of only £0.2bn, a situation which would have been absurd.

The acquisition of Pet

The next stage on GrandMet's route to consolidate its position as a major world branded food and drinks company was to build on the success of Pillsbury in the USA with the acquisition of Pet in February 1995 for £1.8bn. Investing in brands, reducing costs, new product development, and add-on acquisitions had greatly improved Pillsbury's sales, profits and cash generation. Based in St Louis, Missouri, Pet was a prominent branded US food company; its main products were Mexican and Italian foods together with frozen and bakery products. Its major US brands included Old El Paso, the number one brand in Mexican foods, and Progresso, the number two brand in ready-to-serve soups.

This acquisition again significantly affected GrandMet's balance sheet:

	£bn
Brands	3.8
Other assets	7.3
Liabilities	(7.7)
Net assets	3.4

BASIS OF VALUATION

Valuations of intangible assets are bound to be subjective. Most valuations are economic-based, since market-based values are not available for most types of intangible assets. The purest method is the capitalisation of net cash flows forecast to be generated by the intang-ible asset, discounted to present value. In practice, valuations of established and mature intangible assets often use a multiple of maintainable earnings or cash flows as a surrogate for the detailed cash flow forecasts. This is acceptable provided prudent assumptions are made.

GrandMet's acquired brands were valued at the dates of acquisition using the multiple of earnings method; some of those valuations were carried out by external professional valuers such as Interbrand. The contribution that is maintainable and attributable to each brand acquired is that directly generated by the brand and excludes any exceptional factors in the period. The multiple is varied according to the strength and potential of the brand. The 1996 Accounting Standards Board proposals require net present value calculations, and GrandMet will be using this basis in the future.

AMORTISATION

GrandMet has retained its brands on the balance sheet at what is effectively the price that was paid to acquire them, a policy consistent with the way in which production plant is valued at acquisition but not revalued thereafter. However, it is necessary to ensure that the brand has not declined in value. The standard accounting methodology to deal with a decline in value over time is a systematic depreciation charge, to write down the asset over its remaining useful life. Though this works well with wasting assets like plant and machinery, it is often inappropriate for intangible assets.

Some intangible assets have indefinite lives. That is, their lives cannot be pre-determined, but are dependent on how well they are developed and supported. This is especially true of consumer food and drinks brands. It has been calculated that the average age of the world's top 100 spirits brands is almost 100 years. These intangible assets, which are maintaining or increasing their values through considerable advertising support, should not be amortised over an arbitrary life through the profit and loss account. A more appropriate method of ensuring that any diminution in value is reflected in the accounts is to carry out an annual review of the value of the brand. This is done by reference to historic and forecast contributions. Any shortfall in the value would then be written off for balance sheet purposes and charged against profit.

CURRENT SITUATION

GrandMet's action in putting its acquired brands on its balance sheet in 1988 precipitated the long hard look at accounting for intangibles that has culminated, eight years on, in last year's ASB exposure draft.

GrandMet welcomes the ASB's proposed measures: they are, in effect, validating what it and a number of other companies have already been doing over the past few years. But, the £3bn of net assets GrandMet carries on the balance sheet at present is a better mirror of commercial reality than the negative assets it would show if it did not capitalise its brands. The balance sheet tells only half the story. Long-established brands, such as Baileys Original Irish Cream liqueur and J & B Rare Scotch whisky, though, like Smirnoff or Green Giant, very valuable, they are not reflected on the balance sheet – the first because it was home-grown, the second because it was acquired long ago at very little cost (*see Table 2.1*). Even those brands that are capitalised are not carried at their current values. The net result is that the balance sheet reflects a mix of accounting for brand values. This results in an incomplete asset amount reported on GrandMet's balance sheet.

This is an anomaly of which the ASB is well aware. Its draft statement of principles, issued in November 1995, considers, among other things, an evolution towards the greater use in the balance sheet of current values rather than historical costs, subject to the constraints of reliability and cost. The draft, which suggests that current values may be most relevant to the decisions of users, has provoked heated debate. Clearly the distinction between acquired and home-grown intangibles would be meaningless if a current value balance sheet were adopted. However, current values are inevitably more subjective and involve the preparers in much more work. Their use would probably also involve changing the profit and loss account and, thus, perceptions of how performance should be assessed. It could be some time before UK companies are ready to go down this route. In any case, there is a wider debate about the purpose of financial statements to be resolved before the decision will be taken as to whether self-generated brands should be capitalised, and whether they and acquired brands should be regularly restated to current values.

In the meantime, what is certain is the importance of brands to GrandMet's operations: a focus of the company's business strategy is to strengthen and increase the international consumer appeal of its key brands. Advertising, marketing and promotion expenditure

TABLE 2.1: GrandMet's top spirits brands

Brand	Age	Top 100 position*	Cases (million per year)
Smirnoff	1860s	2	15
J & B Rare	1760s	5	6
Baileys	1974	15	4
Popov		20	3
Gilbey's London Dry Gin	1872	33	over 2
Black Velvet		38	over 2
Malibu	1981	70	1.5
Christian Brothers Brandy		74	over 1
Metaxa	1888	100	over 1
Croft Port	1678		
Delaforce Port	1868		
Ouzo 12	1880		
Dreher Brandy			4
Cinzano sparkling wine	1757		2

Impact International annual international survey of top 100 premium spirits.

in the year 1994/5 topped £1bn for the first time, and approximately one-quarter of this was advertising.

The impetus and primary reason for brand valuation at GrandMet has been for balance sheet purposes. Only acquired brands which are 'material' – that is, they have a value exceeding £50m – are capitalised. There are, currently, about ten major brands on the balance sheet, including Smirnoff, Pillsbury, Green Giant, Burger King, Häagen-Dazs, Old El Paso and Progresso. These brands are assessed annually, but this is very much a financial tool. The sole purpose is to prove, through the impairment test, that the value of each of the brands has not fallen. In terms of internal management information, this is not very helpful. However, for internal purposes management has developed measures which will provide more useful management information on brands – the so-called 'brand equity monitor' – in order to give a better idea of how they are growing the business, economically as opposed to reported profits.

In 1995 the first brand equity monitor was carried out – an extensive evaluation of the health of all the key brands in each of their key markets. This comprises monitoring a large number of different measures, both financial (such as contribution, pricing, advertising investment) and marketing (eg brand awareness and market share movement).

The brand-equity monitor measures the key drivers of a strong consumer franchise and is an essential element of GrandMet's practice of measuring brand equity. For example, good awareness, trial and loyalty will lead to a strong share and the ability to command a price premium. It is this price premium that in turn measures the value of the current brand strategy to the business – and the value to shareholders. Measures include awareness, penetration, loyalty, price elasticity, value for money, perceived quality, overall consumer rating, key image rating, advertising investment, trade distribution and share of display.

These checks are used by brand managers and the directors to measure the trends in brand equity – is it being built or eroded? This information is not made available to users of financial statements – it is too commercially sensitive and too detailed. But, the commitment to this process indicates the importance of brands to the business, even if for the moment this is not fully reflected in GrandMet's financial statements.

This, so far, has been a marketing rather than a financial tool, but in future these indicators may be used to help assess the net present value of the brand. Already the exercise has helped bring financial and marketing people closer together, and the process will accelerate.

CONCLUSION

Our brand equity monitor, taken together with valuing our brands, has helped us manage our brands and our brand strategy development. Now that we are clearer about what each of our brands is worth, it is far easier for us to work out where investment needs to be made. We are taking informed decisions rather than taking shots in the dark, and understand what it is we are trying to achieve.

3

ALTERNATIVE METHODS
OF BRAND VALUATION

CHRISTOPHER GLOVER,
INDEPENDENT COMPANY VALUATION SPECIALIST

A brand must be separable from the rest
of the company if it is to have a market value.
But the inevitable blurring of the distinction between
the brand and the product has implications for the
brand-valuation method. This chapter examines some
of the different brand valuation methods available,
and provides a guide to the most appropriate
method in a number of given situations.

Today, a brand generally takes the form of a name or symbol, and the design and packaging may well be an integral part. A narrow definition would be the intellectual property rights, such as trade mark, copyright and design rights, in the brand itself. However, it often happens that the success of a brand cannot be divorced from various aspects of the production, sales and marketing process. This may mean that a sale of the intellectual property rights on their own would realise only a fraction of the value of the brand.

It is axiomatic that for a brand to have market value it must be separable from the rest of the company, since only if it is separable can it be sold. To meet this requirement of separability it will generally be necessary to widen the definition of the brand beyond the intellectual property rights so as to embrace the essential production, selling and marketing attributes. This may mean that the conceptual distinction between the brand and the product becomes blurred. Perhaps the brand and the product – like the mind and the body – are conceptually distinct but inseparable elements. This inevitable blurring of the distinction between the brand and the product has implications for brand-valuation method.

BRAND SEPARABILITY

The Black Company, for example, is well known for its Sooty reconditioned toner cartridges used in photocopiers. Customers exchange their spent cartridges for a refurbished Sooty one supplied by the Black Company at a considerably lower cost than that of a replacement cartridge from the original equipment manufacturer. There are a number of competitor businesses supplying reconditioned cartridges but Sooty is the clear market leader and is generally considered to have the best product. Its superior quality makes it cheaper to use than a replacement OEM cartridge. To maintain this advantage, the purchaser of the brand would expect to be given the technical specification and production know-how. Furthermore the brand cannot be properly exploited without the customer list. This reveals the identity of those who already use the Sooty cartridge and are likely to replace it with another one. The Sooty brand would therefore have little appeal, and hence value, without the customer list and the technical specification. The definition of the brand would accordingly have to embrace these aspects.

It would also be necessary to assess the severance effects implied in a sale of the brand. The Black Company also has an office supplies business and many of these customers buy Sooty cartridges. In these circumstances the Black Company could hardly contemplate a sale of the Sooty brand to a purchaser who was also in the business of office supplies. This narrows the field of potential purchasers and could render the brand unmarketable.

SOURCE OF VALUE

The value of a brand in the narrower sense of the intellectual property rights in the name and product get-up does not lie so much in the earning power of the brand as in the power of the brand to attract sales, that is, its customer recognition and appeal and its ability to command a premium price. The two traditional methods of brand valuation, namely, the premium-pricing technique and the royalty method, reflect this reality. The premium-pricing technique looks to the price premium that the branded product commands compared to the unbranded equivalent product. The royalty method values the brand by reference to what others are prepared to pay for the privilege of using it.

Once the definition of the brand is widened to embrace important attributes of the product, the branded product's earnings inevitably become a factor in the valuation. However, earnings will never be the sole determinant of value. If they were, it would suggest that unprofitable brands had no value. It would also imply that actions which increase profits, such as, improved manufacturing efficiency or cheaper sourcing of materials, increase the value of the brand. By contrast actions which depress profits, eg, price discounts, rent reviews and pay awards, would depress the brand's value. Few would accept such a rigidly linear relationship between brand profit and brand value.

The valuation of brands, as indeed of intellectual property generally, is popularly seen as a highly specialised, even esoteric, discipline, shrouded in mystique. There is no warrant for this. Brand valuation is based on the same fundamental precepts as all economic valuations. The most fundamental as well as the most obvious precept of all is: the value of something is what you can get out of it. All economic valuation is therefore predicated on the creation or maintenance of some future state of affairs. The second fundamental precept of valuation is: the value of something cannot be stated in the abstract. The questions 'to whom?' and 'for what purpose?' must always be asked.

OWNER VALUE

In the example above the Sooty brand probably has a greater value to the Black Company than it does to anyone else. Mainly because of the severance costs, it would not pay the Black Company to sell its Sooty brand. In other words, the owner value – measured by how worse off the Black Company would be if it were deprived of its Sooty brand – exceeds the market value. It is normal for the value to the owner to exceed market value. If it was not the general rule, everyone would want to dispose of their property; prices would fall and exchange would eventually cease.

If circumstances change for the Black Company – say it decides to close down its unprofitable office-supplies division and concentrate on its mainstream activities – then the owner or deprival value of the Sooty brand might fall below market value in which case the Black Company's only interest would be to dispose of its Sooty brand to the highest bidder. In valuing the brand for this purpose it would be essential to envisage the likely purchaser or class of purchasers and assess the value of the Sooty brand to them. This in turn will be a function of their individual circumstances. An assessment of the owner values of prospective purchasers is essential in determining the likely sale price, ie, the market value of the brand.

If the Black Company wants a valuation of its Sooty brand for balance sheet purposes, the market value definition would probably be unsuitable, particularly if a sale of the brand is out of the question. The owner value or deprival value of the brand would probably be a more relevant figure. Obviously, there would have to be a full disclosure of the value concept adopted and the elements included in the definition of the brand. If a valuation is required for tax purposes, the taxing statutes will no doubt specify certain rules to be followed and this will determine how the valuation is done. Thus it can be seen that the purpose of the valuation affects the valuation itself.

PREMIUM PRICING TECHNIQUE

The premium pricing technique is traditional in the valuation of intellectual property, particularly of patents. Patented drugs, for example, can command huge premiums. Examples of drugs leaving patent protection indicate that prices can fall by up to 90 per cent. A consumer brand would not command a premium anything like as high as this. With a branded product there is unlikely to be an unbranded equivalent; goods are always sold with some identifying mark. Problems abound in measuring the premium. Does one base oneself on the price of the supermarkets' own-label product or on the price of less-well-known brands sold elsewhere? The selling price of the branded product in question will itself be variable. Prices will vary across different size packs; promotional discounts will be offered from time-to-time and unit selling prices to larger customers, such as supermarkets and large retailing chains, will probably be discounted for volume. Assessing the price premium will therefore be a highly subjective exercise.

Once the price premium as a percentage of sales has been ascertained, it can be applied to actual and prospective sales over the estimated life of the brand. The annual benefits are discounted at a suitable rate of return in order to obtain the brand's present value. Given that most products are in one sense or another branded, the strength of a particular brand reflects the extent to which consumers prefer it to some alternative. This does not necessarily mean that the product sells for a premium price; rather it enables the branded product to sell better than the alternatives. Because of this and of the pitfalls in measuring the premium, it would be dangerous to use the premium-pricing technique on its own. At best, it provides a useful cross-check. In many cases it will be impractical to apply.

ROYALTY METHOD

The royalty method, like the premium-pricing technique, has an honourable and ancient pedigree in the valuation of intellectual property. The amount a third party is prepared to pay for the use of a patent or trade mark provides objective independent evidence of its value. The same is true of a brand. Generally speaking, consumer brands are only licensed overseas, often where the market is undeveloped. The licence or distribution agreement will usually stipulate minimum sales levels and commit the local distributor to maintaining a certain level of advertising and marketing expenditure. Often the product itself will be supplied by the brand's owner. The price charged may or may not include a margin of profit. All these conditions have a bearing on how the royalty rate is fixed and, hence, its relevance.

With the royalty expressed as a percentage of the brand's sales, the annual pre-tax benefit from the brand can be assessed. A view has to be taken on the life of the brand and the likely course of sales over that period. These annual pre-tax income increments are then discounted to the valuation date and a present value is obtained.

As the owner of a successful brand will want to exploit it himself, licensing or distribution arrangements may well not exist. Where they do, they will cover only a small fraction of total brand sales. Furthermore, the economic and market conditions in the overseas territories will probably differ markedly from those in the main markets where the bulk of brand sales are made. In these circumstances, the royalty method, like the premium-pricing technique, will probably be an unsuitable primary valuation method. It can, however, provide a useful cross-check.

EARNINGS BASIS

For the majority of branded products the earnings basis will provide the most realistic valuation. This is because of the way consumer preference for the brand arises. It may be because the product has a superior formulation or technical specification; it may be because the packaging is particularly attractive; perhaps it is more widely available (ie, superior distribution); finally, it may be because of clever advertising and marketing. Often it will be a combination of some or all of these product-related factors. The appeal of the brand cannot therefore be distinguished from the appeal of the product. The same difficulty is encountered as with the Sooty business-to-business brand. Although the brand and the product are conceptually distinct, for valuation purposes they are inextricably linked. Once the product becomes part of the valuation the earnings must become the dominant factor. The brand exists to promote sales of the product; the product, on the other hand, is there to make a profit.

The profit attributable to the branded product needs to be adjusted to eliminate profit arising from factors not included in the definition of the brand. Thus, the benefit of the fixed and working capital employed in the manufacture and sale of the product has to be removed from total profit. This is not a straightforward calculation. Indeed, the calculation of brand profit itself will be affected by assumptions used in the allocation of costs – particularly, overheads and advertising and marketing spend – between different products. A suitable capitalisation rate is applied to the brand's profits to produce the brand's value. If profit after tax is used the capitalisation rate may be derived from the company's own price/earnings (p/e) ratio or that of quoted companies with similar brands. The better approach, in the author's view, is to use a pre-tax rate of return. This will enable the risk premium to be assessed. Furthermore this rate of return can be checked with the company's hurdle-rate for capital investment projects. Best of all is the discounted cash flow approach. But this requires prophetic foresight of a myriad number of variables and is generally out of the question.

VALUATION BASES COMPARED

One can now bring together these alternative methods of valuation in a concrete example. Odour is a branded mass female fragrance with annual sales of $200m. Its operating results are summarised in Table 3.1 below..

Approximately half the overhead cost is fixed. The rest is assumed to be directly variable with sales. The capital employed, comprising fixed assets and net working capital, is $80m.

There are two overseas licensing agreements, the royalty rate in both cases being 12.5 per cent. Odour's owner itself acts as a distributor for Skunk, an imported men's toiletries brand. Under the agreement, which runs for five years, a royalty rate of 7.5 per cent is payable. Enquiry reveals that there is no unbranded (or branded) equivalent to Odour. Its competitor fragrances are all distinctly different. The premium pricing concept is, therefore, not applicable in this case.

TABLE 3.1: Summary of Odour operating results

	$m	%
Sales	200	100
	—	—
Gross profit	102	51
Advertising and marketing	(40)	(20)
	—	—
Contribution	62	31
Overheads	(36)	(18)
	—	—
Profit before tax	26	13

TABLE 3.2: Different Odour valuations compared

	Annual return $000	Value at 15% yield $000	$000
Royalty method			
As licensor	25		166
As licensee	15		100
Premium pricing technique	n/a		n/a
Earnings			
Pre-tax profit	26	173	
Capital employed		(80)	
		—	93
Owner value			
Pre-tax profit	26	173	
Overhead contribution (18 x 3)		54	
Capital employed		(80)	
		—	147

Abstracting from the problems of the capitalisation rate by assuming a 15 per cent required pre-tax profit yield throughout, the alternative brand-valuation techniques produce the values in Table 3.2 above.

In practice, the royalty valuation would be treated as a marker rather than a determinative figure and the earnings-based value would have the greatest weight. The difference between the owner value and the earnings-based valuation lies in the severance cost. Half the overheads, ie $18m, are fixed. If the brand is sold, these overheads would continue to be incurred. In due course, either a replacement product would have to be found or the manufacturing facilities would have to be closed down. This severance cost has been included at three times the annual fixed overhead. This is for illustration purposes only; in practice, everything would depend on the circumstances.

On the basis of the above valuations, it would not be in the proprietor's interest to sell Odour for less than $147m. The market value of the brand is $93m but this considers purchases in a general, non-specific way. In an actual sale, the buyer with the highest owner value would be approached. Where recent transactions entailing the sale of brands have occurred these should be examined to see if they can provide a useful cross-check or marker. Often enough, however, the press reports give only the briefest outline of the transaction, making it virtually impossible to extract comparable data.

As will be seen there is considerable variation in the values produced by the different methods. The valuation of brands is highly subjective. It is important to recognise this variability if the valuation is to be credible.

4

VALUATION OF TRADE MARKS AND BRAND NAMES

DAVID HAIGH, BRAND FINANCE LIMITED

RAYMOND PERRIER, INTERBRAND

> Tomes have been written on the subject of asset valuation theory and practice. It is a complex activity which can be undertaken in many different ways using a variety of different assumptions – including the physical, functional, technological, economic or legal life of the asset. This chapter examines a number of alternative methods of brand valuation.

When considering a brand valuation certain key questions must be asked:

- Is the brand clearly identifiable?
- Is title to the brand unambiguous?
- Could the brand be sold separately from the business?
- Is there a premium value over the equivalent commodity product?

If the answer to any of these questions is 'no' there is little point in pursuing the valuation process because the results will be inconclusive.

SELECTING THE BASIS OF VALUATION

An asset may be valued on a 'going concern' or on a liquidation basis. It may be valued on an 'open market' basis or in the knowledge of 'special circumstances'.

For example, the valuer may be briefed to account for the incremental value of an asset to a given business. He may have been commissioned to estimate any one of the following:

- a fair value
- a fair market value
- a commercial value
- an investment value
- a tax value.

Each of these is subtly different from the others. *Inter alia* it is necessary to prepare a valuation after making assumptions concerning the physical, functional, technological, economic or legal life of the asset, each of which will, obviously, be different.

The value of an asset tends to differ depending on the assumptions made in the valuation exercise. It is clear that a taxpayer might want to use assumptions which produce valuations at the lower end of expectations, while a seller might want to use assumptions which produce valuations at the higher end. A professional valuer must use his, or her, independent judgement as to the reasonableness of assumptions used and to disclose them and their effect on the resulting valuation.

In addition to agreeing to the assumptions it is necessary to determine the most appropriate valuation method. There are fundamentally different ways of arriving at a value, and each may be appropriate under different circumstances. The three commonest approaches are:

— cost-based
— market-based
— income-based.

Which of the various bases is most appropriate to a brand valuation?

Cost-based valuations

It is possible to value a brand on the basis of what it actually cost to create or what it might, theoretically, cost to re-create. Such valuations are sometimes used in legal cases where compensation awards are under consideration.

Historical creation cost

In the case of historical creation cost it may be possible to look back over the years since the brand was originally launched and restate actual expenditure to a consistent, current monetary value. This represents the current 'value' of the amount spent on getting the brand to its current state and condition.

For example, it is often possible to look at the history of advertising expenditure in building brand awareness and loyalty, render it into current monetary terms and summarise the total amount invested. The same can be done for each of the other costs which have gone into building the particular brand, and it is possible to arrive at a total figure. Such an approach may be meaningful in the context of a new brand, where the time period for study is short and the costs are readily available.

However, actual costs of creation, even if they are collectible and translatable into a single amount, are of little use in expressing the current value of any particular brand. It would be relatively easy to estimate the development costs of Phileas Fogg, a fairly new brand. However, an exercise of this kind is of limited use. In the case of many brands the actual costs of creation may have been very low while the ultimate value may be high. Above all, historical expenditure is no guide to current value.

Current re-creation cost

In the case of current re-creation cost one argument is that it is possible to estimate the costs involved in re-creating a brand. This could, theoretically, be attempted on a restoration cost basis (re-creating an identical brand) or on a replacement cost basis (re-creating a brand with similar economic value to the owner).

The obvious difficulty is that both these approaches are theoretical, as the objective is to replicate a unique brand. The method is more likely to be found in the valuation of a tangible piece of equipment in a factory. Its application to intangible assets is inappropriate. By definition, unique brands cannot be re-created easily. There is no such thing as a standard, similar or identical brand. Virgin and Body Shop are just two examples of this phenomenon.

The reason brands have such value is because they are unique. By their very nature they are not comparable nor are they replicable. Therefore, attempting to estimate replacement cost is, in general, a futile exercise.

Market-based valuations

This approach is based on the assumption that there are either comparable market transactions (specific brand sales), or comparable company transactions (the sale of specific branded companies), or stock market quotations (providing valuation ratios against which a comparable branded entity can be valued). A valuation may, therefore, be based on:

- disposal of comparable individual brands
- specific branded divisions
- whole companies where adequate information is made publicly available.

Were this sort of information available it might be possible to estimate directly one brand's value by comparison with the value of another brand.

As an example, it is possible to determine a brand value by calculating the total business value (based on comparable stock market multiples) then deducting known tangible-asset values from that implied stock market value, leaving a residual value representing the intangible assets, including the brand. It may then be possible to estimate what proportion of the total intangible-asset value is represented by the brand.

The main difficulty with this deductive approach is that few companies or divisions operate with one brand alone. In practice they frequently trade with several brands, together, possibly, with some unbranded product. Separating out the brand to be valued without access to internal information, therefore, is almost impossible.

Alternatively, it may be possible to simply apply a comparable market multiple to post-tax brand earnings. However, this also presupposes that it is possible to identify individual brand earnings from a divisional, or company, brand portfolio.

In practice, there are few brand sales which are directly comparable. Even where there is information concerning the sale of specific brands or branded businesses, details are not often widely available. The terms of the sale usually remain confidential, although press headlines may suggest otherwise. Without details it is impossible to make sensible comparisons.

In addition, the notion of comparability again assumes that brands are similar or identical, which is unlikely. Using supposedly comparable transactions, eg stock market ratios or multiples is, therefore, unsatisfactory as the primary method for valuing a brand. However, market comparisons can be useful to test the primary valuation method for reasonableness.

Income-based valuations

Again a number of alternative methods are available. The two most frequently used of these are:

'Royalty-relief' method

This approach is based on the theoretical assumption that an operating company owns no brands and needs to license them from a non-operating brand owner. If a brand has to be licensed from a third-party brand owner, a royalty rate on turnover will be charged for the privilege of using the brand.

By owning the brand such royalties are avoided. Ownership of the intangible assets therefore 'relieves' the company from paying a licence fee (the royalty rate) hence the term 'royalty relief'. The 'royalty-relief' method involves estimating likely future sales and then applying an appropriate royalty rate to arrive at the income attributable to brand royalties in future years.

'Discounted cash flows' – DCF

In order to summarise the future stream of revenue into one single value at today's date, it is common investment practice to complete a 'discounted cash flow' (DCF) calculation. The idea is to take the stream of expected cash flows, arising at different times in the future, and identify their value to an investor now. This is conventionally achieved by identifying a discount rate which takes account of the risks inherent in the predicted cash flow. A high-risk cash flow, eg that on sales of Nintendo games, would be discounted much more heavily than the cash flow from a less risky product, for example Lego. The former is highly volatile and a sensible investor would mark down the value of the future cash flows, while the latter is likely to be safe and reliable.

Using the DCF approach the valuer discounts estimated future royalties, at an appropriate discount rate, to arrive at a 'net present value' (NPV) – the brand value.

The advantage of the royalty relief approach is that there are many examples of royalties in use by companies that are licensing brands to one another. The brewing sector abounds with examples of brands licensed between the major players. Some brands which are well known in one industry are also licensed into others. The Dunhill name is famous as a cigarette brand but is also licensed for use on clothes and luxury goods. The franchising sector is another ready source of information on rates charged for franchising certain brands, particularly in the retail sector.

The valuation departments of several major accountancy firms (notably Ernst &

Young and Coopers & Lybrand) prefer the 'royalty-relief' method of valuation. They argue that, after years of compiling comparable royalty rates, they have large databases of appropriate rates from which they can produce reliable valuations. Their view appears to be shared by some courts. The 'royalty-relief' method has, historically, been popular in legal and tax cases because of the belief that comparable data is available to form a sound judgment.

For example, a 1995 case in the US Tax Court, *Nestlé v IRS*, involved the determination of what was an appropriate transfer value for the total world-wide trade mark portfolio of the Carnation Corporation. This had been sold by the US subsidiary (Carnation) to the Swiss parent company (Nestlé). The judge accepted a relief from royalty approach as the basis for final judgment. An expert witness had demonstrated to the court's satisfaction that the range of likely royalties for prepared and packaged food products would be in the range 1-5 per cent. The bottom rate of 1 per cent would relate to weaker brands while 5 per cent would relate to the strongest. The total Carnation portfolio, because of its strength and longevity, was valued on a 4 per cent implied royalty rate.

However, detailed information on royalty rates is not often widely available nor are the terms on which the royalties are based. Rates often incorporate payments for the use of patents, copyrights or shared marketing costs. They vary, depending on tax considerations, expected profits and market circumstances from time to time. They are often highly complex, with differential rates at the varying sales levels, margin split clauses and many other non-comparable terms.

More importantly, the rate charged for an established brand in one sector or geographical region will differ when that brand is being licensed into a new market sector or region. For example, the rate charged for the use of the Shell brand in an established market such as the UK, where the brand is already well known and commands strong consumer loyalty, would be quite different from the rate which would be appropriate in an undeveloped market, eg China, where the Shell brand may be little known. It can, therefore, be extremely difficult, if not impossible, to identify an appropriate royalty rate for a particular brand valuation.

Example valuation – 'royalty relief' method

The simplified 'royalty relief' example which follows is based on the discounted cashflow valuation principles described above. It is also assumed that:

- *Net sales* are expressed in constant *year 0* money.
- *Net sales* exclude unbranded and own-label production.
- The appropriate comparable *royalty rate,* based on market evidence, is 10 per cent.
- The appropriate *discount rate* based on a market, sector and brand *beta* analysis is 15 per cent. (The discount rate is often calculated using the company's 'weighted average cost of capital' as a starting point.)
- *Growth* in the period beyond *year 5* is zero.

TABLE 4.1: 'Royalty relief' method – simplified example

	Year 0	Year 1	Year 2	Year 3	Year 4	Year 5
Net sales (£m)	500.0	**520.0**	**550.0**	**580.0**	**620.0**	**650.0**
Royalty rate	10%	10%	10%	10%	10%	10%
Royalty income (£m)	50.0	52.0	55.0	58.0	62.0	65.0
Tax rate	33%	33%	33%	33%	33%	33%
Tax paid (£m)	16.5	17.2	18.3	19.1	20.5	21.5
Net royalty (£m)	33.5	**34.8**	**36.7**	**38.9**	**41.5**	**43.6**
Discount rate	15%					
Discount factor	1.0	1.15	1.32	1.52	1.75	2.01
DCF (£m)		**30.3**	**27.8**	**25.6**	**23.7**	**21.7**
Value to year 5 (£m)						**129.1**
Annuity (£m)						**144.3**
Growth						0%
Brand value (£m)						**273.4**

Example valuation – 'economic use' method

'Economic use' valuations are the most popular approach to brand valuation. Such valuations consider the economic value of a brand to the current owner in its current use. In other words they calculate the return that the owner actually achieves as the result of owning the brand – the brand's net contribution to the business, both now and in the future.

This can be measured by estimating the increase in gross profit attributable to selling a branded rather than an unbranded product or service. However, brand valuations are more commonly based on net, 'fully absorbed' profits by identifying the excess net earnings attributable to ownership of the brand.

Such valuations draw on internal information, supplemented by external market research. They do not consider the value of the brand in use by a different owner or any 'hope value' based on new uses of the brand.

'Economic use' valuations were used by Interbrand to value the RHM portfolio and have been applied to many hundreds of brands since.

Initially they were based on a multiple of historical brand earnings.

Example valuation – 'historical earnings' method

In the following simplified 'multiple of historical earnings' example it is assumed that:

- *Net sales* are expressed in constant *year 0* money.
- *Net sales* exclude unbranded and own-label production.
- *Tangible capital employed* includes fixed and working capital at current value.
- *Charge for capital* is a 'real' rate, excluding inflation.
- *Branded earnings* have been identified at 75 per cent of total intangible earnings.
- The *weighting factors* produce a best estimate of continuing branded earnings.
- The *multiple* is appropriate to the market, sector and brand at the time of valuation (multiples may be calculated by reference to stock market sector averages or by reference to a brand strength analysis of the type developed by Interbrand).

TABLE 4.2: 'Multiple of historical earnings' method – simplified example

	Year -2	Year -1	Year 0	Year 1	Year 2	Year 3	Year 4	Year 5
Net sales (£m)	**440.0**	**480.0**	**500.0**	520.0	550.0	580.0	620.0	650.0
Operating earnings (£m)	66.0	72.0	75.0	78.0	82.5	87.0	93.0	97.5
Tangible capital employed (£m)	220.0	240.0	250.0	260.0	275.0	290.0	310.0	325.0
Charge for capital @ 5% (£m)	11.0	12.0	12.5	13.0	13.8	14.5	15.5	16.3
Intangible earnings (£m)	55.0	60.0	62.5	65.0	68.8	72.5	77.5	81.3
Brand earnings @ 75% (£m)	41.3	45.0	46.9	48.8	51.6	54.4	58.1	61.0
Tax rate	33%	33%	33%	33%	33%	33%	33%	33%
Tax paid (£m)	13.8	15.0	15.6	16.3	17.2	18.1	19.4	20.3
Post tax brand earnings (£m)	**27.5**	**30.0**	**31.3**	32.5	34.4	36.3	38.7	40.7
Weighting	1	2	3					
Weighted brand earnings (£m)			**30.36**					
Multiple			10					
Brand value (£m)			**303.60**					

This approach is still used, in a modified form, by *Financial World*, a US financial magazine, which produces an estimate of major US brand values each autumn, based on published information.

However, multiples of historical earnings tend to be unreliable because past performance is not necessarily an indication of future performance. Such valuations are also volatile because of the reliance on a small number of years used in the calculation. For example, in 1992 *Financial World* estimated that the Marlboro brand was worth $51.6bn. In 1993, after cutting its price to retain market share, Marlboro was revalued at $33bn. Many observers would argue that Marlboro was actually stronger and more valuable after cutting price than before.

What we really want to know is the value of future earnings stemming from the brand's pact with its consumers. It is, therefore, increasingly common for 'economic use' valuations to be based on the discounted value of future brand earnings. This approach depends on the accuracy of future sales and earnings projections. However, the 'royalty-relief' method noted above is equally dependent on accurate sales forecasts.

Theoretically, the 'economic use' approach should use pure cash-flows from future brand sales. However, it is more straightforward to use an adjusted profit and loss account figure as an approximation of the pure cash flow. This has the benefit of simplicity.

The approach uses the future-earnings stream attributable to a brand after making a fair charge for the tangible assets employed (both maintenance and financing costs). The result is earnings attributable to the intangible assets as a whole. A charge is also normally made for tax at a notional rate. The resulting 'excess' earnings are discounted back to a 'net present value' (NPV) representing the current value of the brand in question.

Typically, such brand valuations are based on five- to ten-year earnings forecasts prepared on an annual basis. In addition, an 'annuity' is calculated on the final year's earnings on the assumption that the brand continues beyond the forecast period, effectively in perpetuity. As brand rights can be owned in perpetuity, and many brands have been around for over 50 years, this is not an unreasonable assumption in many instances.

Just as analysts now value shares on the basis of sustainable cash flows from the business, putting a value on that cash stream, the 'economic use' brand valuation process is essentially a cash flow valuation. In fact, this type of cash flow approach has been endorsed by the Accounting Standards Board.

THE INTERBRAND APPROACH

Interbrand pioneered brand valuations and has always argued for an 'economic use' basis as the only sensible approach. In the early days valuations tended to be based on a multiple of historic-brand profits but the almost universal practice now is to value on the discounted value of future brand earnings.

Interbrand's concept of brand value is based on the premise that brands provide their owners with a security of demand (and thus of earnings) that they would not enjoy if they did not own the brand. In the short-term a manufacturer without a brand might enjoy the same sales, the same economies of scale, even the same premium prices as the manufacturer with a brand. However, the non-branded manufacturer could not rely on the same security of knowing that the brand's customers this year are likely to be customers of the brand next year, and for many years after that.

Given this concept of economic worth, Interbrand argues that an established brand can be valued by assessing what earnings it brings to its owner and how secure those earnings are.

An Interbrand brand-valuation exercise typically comprises a financial analysis (to identify business earnings), a market analysis (to determine what proportion of those earnings are attributable to the brand - the 'role of branding index'), a brand analysis (to assess the security of the brand franchise both with customers and with end-consumers (the 'brand strength score') and finally, a legal analysis (to establish that the brand is a true piece of 'property').

Each of these elements is dealt with in more detail in the following four chapters. A simplified example of the Interbrand method for comparison with the two previous examples follows.

TABLE 4.3: 'Discounted future earnings' method – simplified example

	Year -2	Year -1	Year 0	Year 1	Year 2	Year 3	Year 4	Year 5
Net sales (£m)	**440.0**	**480.0**	**500.0**	520.0	550.0	580.0	620.0	650.0
Operating earnings (£m)	66.0	72.0	75.0	78.0	82.5	87.0	93.0	97.5
Tangible capital employed (£m)	220.0	240.0	250.0	260.0	275.0	290.0	310.0	325.0
Charge for capital @ 5% (£m)	11.0	12.0	12.5	13.0	13.8	14.5	15.5	16.3
Intangible earnings (£m)	55.0	60.0	62.5	65.0	68.8	72.5	77.5	81.3
Brand earnings @ 75% (£m)	41.3	45.0	46.9	48.8	51.6	54.4	58.1	61.0
Tax rate	33%	33%	33%	33%	33%	33%	33%	33%
Tax paid (£m)	13.8	15.0	15.6	16.3	17.2	18.1	19.4	20.3
Post-tax brand earnings (£m)	27.6	30.0	31.3	**32.5**	**34.4**	**36.3**	**38.7**	40.7
Discount rate			15%					
Discount factor			1.0	1.15	1.32	1.52	1.75	2.01
Discounted cash-flow			31.4	**28.3**	**26.1**	**23.9**	**22.1**	**20.2**
Value to year 5 (£m)			**152.4**					
Annuity (£m)			**135.3**					
Growth		0%						
Brand value (£m)			**287.7**					

Example valuation – 'discounted future earnings' method

In the 'discounted future earnings' example on the previous page, it is assumed that:

- *Net sales* are expressed in constant *year 0* money.
- *Net sales* exclude unbranded and own-label production.
- *Tangible capital employed* includes fixed and working capital at current value.
- *Charge for capital* is a 'real' rate, excluding inflation.
- *Branded earnings* have been identified at 75 per cent of total intangible earnings.
- The appropriate *discount rate* based on a market, sector and brand *beta* analysis is 15 per cent. (The discount rate is sometimes calculated using the company's 'weighted average cost of capital' as a starting point or by reference to a brand strength analysis of the type developed by Interbrand.)
- *Growth* in the period beyond *year 5* is zero.

CONCLUSION

There is no single method of brand valuation which is appropriate under all circumstances. Courts sometimes prefer to use a cost or a 'royalty-relief' basis. Tax authorities sometimes prefer a deductive approach, starting with a market-based valuation of the whole enterprise. Bankers generally prefer either a multiple of historic profits, or an evaluation of discounted future cash-flows. In many cases it is necessary to use a number of benchmarks to substantiate the primary valuation basis. However, it seems that the approach which is being used as the primary measure of brand value more and more is the 'economic use' basis calculated by discounting future brand earnings.

5

ACCOUNTING AND FORECASTING FOR BRANDS

DAVID HAIGH, BRAND FINANCE LIMITED

Accounting and forecasting specifically for brands has rapidly become an important management issue over the past ten years. It is now a preoccupation in companies seeking to improve the quality of their management information and marketing accountability systems.
Some have even introduced a new class of accountant – the marketing accountant – to handle such systems.
This chapter examines the process of determining specific brand earnings, right down to a net profit level and sets out the principles of the financial analysis of the Interbrand approach described in Chapter 4.

The catalyst for this change in management thinking was the inclusion of brand values in balance sheets from the late 1980s onwards. Reliable brand valuations depend upon the identification of specific brand earnings, right down to a net-profit level. This implies a fair allocation of all costs, including a charge for the allocation of balance sheet assets to particular brands.

HISTORICAL EARNINGS APPROACH

Initially, brand valuations were based on a multiple of historic profits. It was, therefore, only necessary to analyse historical financial results to identify those profits which related to the specific brands being valued.

The advantage of this historical approach was that the resulting brand valuation was based on absolute data. The brand's historical performance was a firm and reliable stream of earnings which had been audited, reviewed and 'banked'. The disadvantage was that the historical performance of a brand is not necessarily a measure of its future performance. In addition, purchasers are often more interested in the economic cash flows from an asset rather than the accounting profits.

The same criticism had already been levelled at conventional company-valuation techniques; namely that equity valuations based on historical price/earnings multiples were less useful than the discounting of predicted future cash flows. During the 1980s analysts increasingly used the Discounted Cash Flow (DCF) forecasting approach in equity valuations.

FORECAST CASH FLOW APPROACH

Brand-valuation specialists adopted the same technique. Valuations increasingly came to be based on discounted future brand cash flows. Historical profit and loss accounts were used as a means of estimating future revenue, margin and net-profit structures as the starting points for calculating future cash flows of the brand.

Reliable historical profit and cash flow trends remain vital components of the brand-valuation process. This was because the inevitable criticism of a DCF approach was that the earnings stream on which the valuation was based might be inaccurate.

A forecast is always only an estimate and the brand valuer's task is to ensure that the earnings stream selected for the valuation is prudent, reasonable, and reliable because it is based on verifiable historical facts.

It is quite possible to produce a range of brand values, based on different assumptions about the future, then to take a mid-point. In fact, this is frequently done to give an indication of the range of values which might be ascribed to a particular brand. This is clearly a sensible approach in many situations. For example, when selling or licensing to a third party a value range offers the basis for a well-informed negotiation.

Balance sheet valuations must ultimately come down to one number. However, when choosing a specific forecast for the brand valuation the valuer is implicitly taking the mid-point in a valuation range.

It can be seen from this that the accuracy and reasonableness of the forecasting variables is critical to the credibility of any brand-valuation process. Historical accounting is the foundation for reliable future forecasts. If the foundation is weak the fabric of the brand valuation will be shaky.

ACCOUNTING FOR BRANDS

From traditional to modern management accounting techniques

In a sense it is surprising that rigorous brand accounting had not developed before the arrival of balance sheet valuations in the late 1980s. Many companies implicitly recognised the contribution of their brands in building corporate value. However, until the late 1980s the importance of branding, and the differences between brands, had been largely marketing department preoccupations. Boards of Directors had not generally seen the need to 'drill down' to brand level below the summary management accounts.

Sales volumes, values, market share and gross contribution levels were seen to be adequate measures of performance. Complete brand profit and loss (P/L) accounts were not thought to be necessary. Even if there had been a demand for this level of detail, many companies did not have sufficiently sophisticated accounting systems to provide reliable profit data at the brand level.

Several things have dramatically changed the status quo:

- an increasing recognition of the value of brands and their separability as company assets
- the increasing tendency to empower brand managers as intra-preneurs
- the growing tendency to use portfolio investment techniques within a brand portfolio.

Each demands a greater understanding of individual brand profitability.

The impact of new information technology (IT)

However, arguably the most significant impetus to change has been the drastic reduction in costs, combined with the increase in sophistication, of information technology (IT) applications for accounting. It is now possible to capture data and analyse it in many different ways, or to 'drill down' to the level of individual transactions reliably and rapidly.

Activity-based costing systems

The immediate result of this new-found capability has been a huge growth in activity-based costing (ABC) systems. Corporate activity can be reported in a variety of different ways. For example, airlines now have the systems and data to produce P/L statements for individual planes, pilots, airports, destinations, seasons and so on. These can be reconciled back to total figures and provide the basis for culling unprofitable activities. Summary management accounts can be cut in a variety of different ways to achieve this.

The same capability is equally available to manufacturers and retailers. The era of reliable brand profitability statements has finally dawned. Gone are the days when manufacturers could confuse 'cash cows' with 'stars' in their brand portfolios, or misunderstand the impact of own-label activity on branded profit, through lack of financial information.

Defining, coding and analysing the data

While ABC may have liberated management decision-making it must be remembered that it depends upon significant amounts of definition, coding and analysis of transaction data as it enters the financial system. This is time-consuming and prone to error and bad planning. The 'GIGO' rule applies very aptly to ABC systems — garbage in garbage out.

The ABC accounts can only ever be as accurate as the coding of input data that underpins them. If the 'activity' is not clearly defined or, if allocation assumptions are not sensible, the output of these new sophisticated systems will be worthless. The basis of allocation needs to be constantly reviewed. Delegating such allocation decisions to junior members of the management accounting team, as so often happens, can result in misleading brand profitability statements and ultimately to unreliable brand valuations. This throws up a number of practical issues in the preparation of brand profitability and cash flow statements.

Practical problems

The questions which need to be considered when developing ABC systems are precisely the kind of questions asked by the brand valuer when confirming data used in the brand valuation.

Revenue allocation

- Are sales identifiable by brand as well as by pack type or sales channel?
- Are retrospective or volume discounts allocated back to the original sales?
- How are returns and write-offs accounted for?

Cost of goods

- How is the cost of goods allocated; by weight, volume or production run?
- Are cost-allocation assumptions fair to individual brands?
- How are the costs of unbranded or own-label production calculated?
- How are standard costs determined and variances apportioned?

Overhead allocation

- Is there a mechanism for allocating total overhead costs to all brands in the portfolio?
- Are costs apportioned on a 'fully absorbed' basis?
- Can extraordinary items be identified and eliminated?

Marketing appropriations

- Can the corporate marketing spend be fairly split between individual brands?

Current value of capital assets

- Have capital assets been revalued to reflect the true opportunity costs of production?
- What basis has been used for the allocation of depreciation, amortisation and financing costs?
- Does depreciation approximate to annual capex costs?

Allocation of working capital

- Can this be separated by brand?

Summary

These are just a few of the detailed questions which need to be considered in determining that brand profitability statements show a true and fair view of the financial performance of individual brands.

The valuer needs to be convinced that the various assumptions used are fair and consistent from time to time, that costs and assets are fully charged for at their current values, and that the net earnings figure equates to a cash flow figure rather than to an accounting profit. The brand valuer does not audit the data but should always subject assumptions and cost allocations to critical scrutiny.

FORECASTING FOR BRANDS

Management best estimate – fact or fiction?

It must be stressed that brand valuations are always based on management estimates rather than on forecasts constructed by the valuer. The valuer reviews rather than prepares brand earnings forecasts.

In general, brand valuations require three- to five-year projections, although they may be for periods of between five and ten years, depending on the nature of the sector and the brand under review. If it is not possible to forecast at least three to five years there has to be a doubt about the susceptibility of that particular brand to reliable valuation.

The conceptual basis underlying brand valuation is that a brand represents a reliable cash flow stream, arising from the pact between consumer and brand. Brand loyalty generally goes beyond specific product specifications, which may change rapidly from time to time. For example, IT and HiFi products change rapidly but brands like IBM and Sony transcend the changes. Consequently, the flow of branded revenue is often predictable, even in sectors that are subject to rapid product change.

In addition, the discount rate used in the valuation of a brand operating in a highly volatile sector will be greater than the discount rate applied to a brand operating in a less volatile sector. The higher discount rate depresses the valuation, thereby reducing the impact of volatile brand earnings forecasts.

Reconciling forecasting approaches

One perennial problem facing the brand valuer is reconciling different approaches to forecasting within organisations. The reality is that there are, typically, quite different forecasts between departments which change from time to time. How can they be combined into one reliable forecast?

Management approaches to forecasting can be characterised in a number of different ways, examples of which follow.

Central forecasting

Many organisations prepare long-term forecasts centrally, for treasury and for strategic decision-making. They are often produced without much reference to local or specific brand management. The purposes for which they are prepared may not require a great deal of sensitivity to specific brands within a whole portfolio.

Departmental forecasting

Financial and marketing departments frequently produce forecasts quite separately from one another. Sales forecasts are often geared more to the needs of the current sales target than to a medium- or long-term planning horizon. Reconciling assumptions and overcoming departmental biases towards pessimism or optimism can often be difficult.

Which forecast should the valuer depend on? Forecasts are inevitably affected by the attitude of the preparer to risk, by current sentiment in the industry, by the use of the forecast within the organisation, by the time period over which it is prepared and so on. Does this state of affairs make brand earnings forecasts (and therefore brand valuations) a waste of time? Some argue that it does.

However, in the author's view it is possible to synthesise different management forecasts credibly and use them to value brands reliably. It is possible to bench-mark and analyse the data in a number of ways to reduce the margin of error.

Disclosure of assumptions

Disclosure of assumptions is a critical issue. If the user of a brand valuation is aware of the forecast data and assumptions used in producing the valuation it becomes a useful technique for comparing many different brands with different cash flow patterns in a consistent manner. Although brand valuations may change from time to time, disclosure of assumptions allows a clear reconciliation and explanation of changes in brand value. In fact, such reconciliations are often as useful as the absolute valuation itself.

However, the vital safeguard is the brand valuer's critical review. Brand forecasts must be subjected to detailed scrutiny by the valuer to ensure that they make sense in terms of historical data, internal and external market intelligence and relationships within the data.

Some of the critical steps in this review process follow.

External assumptions

- Have the latest and most reputable macro-economic predictions been incorporated into the economic background of the valuation?
- Have independent industry research sources been used to benchmark likely sector growth rates and industry trends?
- Have market share and price predictions been compared with independent industry sources?

Market research data

- Are there price elasticity or advertising elasticity studies available which might indicate the impact on future sales and profits of forecast actions?
- Such historical market studies cannot fully account for the effects of future competitor response. However, they can provide pointers to the realism of forecast management strategies.
- Simple observation of market share data over time is often enough to assess the reasonableness of future market share estimates.

Internal estimates

- Have the various alternative departmental forecasts been synthesised, and is there management consensus behind the result?
- Are the projections consistent with past experience and with production capacity constraints?

Econometrics

- Can historical data relationships be tested using statistical modelling techniques?

In many sectors there is a great deal of detailed weekly or monthly data for sales values, volumes, prices and marketing spends, including competitor information. Using multiple regression analysis and by identifying causal relationships between types of data it is frequently possible to test relationships between elements in the forecast.

Neural networking packages, which identify simple correlations between items of data, can also be helpful in forecasting if a complete econometric modelling approach is not feasible.

Cost-allocation bases

- Are the forecast cost-allocation assumptions credible in terms of past experience and likely structural cost changes within the organisation?
- Are any changes predicted in standard costs, flowing from down-sizing, rationalisation or new investments in production facilities?

Margin structures

- Are forecast prices and margins compatible with past trends and independent market forecasts?
- Do the margin structures reflect cost 'step functions' as volumes vary in the future?

Cost of capital

- Is the cost of capital consistent and credible?

Tax treatment

- Is the predicted tax rate compatible with professional estimates?

Cash flow forecasting

Having answered these and many other questions satisfactorily the valuer can move to a valuation based on management brand cash flow forecasts.

Starting with 'fully absorbed' earnings attributable to all intangible assets, the 'Role of Branding' index is then used to determine the proportion of total intangible earnings attributable to the brand alone. The post-tax, post-inflation branded earnings are then discounted to a 'net present value' using a discount rate determined by a 'brand strength' scoring process.

Sensitivity analysis

In addition to testing assumptions and facts in a number of ways prior to producing three, five- or even ten-year forecasts the brand valuer typically reviews the results by considering the sensitivity of the forecast to changes in the assumptions. Some changes in assumptions have minimal impact on the outcome of the valuation. Others have a major impact. These are tested and reviewed both internally and externally to arrive at the most sensible result

---

FIGURE 5.1: Template for an Interbrand 'economic use' brand valuation

---

	Gross sales
Less costs of:	Duties
	Discounts
	Production
	Distribution
	Selling
	Marketing
	Tangible asset replacement/depreciation
	Central overheads
Less financing charge for:	Tangible assets employed
	Working capital employed
Exclude:	Amortisation of intangibles
	Extraordinary items
Resulting in:	Fully absorbed intangible earnings

---

in terms of both forecast and ultimate valuation. It is usual to discuss and reconfirm sensitive assumptions with management before completing the exercise.

The forecasting and valuation process becomes an iterative one in which information is checked and rechecked in a number of ways before a final conclusion is drawn.

CONCLUSION

So, the brand forecasting and valuation process is an iterative one in which information is checked and rechecked in a number of ways before a final conclusion is drawn.

Once obtained the results need to be used with care by an informed user. It can be argued that the subjectivity involved in brand accounting (caused by judgemental cost allocation) and in brand forecasting (caused by different internal and external estimates) render the resulting brand valuations of questionable value.

In the author's view brand valuations are an extremely useful management tool. However, they need to be prepared with care by experienced valuers and the resulting valuations need to be interpreted in the context of the assumptions which have produced them. Using a brand valuation without an understanding of how it was arrived at, may still be useful for declaring an absolute figure in the balance sheet, in the courts or for tax declarations. But, for management purposes, it is crucial to understand the assumptions which lie behind the bald figure.

If interpreted correctly, brand valuations provide a focal point for a range of accounting and forecasting information. They allow a holistic understanding of brands which was simply not available even ten years ago.

CHAPTER

6

THE ROLE OF BRANDING

RAYMOND PERRIER, INTERBRAND

As has been described already, the principal approach to valuing a
brand is to capitalise historic brand earnings or discount future
brand earnings. But, what *are* brand earnings? This question is
the key to the whole subject of brand valuation. This chapter
therefore sets out the principles of the market analysis of the
Interbrand approach as described in Chapter 4.

We start from the supposition that earnings made by a going-concern business are a function of the various assets that it employs. From the businesses regularly examined it seems
that in the majority of cases there are three distinct types of assets that can be identified:

- tangible assets
- brands
- other intangible assets.

The task for the brand valuer, therefore, is to identify what proportion of the earnings can
be attributed to the brand (*see Figure 6.1 on the following page*).

Allocating earnings to tangible assets has been described in the previous chapter. A
straightforward value of the assets is identified – the fixed assets, stock, and creditors net
of debtors – and a charge made for the use of these. This charge is designed to reflect the
opportunity-cost of employing these assets in the production and distribution of the
branded item. It can be calculated as the notional interest charge or remuneration rate
on the value of the assets. After deducting this charge we have, by definition, the return
on the intangibles of the business. We call what is left the 'earnings from intangibles' or
'residual earnings'.

In some cases it is assumed that virtually all of the residual earnings are due to the
brand. If there are no other intangible elements in the business, or if those that exist are
inextricably linked to the brand – it can be argued that the brand earnings are virtually
100 per cent of the residual earnings.

FIGURE 6.1: Relative importance of brands and other assets

	Tangibles	Brand	Other intangibles
Utilities	70%	0%	30%
Industrial	70%	5%	25%
Pharmaceutical	40%	10%	50%
Retail	70%	15%	15%
Info Tech	30%	20%	50%
Automotive	50%	30%	20%
Financial services	20%	30%	50%
Food and drink	40%	55%	5%
Luxury goods	25%	70%	5%

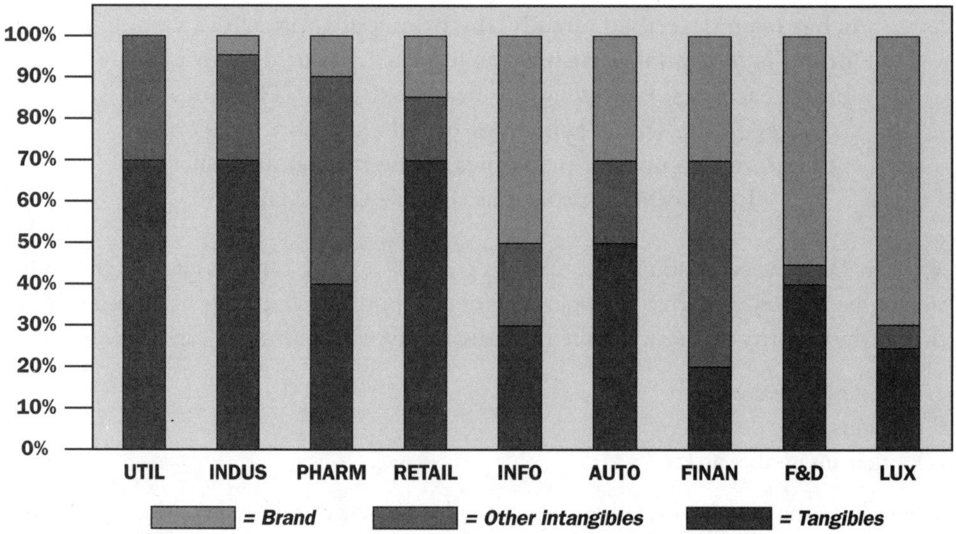

UTIL	= UTILITIES	RETAIL	= RETAIL
INDUS	= INDUSTRIAL	INFO	= INFO TECH
PHARM	= PHARMACEUTICAL	AUTO	= AUTOMOTIVE
FINAN	= FINANCIAL SERVICES		
F&D	= FOOD AND DRINK		
LUX	= LUXURY GOODS		

As an example, Yves St Laurent is a branded business which makes a significant return, over and above a normal return, to cover the opportunity cost of its capital employed. To what is this due apart from the brand? It could be claimed that the business has a good distribution network, but it enjoys this precisely because of the brand. Lose the brand and you lose the distribution. Or it might be argued that the business owns unique recipes and formulations. However, would these be at all effective if the company did not own the brand to exploit them? It appears that with a brand such as YSL, as with many other consumer goods, the brand is the sole intangible that is driving the business.

ALTERNATIVE INTANGIBLES TO THE BRAND

It is not always the case that the brand is the main driving force in a company. Some businesses have a wide range of different intangible assets that they employ and which would give a return over and above a base return on the tangible assets.

The most obvious examples of such companies are large industrial concerns such as the Dow organisation which has some well-known and well-regarded brands. These include the Dow name itself and also 'ingredient' brands such as Coming. Even without these the business would still have significant intangible value particularly in its patents, stemming from its technical know-how. Its personal relationships with key customers is also of great importance. These contribute to the earnings of the business and would, in many instances, continue to exist and be effective (although perhaps less effective) even if the brands were lost.

This would be especially true in the case of businesses that enjoy specific intangible assets other than brands. A pharmaceutical company almost certainly has much more invested in its patents than in its brands. For as long as the product is under patent, the anti-ulcerant, ranitidine, that Glaxo-Wellcome markets under the name Zantac would sell as well under a different name.

Service companies can also enjoy substantial intangibles. For example, while British Airways (BA) and South African Airways (SAA) are the only airlines with the landing rights to run services from London to Johannesburg, the value of either of the brands is limited to establishing a simple preference for one over the other. Thus, for this route at least, the landing rights are so exclusive that they are the key source of intangible value.

What is instructive, even about these two examples, is that the brands' owners are investing significant amounts in brand building. Why would they do this when the patent or the landing rights establish the intangible value in the business? The reason is that in neither case can the brand owner rely on these rights to last indefinitely. Patents have a finite life, usually of 20 years from filing, which, given the procedure of gaining approvals, now means a commercially-useful life in the pharmaceutical industry of some 15 years. Glaxo's patent on ranitidine has a definite end-date even if the company is successful in extending it with further patents. Also, BA and SAA know that at some point in the future they will lose the exclusive right to exploit the London-Johannesburg route. Thus, these companies are preparing for future competition, from rival pharmaceutical manufacturers of unbranded generics of ranitidine in the former example, or against Virgin Airlines in the latter. Investment in brands today, while competition is being kept at bay at least temporarily, can help these companies establish equity that will serve them well in the future.

When assessing brands like this, the valuer needs to take into account the fact that these brands may have only a marginal role to play at the moment while their markets are protected but that they will have a more significant role to play in the future when the markets are opened up. For example, Glaxo-Wellcome also have the advantage of using the Zantac name on an 'over-the-counter' anti-ulcerant, a milder form of the prescription drug (*see Figure 6.2 on the following page*).

FIGURE 6.2: Increasing role of branding in the airline industry

	Tangibles	Brand	Other intangibles
1960	40%	5%	55%
1970	40%	10%	50%
1980	40%	15%	45%
1990	40%	20%	40%
2000	40%	30%	30%
2010	40%	45%	15%

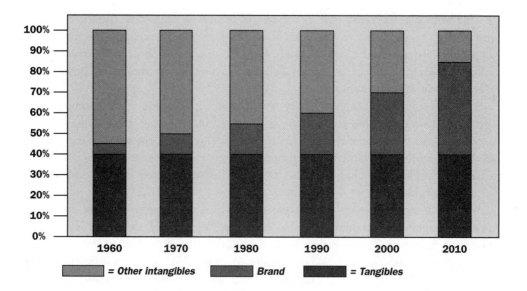

THE SHELL EXAMPLE

The question of the role of the brand is even more complex when dealing with a brand that is used in many markets and for many consumer groups. Take Shell. It is used by the company variously, for selling:

- petrol to members of the general public through service stations
- packaged lubricants through supermarkets
- high specification air fuel to airlines
- lower grade lubricants to the shipping industry
- bulk chemicals and speciality chemicals to other manufacturers.

In all of these the corporation is using the same Shell name but the role that the brand plays varies enormously between these different markets.

This role will depend on a variety of factors:

  – the degree to which price is the determinant in selling the product
  – whether it is a high value-added or a commodity product
  – whether the customer buying group is highly knowledgeable or not
  – whether the product is sold as an end in itself or as a component part of something else
  – whether other brand names are used alongside
  – whether the product is technically distinct from competitors or generally interchangeable.

On examination it is probable that branding, when selling lubricants to car owners through supermarkets, is found to have a much higher significance than when selling marine fuels by direct delivery to a shipping company. In the first case, a relatively unknowledgeable customer is faced with a number of directly competing products on a supermarket shelf. Though price may have some impact, his or her choice of Shell is unlikely to be driven by price since Shell will not be the cheapest option available. One of the reasons why price is less important is that the relatively small amount spent on the product, if mis-spent, could result in a very expensive impact later, through damage to the car. The consumer is far more influenced by the perceived quality of the product and – in the absence of a laboratory at home in which to test the product – relies on the brand name and the quality of the packaging to choose between the options.

On the other hand, the purchaser of marine fuels is likely to have a specific need for a large amount of fuel at a certain time and in a certain location. He or she will probably call a number of suppliers to find out who can actually deliver as required and also to establish relative price. If Shell were to claim superior product quality over the competition such a claim is unlikely to be accepted without a detailed test conducted by the purchaser's technical staff. Assuming a number of suppliers can deliver and they are all offering the same quality of product (which is probable), the key factor then will be absolute price. The perception of intangibles, eg after sales service, reliability of delivery and financing terms – areas in which the strong Shell brand could be perceived as superior to an unbranded supplier – may have only marginal impact.

Thus, it can be seen that, for the ordinary member of the public buying lubricants, the factors that enable a choice to be made have strong links to the brand; in the latter case they are not. In other words, the first customer when offered the same product at the same price but without the presence of the Shell brand (or an equally-trusted brand), is very unlikely to buy the product. The latter customer, if offered the same delivery at the same price (probably the lowest) and the same terms of payment but from an unknown brand, is more likely to be prepared to buy as before (see Figure 6.3 on the following page).

The question that needs to be asked when determining the role that branding plays for establishing a stream of earnings is the question of deprival: what would happen if the brand were removed but all other elements remained the same? (In asking this it is impor-

FIGURE 6.3: Activities: Role of branding index

Retail fuels	40%
Air fuels	20%
Marine fuels	10%
Consumer lubricants	70%
Bulk chemicals	2%
Added-value chemicals	8%
Commercial lubricants	40%
Commercial fuels	25%

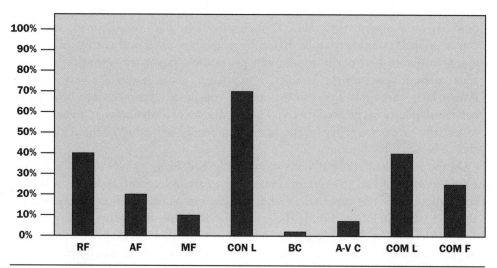

RF	= RETAIL FUELS	BC	= BULK CHEMICALS
AF	= AIR FUELS	A-V C	= ADDED-VALUE CHEMICALS
MF	= MARINE FUELS	COM L	= COMMERCIAL LUBRICANTS
CON L	= CONSUMER LUBRICANTS	COM F	= COMMERCIAL FUELS

tant to realise that the brand cannot be replaced by a similar brand but by a non-brand: not what happens if we replace Shell with Mobil but what happens if we replace Shell with nothing?) Even when this question is examined in detail the answer is not always obvious. For example, we cannot assume that the brand plays an important role when selling to ordinary consumers but that it plays less of a role in a business-to-business context. This is not always true. An example that will highlight this is the sale of petrol through retail sites to ordinary drivers.

The role of business drivers

First of all it is necessary to consider what it is that would influence Shell's success in this business activity. There are a great many factors or business drivers which enable the company to make a return, over and above a base return on capital employed. Not all of these are dependent on the brand. The quality of the locations themselves and the convenience of individual sites is critical (and not normally directly reflected in the value that the locations hold on the balance sheet, especially if they are leased). In many circumstances consumers habitually use a service station because of its convenience to their home or place of work or its position at a traffic junction or on a busy motorway.

Not only are individual sites important but so is the accumulation of sites in a network. Research in many countries suggests that a network of 100 sites in a given area is more than twice as effective as a network of 50 sites, even when the average quality of individual sites is the same. The actions of Mobil and BP in joining their retail networks in Europe under one common brand is clear evidence of belief in this benefit.

Further factors might include the level of customer service, the quality (or perceived quality) of the petrol products, the provision of other services (convenience stores, car wash, oil change) and the design and cleanliness of the site. With these factors it may be that they simply establish a certain level of competence in the market (provision of unleaded petrol is now something that everyone does) while with others they can actually create a competitive advantage. Thus, when there were some networks with faded, ill-lit and old-fashioned station designs, the ones that had modernised (or 're-imaged') had a point of difference. Now that virtually all networks have gone through this process the advantage of one over another is perhaps no more than a preference for green over black over blue.

In some markets prices are regulated and so there can be no competition on price. However, in others price can be a vital factor. Shell may have an excellent network of sites, great service and wonderful products, but if the price is too high, customers are likely to go elsewhere. Finally, there is a role in consumers' choice, for various forms of advertising, sponsorship and promotions.

TABLE 6.1: A summary of the drivers in retail petrol business

Location
Network
Price
Design of site
Cleanliness of site
Provision of car-related services (car wash, etc)
Provision of other services (convenience store)
Promotions
Advertising and sponsorship
Quality of product
Acceptance of credit cards
Provision of premium petrols

The role of the brand

What role does the brand play in all of this? Overall, a fairly limited one. The question that we should ask is what would happen if the brand were changed to something new, or abandoned entirely. It is helpful to answer this in relation to the business factors or drivers identified above.

In some cases, the effectiveness of the driver would be in no way diminished if the brand were lost. A station on a major junction would still be on that junction even if the brand were lost. Similarly, a station selling at the lowest price in town would still be selling at the lowest price even if the brand were lost. On the other hand there are some factors that are entirely dependent on the brand for their effectiveness. Consumers may be concerned about the quality of their petrol (and are suspicious that some petrols may not be as good as others). They can only use the brand to make a judgement about quality since they cannot tell by looking at the product or, even in most cases, by seeing the results of the product (since this is hidden within the complexities of the car's engine). Then again there are some factors that are partly dependent on the brand and partly independent. For example, customer service can be judged by the customer from their own individual experience of the site. If the same quality of service were offered but, without the support of the brand, for many customers it would appear to be as good. But, a brand can establish higher expectations of customer service and especially create expectations for other sites in the network.

ASSESSMENT OF THE ROLE OF BRANDS

There are then two distinct steps in assessing the role that branding plays. The first is to identify what it is that drives the business (what contributes to competitive success) and weight these for their relative importance. Each 'driver' is analysed, weighted and ranked relative to all the others in the business. The second is to ask the question, 'to what extent is this driver dependent on the brand?'. One of the best tests to apply during this process is to consider how effective, or otherwise, the driver would be were the brand to be taken away. If the driver would be just as effective without the brand then that is a fairly strong indication that the brand has no role. If, on the other hand, the driver would be neutralised, then it suggests that the brand plays a very strong role.

Importantly these questions need to be examined in relation to a homogenous market or product segment. Even within a defined segment there may be substantial differences between territories or customer groups. The chart (*see Figure 6.4*) shows how the role of a brand might be calculated for Esso's retail petrol business in three countries: the UK, the USA and Chile and it can, therefore, be seen how this can, and does, change, depending on the circumstances of particular markets.

From this analysis it is seen that the role of branding, when selling petrol in a highly price-competive market like the UK, is lower than in a market such as the USA where there are concerns about the quality of 'unbranded' petrols and lower still than in Chile where prices are set and competition can only be on other intangible factors.

FIGURE 6.4: Retail

United Kingdom	Weighting	Relative importance	Dependence on brand	Role of branding
Location	100	31%	0%	0%
Network	40	12%	80%	10%
Price	80	25%	0%	0%
Design of site	10	3%	60%	2%
Cleanliness of site	10	3%	40%	1%
Provision of car-related services	10	3%	20%	1%
Provision of other services	20	6%	20%	1%
Promotions	20	6%	20%	1%
Advertising and sponsorship	15	5%	100%	5%
Quality of product	10	3%	100%	3%
Acceptance of credit cards	5	2%	40%	1%
Provision of premium petrol	5	2%	40%	1%
	325	**100%**		**26%**

United States	Weighting	Relative importance	Dependence on brand	Role of branding
Location	100	27%	0%	0%
Network	30	8%	60%	5%
Price	60	16%	0%	0%
Design of site	10	3%	60%	2%
Cleanliness of site	10	3%	40%	1%
Provision of car-related services	10	3%	20%	1%
Provision of other services	30	8%	40%	3%
Promotions	20	5%	20%	1%
Advertising and sponsorship	15	4%	100%	4%
Quality of product	50	14%	100%	14%
Acceptance of credit cards	30	8%	70%	6%
Provision of premium petrol	5	1%	20%	0%
	370	**100%**		**37%**

Chile	Weighting	Relative importance	Dependence on brand	Role of branding
Location	100	29%	0%	0%
Network	20	6%	80%	5%
Price	0	0%	0%	0%
Design of site	40	11%	60%	7%
Cleanliness of site	30	9%	40%	3%
Provision of car-related services	30	9%	20%	2%
Provision of other services	40	11%	20%	2%
Promotions	10	3%	20%	1%
Advertising and sponsorship	30	9%	100%	9%
Quality of product	50	14%	100%	14%
Acceptance of credit cards	0	0%	40%	0%
Provision of premium petrol	0	0%	40%	0%
	350	**100%**		**43%**

Subjectivity

Clearly this process is one which relies on a considerable amount of judgement and expertise. Though still including a high degree of subjectivity, a professional approach to the question can ensure that the results are not arbitrary and are defendable. Interbrand has developed a proprietary process for assessing this role of a branding index. Thus, one can say with some certainty what proportion of the intangible profits of a business relate to the brand, as opposed to the other intangible assets in the business.

One way of reducing subjectivity is to ensure that the valuer refers to independent market research to assist in this task. Independent research can be invaluable in identifying what it is that drives consumer purchase and the extent to which consumers believe that the brand helps them in that regard. Research techniques today are far more sophisticated than yesteryear and analysing research to support the role of branding analysis is becoming an increasingly important element of the valuer's skillbase. The valuer must identify as much relevant and supportive research data as possible in order to reduce the inevitable subjectivity of the role of the branding process.

Consumer behaviour

In addition the valuer can make use of management interviews, market visits (eg site visits in the petrol-retail example analysed above) and comparisons with other industries and competitors. The best test must be a proper understanding of the way that the market operates. For example, it was believed that perceived quality in the retail petrol market and how dependent that might be on the presence of a well-known oil brand was given a jolt by the huge success of supermarket petrol sales (now 30 per cent of the total). If consumers really did believe (as they do for example in the USA) that the quality of unbranded petrol is lower than that of petrol carrying the brand of an established oil company they would not have been so willing to switch allegiance. Consumer surveys may still show people claiming that product quality to be a determining factor even when consumer behaviour belies this or suggests that consumers no longer rely on an 'oil' brand as a guarantee of product quality.

Consumer behaviour must also help to make a judgement about the dependence of the driver on the brand. Oil companies may wish to claim that they have a reputation for being competitively priced but those consumers who are influenced by price will have a very clear idea themselves what the price from a certain service station is and will not rely on the brand to tell them this – they can read it from the sign outside. On the other hand, the same price-sensitive consumers, when choosing a supermarket for their grocery purchases, are likely to be able to compare the prices of only a very small proportion of the goods they are going to buy. In this case, they rely more on the brand to give them a reassurance of good pricing (which they may then test for certain lead products).

CONCLUSION

Once the role of the brand has been analysed in detail, it is then possible to identify the earnings that relate exclusively to the brand rather than any of the other intangible assets.

Figure 6.3 shows how this analysis might translate into a Role of Branding Index for a number of markets (though in reality these indices would themselves vary depending on the territory or, in some cases, depending on the brand).

The reality of the Role of Branding Index expresses the importance of the brand (as opposed to other intangibles) in securing volume and profitability. It thus represents the proportion of Residual Earnings (the profit from intangibles in the business) that can be fairly ascribed to the brand. By taking the Role of Branding Index as a percentage of Residual Earnings we thus identify 'Brand Earnings'.

This definition of Brand Earnings can then be used in one of two ways. It forms the relevant stream of cash (after adjustments for tax and, in some cases, capital expenditure) when calculating Brand Value. But since we have through this process isolated the earnings which are due solely to the brand we have the basis on which to determine a royalty rate to be charged for the use of the brand. Brand Earnings could be expressed as a percentage of sales, or of profit as an amount per litre or per kilo, and this could then be used for setting an appropriate royalty rate.

CHAPTER

7

BRAND STRENGTH ANALYSIS

DAVID ANDREW, INTERBRAND PACIFIC

As noted in Chapter 4 'Valuation of Trade Marks and Brand Names', Brand Strength Analysis is the third of the four phases of analysis that make up the Interbrand Group's brand valuation methodology. The value of a brand reflects not only what earnings it is capable of generating in the future, but also the likelihood of those earnings actually being realised. This chapter analyses the criteria used to judge brand strength and points to the wealth of diagnostic information the exercise yields.

Once the Financial Analysis phase has isolated the intangible earnings generated by the branded business under review, and the Market Analysis has identified the proportion of those earnings attributable to the brand (as opposed to the other intangible assets of the business), it is necessary to identify the risk profile of the brand in order that the discount rate to be applied to forecast brand cash flows can be calculated.

Two brands that demonstrate identical earnings forecasts may well have completely different values. If one is a powerful, broadly-based, well-established market leader and the other is a highly fashionable brand launched recently in only one category or market, it is the former that will have the greater value. This is because the risk profile of the new brand is much greater than that of the more established, proven performer.

The value of a brand reflects not only what earnings it is capable of generating in the future, but also the likelihood of those earnings actually being realised.

Assessing Brand Strength

The brand's strength is the primary determinant of its risk profile as a marketing asset. The stronger the brand is, the lower the risk that its projected cash flow will not be realised. The weaker the brand, the less secure those future cash flows will be.

Accordingly, the valuer needs to carry out an extensive analysis of the strength of the brand. In the Interbrand methodology this takes the form of a brand audit conducted in conjunction with the marketing director and brand managers, and commences with the completion of a detailed questionnaire by the brand team. The questionnaire collects all relevant brand information in a structured and comprehensive way, and is supplemented with a review by the valuer of existing research, the competitive context, and the brand's advertising and promotional history, as well as with visits to production and distribution facilities, retail outlets, and advertising agencies.

Scoring against key dimensions

Thus equipped, the valuer can proceed to score the brand against the seven key dimensions of brand strength, using a notional ideal 'risk-free' brand as the standard. While scoring in this manner requires a series of informed judgements, the approach is no different in principle from that employed by, say, a professional real-estate valuer who, calling on relevant valuation experience, conversancy with the latest market trends, and familiarity with analogous properties in the category, can confidently express a value for any given property under consideration.

In carrying out a Brand Strength Analysis, Interbrand similarly relies upon expertise in brands and branding acquired over the 20 years it has dedicated to providing brand-related services to the world's premier branded goods and services companies. The wide variety of brands the Group has valued also means that whatever the category concerned – telecommunications, confectionery, airlines, financial services – there are always precedents to serve as a point of reference for the valuer, and colleagues who have had valuation experience with the product or service in question.

The seven dimensions of brand strength – representing Interbrand's view of the key determinants of a brand's risk profile – were designed into the methodology at the inception of the Group's valuation service in 1987. Nine years and over 1,200 valuations later the identical seven dimensions still form the basis on which the brand's strength is assessed. The dimensions are weighted to reflect their relative contribution to the ideal, and the brand is scored on each in accordance with clearly-established and consistent guidelines. A summary of the dimensions follows:

Market   Weighting: 10/100

Brands in markets such as food, drinks and publishing are *prima facie* stronger than brands in, eg high-technology or clothing areas, as these latter markets are more vulnerable to technological obsolescence or fashion changes. A brand in a stable but growing market with strong barriers to entry will score particularly well on this dimension.

Stability   Weighting: 15/100

Long-established brands which command consumer loyalty and have become part of the 'fabric' of their markets are particularly valuable and are afforded higher scores on stability than brands only recently launched, or those with a history of being managed in erratic fashion.

Leadership   Weighting: 25/100

A brand which leads its market sector is generally a more stable and valuable property than a brand lower down the order. To score highly in the area of Leadership a brand must be a dominant force in its sector, with a strong market share. It must, therefore, be able to influence its market significantly, set price points, command distribution, and resist competitive invasion.

Internationality   Weighting: 25/100

Brands which have proven international acceptance and appeal are inherently stronger than national or regional brands. Substantial investment will have been incurred in the geographical development of such brands, and they are less susceptible to competitive attack. They are, therefore, more robust and stable assets. Likewise, being broadly based across a number of markets means that they are less vulnerable to the vicissitudes of any single market – which might well sink a brand based *only* in that market. Moreover, not all brands are capable of crossing cultural and national barriers, so that those which have demonstrated they can do so must be considered as particularly valuable assets.

Trend   Weighting: 10/100

The overall long-term trend of the brand is an important measure of its ability to remain contemporary and relevant to consumers, and hence of its value. Brands which demonstrate consistent volume growth and have the ability to win share from major competitors over time score well on trend.

Support   Weighting: 10/100

Those brands which have received systematic investment and focused support usually have a much stronger franchise than those which have not. While the amount spent in supporting a brand is important, the quality and consistency of that support are equally significant.

Protection   Weighting: 5/100

A registered trade mark is a statutory monopoly in a name, device, or combination of these two. Other protection may exist in common law, at least in certain countries. The strength and breadth of the brand's protection is critical in assessing its strength. Indeed, if the legal basis of the brand is suspect it may not be possible to apply a value to the brand at all for balance sheet purposes.

Scoring as a whole

For the experienced valuer the process of awarding a score to a brand on any particular dimension involves working through a check-list of sub-attributes and accessing market information from a wide range of sources – market research studies, Nielsen data, advertising expenditure and awareness reports, etc. – to assess the brand's performance against each.

For example, in arriving at a score for the Leadership dimension the valuer would take into consideration such aspects as:

- the market and segment rankings of the brand
- its share of both market and segment, by volume
- its price relative to that of the competition
- the extent to which the brand was a leader rather than a follower on price
- the level of distribution it commanded relative to competition
- the overall calibre of the competition
- the saliency or dominance the brand exhibited
- the degree to which such dominance served to protect the brand against competitive attack.

The brand strength score would normally then be discussed in detail with the brand team – and agreed – before embarking on the next phase of the valuation. The relationship between the stature of the brand and the score it will generate is given in Table 7.1. For example, an 'average' brand will score 30 to 40 per cent, not, as might be expected, around 50 per cent.

TABLE 7.1: Typical score by brand type

Type of brand	%
Leading international brand	70 +
Strong international brand	50 – 70
Leading national brand	50 – 65
Strong national brand	40 – 50
Average brand	30 – 40
Below average brand	up to 30

The reasoning behind the scoring of different brands is discussed in four examples:

Brand A

This is a leading international toiletries brand operating in a 'mainstream' and stable market sector. The brand has been established for many years and is brand leader or a strong 'number two' in all its major international markets.

Brand B

This is a leading food brand which operates in a traditional and stable market but one where tastes are slowly changing with a move away from traditional products and towards convenience foods. The brand has limited export sales and its trade mark protection, though quite strong, is based mainly on common law rather than registered rights.

Brand C

This is a secondary but aspiring national soft drink launched just five years ago. The market is dynamic with strong growth. The brand has been very heavily supported and much has been achieved. There is, however, still room for growth. Even though export sales are still very small, the brand name, 'get up', and positioning have all been developed with international markets in mind. The brand still has some trade mark registration problems in its home market.

Brand D

This is an established, but quite small, regional brand in a highly fragmented yet stable market.

Based upon careful dimension-by-dimension analyses, the scores attributed to each brand might be as follows:

TABLE 7.2: Sample scores

Strength dimensions	Maximum score	Brand A	Brand B	Brand C	Brand D
Market	10	7	6	8	6
Stability	15	11	10	7	11
Leadership	25	18	19	9	6
Internationality	25	17	5	2	0
Trend	10	6	6	7	5
Support	10	8	7	7	4
Protection	5	5	3	4	3
Total	100	72	56	44	35

Although the scores are hypothetical, they demonstrate the basic building blocks with which an overall brand strength assessment can be constructed.

Global Brand Considerations

A brand that is a truly global brand presents the valuer with additional variables that must be taken into account. First and foremost, no matter how well established the brand may be in multiple markets around the world, its brand strength is likely to vary significantly from one country to another. This is because, for example, the nature and dynamics of each market will differ; the brand's longevity in each will be greater or lesser; the competitive environment and the brand's market ranking will vary; and the trajectory of its performance from country to country will not be consistent. Accordingly, in such cases it is necessary to determine a risk profile – and hence carry out a Brand Strength Analysis – for *each* market, with an aggregate brand value being built up from the application of the consequent scores/discount rates to the respective brand earnings for each market.

To be fair to a global brand treated in this way it is then necessary to normalise its score for Internationality in its 'home' market across all other markets so as not to disadvantage the brand for its development outside its country of origin.

CONCLUSION

It should be clear, therefore, that while the primary role of brand strength analysis is to establish the risk profile of the brand, it yields in the process a wealth of diagnostic information pertinent to a deeper understanding of the brand, and hence more informed brand management. Specifically, since the technique effectively permits the ranking of brands within a given portfolio in terms of brand strength, it gives rise to useful brand-by-brand comparisons, and highlights those areas where the management could most readily direct its efforts to enhance brand strength, and ultimately, brand value.

As brand value (in Interbrand's measured financial sense) gains increasing credence as a key index of brand-building performance, there is a tendency to interpret the underpinning brand-strength score as a measure of brand equity – which it is not. While a Brand Strength Analysis considers a number of the factors that contribute to a brand's equity, it should be remembered that its main thrust is to assess the brand's capacity to deliver future earnings. As such it devotes much more attention to the brand's operating context, its performance dynamics, and the security of its competitive advantage, than to what the consumer sees in the brand. The bottom line is that if one accepts a definition of brand equity as 'the set of brand-related assets and liabilities that add to, or subtract from, the value (in the non-financial sense) provided to the customer by the product or service itself', then brand equity represents an assessment of the brand's influence from a *consumer* perspective while brand strength represents an assessment of the brand as an engine of profit from a *management* perspective.

8

BRANDS AS INTELLECTUAL PROPERTY

JANET FOGG, MARKFORCE ASSOCIATES

This chapter outlines the legal considerations relating to the selection, protection and enforcement of trade marks, the final phase of the Interbrand approach to brand valuation. Even though registration of trade marks has been possible in the UK and other countries since the last century, and many companies do indeed recognise the importance of protecting their valuable trade mark rights, this is still not always the case. With increasing awareness of the value of brands and globalisation of businesses, choosing the right trade mark and ensuring that it is properly protected will enhance the chances of success in the market place.

WHAT IS A TRADE MARK?

A trade mark is defined in the UK Trade Marks Act 1994 as 'any sign capable of being represented graphically which is capable of distinguishing goods or services of one undertaking from those of another undertaking. A trade mark may, in particular, consist of words (including personal names), designs, letters, numerals or the shape of goods or their packing'. While in practice most trade marks consist of a word or words, logos, labels or a combination of these, trade marks can also consist of one or more of the following:

- slogans
- shapes
- sounds
- smells
- the overall get-up of a product.

A trade mark has three functions:

– to distinguish the goods or services of one business from those of another
– to indicate the source or origin of the goods or services
– to serve as an indication of consistent quality (whether good or bad).

WHAT CAN BE REGISTERED?

Although the criteria for registrability of a trade mark can differ quite substantially from country to country, the UK and other European Union (EU) countries have had to comply with a Directive intended to harmonise to a large extent (although not entirely) their laws relating to trade marks. The UK complied with this Directive through the Trade Marks Act 1994, which dramatically changed the law which had previously been in force in a number of areas including what is now registrable as a trade mark. In addition to being 'a sign capable of being represented graphically which is capable of distinguishing goods or services of one undertaking from those of other undertakings' to qualify for registration a trade mark must *not*:

– be devoid of distinctive character
– be recognised in the relevant trade as denoting the kind, quality, quantity, intended purpose, value, geographical origin, the time of production of goods or of rendering of services, or other characteristics of the goods or services
– be generic in relation to the goods or services
– consist of the shape of the goods themselves, the shape of goods which is necessary to obtain a technical result, or the shape which gives substantial value to the goods
– be contrary to public policy or to accepted principles of morality
– be deceptive.

However, it is possible to overcome objections from the Registrar of Trade Marks on these grounds if the trade mark owner can demonstrate that through use of the trade mark, it has become distinctive of his products or services exclusively. As well as fulfilling the registrability criteria set out above, a trade mark must not conflict with an earlier trade mark, and it is here that most of the problems arise as will be discussed later in this chapter.

SELECTING NEW TRADE MARKS

From the trade mark owner's view the most attractive trade mark is the one which best describes his goods or services. The more the trade mark indicates what the product is, the less the owner will have to spend to get his message across to the consumer. From a legal viewpoint, however, distinctiveness is the key to a strong trade mark. The more distinctive the trade mark, the more likely it is to be legally available, and the stronger the rights which will be obtained through use and registration. The disadvantage of a very distinctive trade mark is the investment the trade mark owner will have to make in marketing his product and service. But once consumer awareness has been established, there should be far fewer problems in maintaining a monopoly in the trade mark. In practice very distinctive trade marks often consist of invented words, examples of which are Kodak, Zeneca and Xerox, household names in the UK and many other countries.

THE TRADE MARK SEARCHING PROCESS

Registers of trade marks protect the rights of third parties. Before adopting a new trade mark it is, therefore, essential to carry out searches. While trade mark searches in one country are relatively quick and inexpensive, searching internationally is both time-consuming and expensive. This is because the registers are becoming increasingly crowded making it more and more difficult to find attractive and appropriate marks, which are legally available, especially in the areas of toiletries, pharmaceuticals and computer technology. Most obvious and attractive names will almost certainly have been registered already, in at least one of the relevant countries.

Consequently, it is usually necessary to search a number of names before a decision is made. The searching process can be time-consuming and expensive. The cost-effective way of tackling the process is to conduct preliminary computerised searches in the Trade Marks Registers which can be accessed on-line to eliminate, at the outset, names which have obvious problems.

More detailed searches should then be carried out, including obtaining the opinion of a local expert. Again to keep costs down, and if time permits, it is advisable to search the relevant Registers sequentially starting, for example, with a list of 20 to 30 names in the trade-mark owner's home country. The surviving names can then be searched in the remaining countries of interest. These countries are divided into several batches. Such a phased process can take much longer than searching all the short-listed names in parallel. It means that names encountering serious obstacles can be eliminated at each stage, thereby avoiding unnecessary costs.

Even if the searching process is handled in this way, it is unusual for a trade mark to emerge completely unscathed with no potential problems in any of the countries searched. More often the selected name will have at least one or two minor obstacles which need to be resolved before the trade mark is brought into use. For example, it may be advisable to seek consent from the owners of a similar mark, or to check whether a conflicting mark is being used in the same or similar area of business, or whether the registration might be vulnerable to cancellation for non-use. In cases where an approach for consent is necessary, this can often take some time, since the trade mark's owner will have to wait until the party who has been approached has considered the matter internally and is ready to respond. This again illustrates the importance of starting availability searches as early as possible before the proposed launch of the new product or service.

In the UK and other common law countries in which rights to a trade mark are acquired through use, as well as by registration, it is a good idea to carry out searches, not only of the Trade Marks Registers, but also to check the index of company names, relevant databases and telephone/trade directories.

REGISTERING TRADE MARKS AND
THE IMPORTANCE OF REGISTRATION

Although to a limited extent rights to a trade mark in the UK are acquired through use, in most countries the rights belong to the first applicant for registration. Registration of a trade mark gives the owner a statutory monopoly in the trade mark for the goods or services covered by the registration, and in many countries for similar goods and services too. The owner can, therefore, take action in the courts to prevent the unauthorised use of his trade mark (or of a mark which is confusingly similar) and, if successful, will obtain an injunction and damages.

In the UK and other common-law countries it may be possible to prevent use of the same or similar trade mark by a competitor by means of an action for 'passing off', even if the plaintiff's mark is not registered. But, to succeed, the plaintiff has to establish to the court's satisfaction that he has acquired a reputation and goodwill through use of his mark. Also, that the defendant's use of the same or similar mark amounts to a mis-representation, which is confusing or likely to confuse a substantial number of people, thereby damaging the plaintiff's business. Common-law rights are therefore difficult, time-consuming and expensive to enforce and the outcome of 'passing off' actions is often unpredictable. By contrast, the rights granted through registration of a trade mark are relatively straightforward and inexpensive to enforce, and the outcome tends to be more certain.

The advantages of registering a trade mark may be summarised as follows:

- the trade mark's owner obtains a statutory monopoly which is legally enforceable against infringers
- filing a trade mark application reserves a trade mark before it is brought into use
- a trade mark registration can act as a strong deterrent to competitors considering the adoption of the same or similar name because it will be entered on the Trade Marks Register and revealed by searches as a potential obstacle
- the owner of a trade mark registration can lodge a notice with Customs and Excise authorities to prevent the import of infringing goods by specifying the expected time and place the consignment will arrive.

THE REGISTRATION PROCEDURE

The procedure differs substantially from country to country, even among EU countries, notwithstanding the Harmonisation Directive. In the UK once an application has been lodged at the Trade Marks Registry and a filing receipt issued, it will then be examined as to inherent registrability according to the criteria outlined earlier in this chapter, and for conflict with earlier trade marks. An examination report will be forwarded to the applicant or his attorneys stating either that the application has been accepted or, more often, that official objections have been raised. It is sometimes possible to argue suc-cessfully against official objections through correspondence with the Registry, although if these arguments fail the applicant has the option of attending a hearing before one of the Registry's more senior officials at which the objections are reconsidered.

Following examination and subsequent arguments, the application may be rejected, in which case the applicant can appeal to the High Court. Alternatively, it is accepted. If so it is ready to be published in the *Trade Marks Journal*.

Following publication there is a period of three months within which anyone may object by filing formal opposition. Provided no oppositions are lodged the application will be registered and the registration certificate issued. Typically, this whole procedure from application, takes about a year to 18 months, assuming no serious problems. Once a trade mark is registered (but not while it remains pending) it can be used as the basis for an infringement action. Since the rights obtained are backdated to the date of application, it may be possible to claim damages for the period in which the application was pending, provided the infringer was placed on notice.

As long as a trade mark is used within five years of registration and use continues for a period of five years or longer, the registration should remain valid and can continue in force indefinitely. The appropriate renewal fees need to be paid every ten years to maintain its validity.

Many countries have systems which are similar to the UK which provide for a full examination as to inherent registrability and conflict with prior marks. At the other end of the spectrum there are countries, such as Benelux (Belgium, The Netherlands and Luxembourg) and Italy. These countries operate deposit systems of trade-mark registration, whereby the application is filed and there is no official examination or opposition procedure. The registration certificate is issued notwithstanding that the trade mark may not be inherently registrable according to their laws, or conflicts with earlier trade marks already on the Register. In the absence of an opposition procedure anyone wishing to raise objection in these circumstances has to wait until after registration and then apply for cancellation.

PROTECTING AND MONITORING TRADE MARKS

To maintain a monopoly in a trade mark it is essential that it should be used for the registered goods or services. Failure to do so means that the trade mark registration will become vulnerable to cancellation for non-use, in most countries five years after registration, and that the right to future use of the trade mark will be lost. To avoid possible invalidity of a trade mark registration it is important that the mark is used in the form in which it is registered and that it is used for the goods or services covered by the registration. If a trade mark is updated (and this applies in particular to logos or labels) advice should be sought as to whether any amendment of the mark covered by the existing registration is possible. If not, a new application for the updated version of the trade mark should be filed. Similarly if it is proposed that the trade mark will be used on goods or services outside the scope of the existing registration, appropriates searches should be carried out and new applications filed.

CORRECT USE OF TRADE MARKS

It is also important to ensure that the trade mark is used correctly. It must not become the generic name for the goods or services, thereby leaving the registration vulnerable to cancellation on these grounds. The following are guidelines for the correct use of trade marks:

— whenever they appear in text, trade marks should be distinguished from the surrounding text by, eg showing the trade mark in capitals, italics, in bold type, in a different colour, or placing it in quotation marks
— trade marks should always be followed by the generic name of the product or service, as in "Xerox photocopiers"
— trade marks should be used as adjectives and not as nouns or verbs
— trade marks should be used consistently in the same spelling and format
— the trade-mark owner should give notice to others that a trade mark is in fact being claimed as a trade mark, by use of the TM symbol if the trade mark is not registered or the R in a circle symbol if it is. In addition it is a good idea to include a footnote in printed matter to the effect that 'X is a (registered) trade mark of Y company'.

POLICING OF TRADE MARKS

To maintain a monopoly in a trade mark it is important to act quickly when infringements come to light. Failure to do so will lead to a dilution and possibly the eventual loss of a trade mark owner's rights. As soon as an infringement comes to the trade mark owner's attention he should seek professional advice with a view to taking appropriate action. It is, therefore, important to monitor the activities of competitors and of the market-place generally.

It is also possible to subscribe to a watching service for trade marks. The owner is informed of the publication of any applications to register trade marks which are the same or similar, so that objections can be raised.

THE EFFECTS OF THE UK TRADE MARKS ACT 1994

The main effects of the Trade Marks Act 1994 are summarised as follows:

— the definition of a trade mark is extended to include marks which would have been unregistrable under the old law such as shapes, sounds and smells and any mark established as being factually distinctive through prior use
— the cost of obtaining registration of a trade mark has been reduced by allowing for applications covering any number of goods or services, where previously separate applications would have been necessary
— the infringement rights granted by registration have been extended to include, in certain circumstances, similar goods or services where before, protection applied only to the precise goods or services covered by a registration
— the Act provides protection for famous marks, even against their use on dissimilar goods or services

– protection for trade marks in use but not registered has been limited making it more important than before to ensure that a mark is correctly registered

– the licensing and assignment provisions have been simplified.

The 1994 Act replaced the Trade Marks Act 1938 which was generally regarded as out-of-date, cumbersome and inappropriate for the current needs of trade mark owners. The changes brought about by the new Act are to the benefit of owners because they simplify the registration process and bring the UK more into line with its European counterparts.

DEVELOPMENTS IN EUROPE

The Community Trade Mark

The Community Trade Mark system has been in the pipeline since 1964 when it was first proposed by the European Commission. An EU Regulation for the Community Trade Mark was not eventually finalised until 1993 – almost 30 years later. The system is now operational and the Community Trade Marks office, based in Alicante, Spain, started accepting applications on 1 January 1996 with the official commencement date being 1 April 1996. Applications filed during the period 1 January to 31 March 1996 have an effective filing date of 1 April 1996.

The purpose of the Community Trade Mark system is to establish a single trade mark registration covering all the member states of the EU. However, the Community system will not replace existing national registrations which will continue in parallel.

Applications to register a Community Trade Mark can be filed, either directly at the Community Trade Marks office in Alicante, or at any one of the national Trade Marks registries. Applications can be filed in any of the official languages of the EU although the working languages for the Community Trade Marks' office are English, French, German, Italian and Spanish. Applicants are also required to designate a second language which must be one of the five working languages of the office.

The registration procedure involves official examination of the application to see whether the trade mark is registrable. The criteria which apply are effectively the same as under the UK Trade Marks Act 1994.

The Community Trade Marks Office also carries out an official search of the Community Trade Marks Register and draws the applicant's attention to any prior marks which appear to conflict. However, an application will not be refused based on the results of the official search. The onus is, therefore, on the applicant to decide whether or not to proceed, bearing in mind that the owners of conflicting marks will be able to oppose the application. Similar searches will also be carried out in the national registers of those countries who wish to conduct official searches. Again, however, the application will not be rejected on the grounds of conflict with any prior marks found and those marks will merely be drawn to the applicant's attention.

Once accepted, a Community Trade Mark application is published for opposition purposes and there is a period of three months from the date of publication within which interested third parties may raise objections. In the absence of oppositions, the application proceeds to registration for an initial period of ten years, renewable indefinitely for further ten-year periods.

In the case of a trade mark which is available throughout the EU, the Community Trade Mark system is a simple and cost-effective way of obtaining a registration applicable in all member states. However, in practice, given that the registers in all member states are very crowded, many Community Trade Mark applications could encounter third party oppositions, apart from well known trade marks already covered by existing national registrations. It is therefore worth noting that, when a pending application is refused or successfully opposed, the applicant has the option of applying to convert to separate national applications, clearly an attractive feature of the system.

The Madrid Agreement and The Madrid Protocol

The Madrid Agreement for the International Registration of Trade Marks, known as the Madrid Agreement, has provided an international registration system since 1891. An applicant, who should be a national of a member country or have a real and effective commercial establishment in a member country, first obtains registration in its home country. It then applies to the World Intellectual Property Organisation (WIPO) in Geneva for an international registration by designating the member states in which protection is required. The next move is to send the application to the national office in each designated country which examines and prosecutes the application according to its national laws. The outcome is an international registration covering a number of countries, which is obtained more quickly and cost-effectively than by filing separate national applications in the countries concerned.

Although the Madrid Agreement has worked very well over a considerable period of time, important countries such as the USA, Japan and the UK have not joined. There are several reasons for this.

- The Madrid Agreement requires an international registration to be based on a national registration which puts these countries at an immediate disadvantage because of the length of time normally taken to obtain registration.
- The Agreement includes provisions for 'central attack', whereby the international registration is dependent upon the national registration on which it is based for the first five years, during which time, if the national registration is cancelled the entire international registration is also cancelled.
- The national trade mark offices are required to notify WIPO of objections to international registrations within a period of twelve months, considered to be too short a timescale.
- The fees payable to national registries for handling Madrid Agreement applications are considered too low.

The Madrid Protocol of 1989, technically a modification of the Madrid Agreement, is a parallel system which came into force on 1 April 1996, which will also provide for the international registration of trade marks and is intended to attract those countries for which the original Madrid Agreement was unacceptable. However, the Protocol is different from the original Madrid Agreement in the following ways:

- protocol applications can be based on national *applications* rather than national *registrations*
- national trade marks registries will have up to eighteen months to examine applications and notify WIPO of objections
- the fees are higher and generally equate to national application fees in the relevant countries.

A further advantage of the Protocol over the Madrid Agreement for English-speaking countries is that the official language of the original Agreement was French, whereas under the Protocol applications may be made in either English or French.

As a result of recent developments in Europe applicants in some countries will have the option of applying for registration of trade marks through their national trade marks office, via the Community Trade Mark system, the Madrid Agreement or the Madrid Protocol. It will depend on the particular circumstances of each individual case as to which route is appropriate. In view of the complexities of trade mark registration and the number of different systems which operate around the world, it makes good sense for the owners of trade marks to obtain professional advice.

PART TWO

APPLICATIONS

CHAPTER

9

BRANDS FROM THE STANDARDS SETTERS' PERSPECTIVE

TERRY HARDING, ERNST & YOUNG

Both the UK Accounting Standards Board (ASB) and the International Accounting Standards Committee (IASC) are in the process of developing standards to deal with the recognition of intangible assets, including brands, in published financial statements. This chapter deals with the way in which standards setters tackle the process, the current practice internationally, the alternative views on the four main issues, and the differing conclusions drawn by the ASB and the IASC based on, apparently, similar information. It does not seek to support or attack any particular position, but attempts to set out some of the reasoning behind what some describe as the setters' overly cautious approach to the problem.

Both the ASB and the IASC have been working on these projects for some time, the IASC since 1989. During the process, both have been criticised by large corporations for taking positions which are out of step with commercial reality; the ASB by sub-suming brands within goodwill (it has since changed its position) and the IASC for a highly restrictive approach which would prohibit revaluation of brands on the balance sheet and require amortisation over an arbitrarily short period. So how can there be such a divergence of opinion?

From the standards setters' perspective there are only four real issues:

- should purchased brands be recognised on the balance sheet?
- should internally-generated brands be recognised on the balance sheet?
- should brands be re-measured and carried at fair value?
- over what period (if any) should they be amortised?

THE REGULATOR'S APPROACH TO STANDARDS SETTING

How does a regulator approach such a topic where there are few, if any, existing requirements or guidelines? Essentially, the aim of the standards setter is to strike a balance between a number of (often competing) objectives and influences.

Conceptual frameworks

Most standards setters have developed and approved explicit frameworks, the main objective of which is to guide them in developing new standards. In practice, standards setters place great emphasis on the framework when considering alternative proposals for new standards. Those drafters that do not have explicit frameworks, nevertheless work within implicit frameworks based on existing practice and common experience. Both the ASB and IASC have similar frameworks: the IASC framework is explicit and has been approved by the IASC board for use in developing standards; the ASB's is an implicit one, although it is in the process of developing an explicit framework which differs in some important respects.

The three significant features of the IASC frameworks as they apply to brands are:

- The objective of financial statements is to provide information which is useful to those making economic decisions. Although there is a wide range of users, in most contexts the focus is on equity investors and their advisers who use financial statements as one basis for forecasting a company's future cash flows and thus determining its share price. The emphasis is on the needs of the capital markets
- Assets are defined as resources giving rise to future economic benefits, and are recognised on the balance sheet when those future benefits are probable and their amount can be measured reliably
- Assets are initially measured at cost, those of a long-term nature are amortised over their useful lives and they may be revalued to fair values when those values can be reliably measured.

In essence, the objective is to provide information which is relevant but only to the extent that it is also reliable as a basis for assessments about the future. Most of the arguments about brands centre on reliability – can their cost be measured with sufficient reliability that they should be recognised in the balance sheet? Can the useful life of brands be reliably estimated to be very long or indefinite, such that they need not be amortised? Can the value of a brand be measured reliably enough to permit revaluations on the balance sheet?

A range of existing practices and ideas

The standard setters must reconcile the treatments suggested by the framework with existing practices, including practice by companies in the UK and, for the IASC, with international practice. They must take account of inconsistencies and conflicts in existing practice, as well as academic and other research in the area.

Having developed an approach which reconciles conflicts between the framework and various practices and ideas, setters issue discussion papers and exposure drafts for comment by interested parties, in this case ranging from brand valuers through companies with significant interests in brands, auditors, financial analysts and academics. Inevitably, the end result represents a compromise between all these views, but, at least within the IASC, the framework, and particularly the objective of providing relevant but reliable information, remains the benchmark against which all proposals are tested.

Compromise solutions

In considering how proposals are developed within the IASC, it is important to remember also that the IASC's constituency and Board representation is very broad. The IASC board includes representatives from 15 countries and organisations, including companies, financial analysts and auditors. Many of the representatives are from traditionally conservative countries, eg Germany, France, Switzerland, India, Malaysia and Japan, where they place more emphasis on prudence than has been the case in recent years in the UK. Other countries, such as the USA and Canada, remain committed to historical cost as the basis for financial statements, leaving them either neutral or opposed to revaluations in financial statements. Although each country is encouraged to leave its own national framework behind and to argue on the basis of the agreed IASC framework, national prejudices and politics inevitably play their part in the compromise solutions that result.

The ASB, with its smaller board and narrower constituency, is perhaps less inhibited in this way, and therefore more likely to pursue a more progressive path, as is evident from its revised approach to goodwill and brands, as well as its proposed framework. Some argue that the ASB's proposals are out of line with international practice; others argue that the proposals are sensible and the UK should lead the way in developing an international solution which is acceptable to companies and the accounting profession.

INTERNATIONAL COMPARISONS

International comparison is difficult because there are few countries with well-established and clearly-defined rules for the recognition, amortisation and revaluation of intangible assets, including brands. The IASC is a growing force in world standard setting. Other countries, eg Australia, New Zealand, South Africa, Hong Kong and, perhaps, the USA and Canada, are likely to adopt requirements similar to the IASC proposals once the IASC standard is approved. The influence of the IASC on UK accounting is also growing, so that there is some, but not yet overwhelming, pressure for the ASB to move towards an international solution.

European Union countries have adopted the very broad requirements of the EC Fourth Directive; it permits (but does not specifically require) measurement of both purchased and internally-generated intangible assets at cost, requires those with limited lives to be amortised and requires an annual review for impairment. Within these broad rules, practice varies even within each country and between various types of intangibles. In the UK, for example, there are a number of high profile companies that carry purchased brands at cost, do not amortise them (because they do not consider their lives to be limited) but review the carrying amount for impairment. One or two large companies recognise internally-generated brands at a valuation. But the vast majority of UK companies do not consider purchased brands separately from goodwill and have not considered recognising internally-generated brands.

The USA is one country where the requirements are well established. The US GAAP requires identifiable purchased intangibles to be recognised at cost. It *permits* internally-generated intangibles to be recognised, but does not *require* it. However, it states that the costs of developing, maintaining or restoring intangible assets that are not specifically identifiable, have indeterminate lives or are inherent in a continuing business should be recognised as an expense as incurred. It requires the cost to be amortised over the useful life of the asset, taking into account the effect of obsolescence, demand, competition and other factors, but limits the period of amortisation to 40 years. Acquired assets with indeterminate lives longer than 40 years are required to be amortised over 40 years, not a shorter arbitrary period.

Under these rules, an acquired brand (with an indeterminate life) would be recognised and amortised over 40 years, but an internally generated brand with an indeterminate life could not be recognised. In practice, US companies seem to describe their intangibles as trade marks rather than goodwill and amortise them over periods between ten and 40 years.

The proposals of the IASC and the ASB, together with the requirements and practice in other countries, as they affect brands, are summarised in Table 9.1.

In practice, there are few countries where intangible assets are described as brands on the balance sheet. In most of Europe and North America they are more frequently described as patents, trade marks or, more specifically, newspaper and magazine titles and publishing rights. In such cases, although the assets are recognised, they are likely to be defined narrowly, and, therefore, will include a narrow range of costs and values in the amount recognised. In the UK, Australia, New Zealand and South Africa, where brands are recognised as comprising a wider range of values than those specific to trade marks, they are likely to be given more significance on the balance sheet's list of assets.

THE MAIN ISSUES

Recognition of brands

Brands can be purchased separately, developed internally or, perhaps most commonly, purchased as part of the acquisition of a subsidiary. When it comes to recognising intangible assets, some feel that a wide spectrum should be recognised separately, others believe that a well-defined subset of intangibles should be recognised separately, while a third group insist that all intangibles should be subsumed within goodwill. Some draw a distinction between purchased intangibles and those generated internally, and others believe the distinction is unnecessary.

Should brands be recognised separately from goodwill?

In developing their proposals, both IASC and the ASB have considered why a company would want to capitalise brands. One reason is to strengthen the balance sheet, increasing the share price and making the company less vulnerable to take-overs. Another is to

TABLE 9.1: International comparison of the rules for the treatment of brands

	UK (proposed)	IASC (proposed)	EU*	US/ CANADA	UK (current) Aust/NZ	Japan (proposed)
Recognition:						
Acquired	Yes	Yes	Yes	Yes	Yes	Yes
Internally generated	No	No	Yes	No	Yes	No
Amortisation period (years)	UEL	20	UEL	40	None	UEL
Revaluation	*No*	*No*	*No*	*No*	*Yes*	*No*

UEL = useful economic life (without arbitrary limitation).

* Practice within EU member states varies considerably within the broad requirements of the Directive. In Germany, for example, brands are not recognised separately from goodwill, and in Denmark, Germany, Sweden and Italy, internally-generated brands are not recognised. Amortisation periods in Europe are typically short (5–20 years).

compensate for inappropriate treatments of goodwill, such as write-offs to reserves, which seem to deplete the balance sheet. However, the IASC at least, does not accept these arguments. Instead, it broadly accepts the 'capital markets' view that an expert would make his or her own calculation of future cash flows and the value of the company, irrespective of the company's own 'value' shown in the balance sheet. The market uses these forecasts to determine the share price, so that the value given to brands in the balance sheet should be irrelevant. In practice, market values are affected, at least in the short term, by the announcement of profit figures and 'earnings per share' figures which should be equally irrelevant; if there was no effect on market values, companies would not be concerned.

Nevertheless, standards setters argue that their job is to ensure that financial statements reflect the requirements of users for relevant and reliable information. Users confirm that economic values of brands are neither relevant nor reliable as a basis for forecasting future cash flows and, for this reason, standard setters are reluctant to require or permit their inclusion in balance sheets. The cost of acquired and internally-generated brands is, in the standard-setters' view, useful information as long as the amount shown is a reliable measure of specific costs that can generate specific future benefits.

From the IASC's perspective, the recognition rules should be the same for internally-generated or acquired brands (although the criteria are more difficult to meet for internally generated brands). The ASB's proposals are directed at business combinations and state that internally-generated intangible assets should not be recognised. In terms of the IASC's framework, a brand, in order to be recognised on the balance sheet, must be an identifiable resource, and it must give rise to probable future benefits that can be measured reliably. Two problems are apparent from the definition. Firstly, is a brand an identifiable resource, or a collection of different resources; secondly, it is extremely difficult to measure, or separate, the future economic benefits, ie cash flows or profit, that flow from that specific resource.

Separability is a central issue

The separability of brands is one issue that remains central to the reluctance of the standards setters to permit recognition of brands. Valuers often discuss separability in terms of the ability to sell a package of intangibles (a trade mark with perhaps a patent and related know-how and distribution networks). To the setter, such a package can often seem to be little more than a division of a company – if we valued each division of the company based on its expected future cash flows and added them together, we would have a balance sheet showing the 'value' of the company. This is not the view of the setter for the purpose of reporting. Separability to the standards setter means that there is a separate asset which has a value independent of its earnings in the current activity; that is it could be sold or licensed without also disposing of the remaining assets of that business activity. On that basis, many see brands as collections of assets which are an integral part of a business activity and for which a market price is impossible to establish because each asset is unique.

The solutions of standards setters

These difficulties have led to the requirement proposed in the IASC's exposure draft issued in 1995 that brands should be recognised only when they meet certain strict criteria including:

— they must be subject to a legal right or must be separable
— the role that the asset plays in enhancing future benefits, its ability to perform the role effectively and the intention to use it for this purpose must be demonstrated
— specific expenditures must be capable of being linked with specific future economic benefits which can be measured reliably.

The result is that, for internally-generated brands, recognition is unlikely. For example, although advertising expenditure may contribute to the development of a brand, it is impossible to say what proportion of any particular expenditure is included in the specific revenue streams of the brand, rather than the more general internally-generated goodwill.

In a business combination, brands will be recognised, under the IASC's proposals, when a fair value can be derived from an active market, or when the cost is separately negotiated as part of the acquisition. These circumstances are likely to be rare. In other cases it will be necessary to identify specific future benefits arising from the intangible which can be separated from the benefits arising from the business as a whole. The exposure draft leaves this to the judgement of preparers and auditors in the circumstances, but the wording of the proposals is such that separate recognition should be possible in most cases.

The ASB's proposals deal only with brands when acquired by purchase of the business brand. The proposal is that intangibles should be recognised separately from goodwill when management believes that their fair values can be measured reliably, leaving rather more scope for recognition than in the IASC's proposals. The ASB believes it is important that, even if intangibles and goodwill are recognised separately from one another, the accounting treatment should be similar, so that advantages cannot be gained by designating a balance as an intangible rather than goodwill. It has concentrated on producing identical accounting treatments rather than attempting to define strict recognition criteria for brands.

Valuation

Valuation of brands for accounting purposes is required in two circumstances. Firstly, when a brand is purchased along with a bundle of other assets and liabilities in a business combination, the cost of the acquisition as a whole must be allocated among the various assets and liabilities to be recognised, based on their fair values. If a brand is to be recognised in a business combination, it must have a fair value that can be measured reliably. The recognition of brands in a business combination is dealt with above, but in essence, as long as the accounting treatments for goodwill and intangible assets are similar, the standards setter is unconcerned as to whether that part of the cost of the acquisition is allocated to a brand or to the residual goodwill.

The second circumstance requiring valuation of brands is when a company seeks to revalue a brand that has previously been carried at cost, or which has not been recognised at all. This is more problematical to the standards setter because it involves an increase in the carrying amount (and therefore a 'strengthening' of the balance sheet) which is only justified if the valuation is reliable and long-term. Setters, aware of how often commercial hopes have been dashed in practice, have evolved concepts of prudence which make them wary of bases of appraisal that could be volatile or vulnerable to change. There are strongly differing views on whether a brand really does have a value which can be measured separately from goodwill, and standards setters tend to take the side of those who doubt the accuracy of valuations.

Use of economic values

Those with an interest in valuing brands argue that they can be separated and a value obtained based on discounted-revenue streams. An example is found in the 1992 Arthur Andersen report, 'The Valuation of Intangible Assets', sponsored by 11 major UK companies who believed that much progress had been made, but not acknowledged, in developing acceptable valuation methodologies. The report accepts that most valuations adopt economic-based approaches because of a lack of market information – each methodology seeks to evaluate the net present value of the incremental cash flows or earnings attributable to a brand. The report concludes that it is possible to codify valuation methodologies and improve the general understanding of the valuation process such that users can have more confidence in the incorporation of intangible assets into financial statements. It argues that there is a considerable consensus in the business and professional community regarding valuation methodologies and by the acceptance of valuations in taxation, licensing agreements and fund raising.

The report agrees with the views of the standards setter that separability is one of the main hurdles to be overcome in enabling the value of a brand to be measured reliably. It recognises that the value of an asset, such as a brand, may be dependent on other intangible elements such as goodwill, reputation and relationships, and it must be defined either very narrowly (for example a trade mark) or very broadly (including key people, know-how, distribution systems, etc.). In discussing the separation of brand contribution from the profit or cash flows of the underlying business, it describes most methods as variations on one of the following themes:

- brand contribution (by deducting estimated contribution from unbranded products)
- estimated post-tax royalty under a hypothetical licensing arrangement
- comparative PE ratios to identify the market price of a brand company from an equivalent unbranded company.

Even standards setters would not disagree with a view that such valuations could be useful in some circumstances. Unfortunately, from a setter's perspective, all of these methods are unacceptable as a basis for revaluing assets in the balance sheet because:

- they are too subjective, based on hypothetical and opportunity costs and values (they are not sufficiently reliable measures)
- the broad definition of brands used in such methodologies is indistinguishable from the standard setters' definition of goodwill, being the difference between the fair value of the identifiable (tangible and intangible) assets and liabilities of a company and the fair value of the company as a whole.

What do users want?

In short, many see economic values as no more than measures of goodwill within the business. Whether such valuations are described as 'brands' or as 'goodwill' the view of most standards setters throughout the world is clear. Such amounts should be recognised at cost if they are purchased, amortised over a relatively short period of perceived economic benefit and not measured at economic values in the balance sheet. This is because the purpose of financial statements is not to put a 'value' on the business. This is the *raison d'être* of financial analysts and the markets.

This view is supported by users of financial statements – the analysts themselves. In a 1992 paper 'On the Valuation of Assets', David Damant of the European Federation of Analysts, and a member of the board of IASC, argues that it is the user whose objective is to forecast future cash flows and that the best basis for such forecasts is the cost of an enterprise's assets. The method of valuation in the balance sheet cannot involve any calculation based on future cash flows because the process would be circular – the information would not be useful to an expert user who wishes to forecast future cash flows using his or her own assumptions. An asset is a resource giving rise to future economic benefits – it is not the future economic benefits themselves.

The solutions of the standard setters

These arguments lead to the conclusion, drawn in the IASC's proposals, that intangibles may only be revalued on the balance sheet when a fair value can be obtained from an active market. In this context, an active market requires as many buyers and sellers as possible (so that individual negotiation is not necessary), and publicly available prices. In practice, such markets are likely to exist for few, if any intangibles (and probably for no brands). Companies will be able to report the value of a brand in the notes to the accounts or elsewhere in the annual report. The ASB paper does not consider whether brands should be revalued, but implies that this would not be permitted as it would implicitly capitalise internally-generated intangible assets.

Amortisation

Over 20 years?

The internationally-accepted framework for reporting accepts that all long-term assets (except land) have limited useful lives and that the cost (or revalued amount) should be amortised over that period through the income statement. This is the basis for the IASC's proposals. In its initial proposals, the IASC placed no restriction on that useful life (as with tangible assets, although it does restrict the useful life of goodwill). The emphasis in those proposals was, quite properly, not on ensuring that brands were amortised over the same period as goodwill, but on ensuring that any brand recognised separately from goodwill should be a separable, identifiable asset in its own right.

Later in the process, the IASC's board became less convinced that its recognition criteria were strong enough to prevent goodwill being recognised as brands, and decided to impose a 20-year limit for amortisation of virtually all intangible assets. The result is that the cost of all recognised brands will be required to be amortised over a maximum of 20 years from the date of initial recognition. The reasoning for the 20-year limit on useful life is that, although the useful life of brands may be indeterminate, it cannot be infinite. As the planning horizon of most companies (and national economies) cannot extend beyond 20 years then it is prudent to use 20 years as the longest reliable estimate of useful life. The reason this limit is not imposed for tangible assets is that physical deterioration normally places a similar natural limit on useful lives used.

It would be difficult for any reasonably prudent professional to argue against this position, except that one would expect the effect to be mitigated in some circumstances, for example by:

- the ability to review the useful life regularly and extend the period of amortisation if necessary
- the possibility of reflecting high residual values in the amortisation calculation (thereby amortising only a small part of the cost)
- capitalising 'maintenance' expenditures which extend the useful life beyond the originally assessed 20 years.

But, the IASC proposals allow neither initial estimates of useful life over 20 years, nor any of the three alternatives. For brands, the 20-year period cannot be adjusted as the outlook becomes clearer in future years, since residual values must be assumed to be zero and brand-maintenance costs must be recognised as expenses. The result is that both the arbitrarily-high amortisation expenses and maintenance expenditure are recognised in the income statement each year. The carrying amount of brands is then reduced to zero over 20 years, regardless of whether their value has deteriorated.

Or not at all?

The ASB believes that goodwill and brands can have indefinite useful lives and that it is appropriate not to amortise. Consistent with its emerging philosophy on financial reporting generally, it believes amortisation is not necessary as long as reductions in the 'value to the business' can be measured and reflected in the carrying amount of a brand. Recognised brands would generally not be depreciated unless management believed they had a limited life, and a brand that is secured on a renewable trade mark would, normally, be expected to last indefinitely.

The ASB has developed requirements for impairment tests, based on an assessment of discounted future cash flows, which it believes are strong enough to detect systematic reductions in the value of brands. The proposed annual impairment test formalises a process that should already take place for all non-current assets. In developing its proposals, the impairment proposals were field tested by a number of large groups – most found them to be workable and to provide sensible results.

Those who support the ASB's approach (not surprisingly, perhaps, these are companies with historically successful brands and brand-valuation companies) point to numerous examples of brands that have survived the test of time and can be expected to remain in existence and maintain or increase their values in the future. *The Times* or Coca-Cola are examples often used. The IASC would agree that, in hindsight, this is the case. But they point to other examples such as Triumph or Fry's which could once have been described in similar terms but which have declined significantly in value over time.

The IASC board is unconvinced, at least for the present, of either the 'value to the business' philosophy or of the robustness of impairment testing which, in practice, relies heavily on judgements and assumptions. It believes that although indefinite useful lives may become apparent in hindsight, they cannot be assumed from the outset. The danger with subjective tests based on assumptions about the future is that any write-down would be resisted until it became clear the brand was in deep trouble, resulting in 'big bath' write-downs which fail to reflect the decline in value of the asset. Notwithstanding the arguments for an allocation of cost, the IASC board might consider impairment testing as an alternative to amortisation if it could be convinced that such tests would be sufficiently objective to recognise a fall in value as it occurred. The IASC board has recently begun work on a project to explore the use of discounting in financial statements which will address some of these issues.

Brand maintenance

The question of brand maintenance expenditures is a different issue, but is linked because of the arbitrary amortisation proposals. Most companies with significant brands on their balance sheets spend millions of pounds each year on advertising and other marketing expenditures designed to maintain their market shares and thus to maintain and build the values of their brands. Most would argue that each period's marketing expenditure extends the useful life of the asset and (at least if amortisation is compulsory) should be added to the carrying amount of the asset rather than being recognised as an expense. If they were permitted not to amortise brands, however, many would accept marketing expenditure as a cost of maintaining the value shown on the balance sheet.

In the case of tangible assets, the view of regulators is that maintenance expenditure enables the asset to continue in use but does not increase the useful life of the asset. In other words the useful life of plant, for example, is assessed on the assumption that regular maintenance will take place. The same would be true of brands if their useful life could be assessed beyond the 20-year limit. The ASB's approach is consistent with this view (at least in its practical effect of avoiding the duplication of maintenance and amortisation costs when a brand's value is being maintained). The IASC has considered this issue, but is prepared to accept the duplication in the profit and loss account that results from its approach on the grounds of prudence.

A compromise solution

To permit the capitalisation of marketing costs would go against the IASC's recognition requirements, and it is doubtful whether a residual value can be calculated with any reliability when the useful life of a brand is indeterminate. There is a strong argument, however, that if the planning horizon is the rationale for restricting useful life to 20 years, then useful life should be reassessed at the end of each period, using the 20-year horizon which can be foreseen from that date. This means that a brand would be amortised on a rolling 20-year basis, resulting in an approximation to a reducing-balance basis of amortisation.

TABLE 9.2: Example of amortisation on a rolling 20-year basis

Year	Opening Balance (£000)	Amortisation at 5% (£000)	Closing Balance (£000)
1	1000	50	950
2	950	47	902
3	902	45	857
5	815	41	774
10	630	32	599
15	488	24	463
20	377	19	358

The result would be less conservative than straight-line depreciation over an arbitrary 20-year period. But if, with the benefit of hindsight, a longer useful life could have been justified, then the result in the earlier years is still more conservative than hindsight would suggest was necessary. For example, if, with hindsight, the useful life of the asset proves to be 30 years, then amortisation should have been recognised at a rate of £33,000 per year. Thus after 10 years £330,000 would have been charged. But because this longer useful life could not be reliably deduced until year ten, a more prudent £400,000 of amortisation was charged in the first ten years with the remaining £600,000 amortised over the remaining 20 years.

The use of a 'rolling' 20-year maximum period of amortisation seems a reasonable approximation of the use of the asset over its life and, from the perspective of a standards setter if not a company's, a reasonable compromise between the extreme views of the IASC Exposure Draft and the ASB proposals. It applies a 'front-end loading' to the amortisation process to compensate for the initial uncertainty in measuring useful life beyond a normal planning horizon. It also relies on the ability to assess when the useful life of a brand is no longer indeterminate. It remains to be seen whether the IASC proposals will become more flexible and, perhaps, whether the ASB will move closer to the IASC position in finalising its standard.

THE IASC/ASB CONCLUSIONS

The differences between the approaches of the ASB and the IASC in respect of the four main issues, as they would apply to the treatment of brands, are summarised in Figure 9.1.

How do two different standards setters arrive at such different conclusions while using similar information? The reasons are probably two-fold and based on the various influences on each setter.

One difference is the perceived nature of an intangible asset. The IASC exposure draft and the ASB paper are based on the premise that the range of intangibles can be distinguished by their position on a spectrum. At one end there are intangible assets, such as certain licences, that have readily determinable useful lives and sometimes market-based values. These are similar in nature to property and plant except that they do not suffer physical deterioration. At the other end of the spectrum are assets with indeterminate useful lives and values that cannot be determined except by attempting to separate and discount the cash flows that are expected to be derived from their use. These are, arguably, similar in nature to goodwill; brands fall within this category. The difficulty is in dealing with such a wide range of assets within a single set of rules.

In developing standards, the ASB and the IASC started from different ends of this spectrum. The ASB initially took the view that brands were little more than goodwill in another guise and proposed they should not be recognised separately from goodwill. Recently it has accepted that some intangible assets can be different and that there are certain intangibles with fixed lives that deserve to be dealt with separately from goodwill. Because it sees a close resemblance between brands and goodwill, and only reluctantly recognises that there may be a difference, it focuses on providing accounting treatments which parallel the treatment of goodwill.

FIGURE 9.1: Differences in the approach to the treatment of brands between the ASB and IASC

ISSUE	IASC	ASB
Will brands be recognised when:		
(a) internally generated?	No	No
(b) separately purchased?	Yes	Yes (but not explicit)
(c) purchased in a business combination?	Sometimes – criteria should be capable of being met in many cases	Yes
Can brands be revalued on the balance sheet?	No	Not discussed, but the implication is no
Should brands be amortised?	Yes – over 20 years	No – if indeterminate useful life can be justified
Can brand-maintenance expenditure be capitalised?	No	No

The IASC started with a view that intangibles are similar in nature to property, plant and equipment and it even considered combining the proposed new standard with the existing one on tangible assets. It set out to provide accounting treatments which parallel the treatment of tangible assets and added more restrictive requirements to deal with difficulties inherent in intangible assets. In its latest proposals, the IASC has added restrictions to such an extent that the treatment mirrors that required for goodwill, although the international approach to goodwill differs from the ASB's proposals, so that differences between the two sets of proposals remain.

The second difference is in the frameworks the IASC and the ASB are seeking to apply to financial reporting. Implicit in the IASC framework is the concept that all non-current assets should be recognised at cost and amortised to be matched on a systematic basis against the revenue generated by the asset in each period. As a separate exercise, asset carrying amounts are then reviewed for impairment at each reporting date and written down if necessary. The ASB has chosen to abandon the allocation arguments (bearing in mind also that goodwill is the driving force behind the requirements for brands) with emphasis instead on detailed impairment tests to ensure that 'value' does not fall below the carrying amount. While the ASB believes its proposed impairment tests are strong enough to achieve a systematic write-down over the useful life of brands, the IASC board remains unconvinced.

To many, the IASC's overall approach seems harsh, but it derives essentially from the regulator's concerns about whether brands really are separable, whether they give rise to specific future benefits distinct from goodwill and whether their 'value' can be measured reliably. The IASC has responded essentially to financial analysts and auditors concerns about reliability. The ASB has been more responsive to the corporate view of reliability, but its approach to brands is heavily influenced by the existing treatment of goodwill (which avoids amortisation) and its emerging view of the balance sheet as a measure of current values. The ASB's public hearings, in the autumn of 1995, demonstrated clearly that large corporations in the UK, particularly those whose business is based on brands, support the ASB's approach, while the accounting profession and users of financial statements prefer something more akin to the more restrictive IASC approach.

10

ACCOUNTING FOR BRANDS: THE PRACTITIONER'S PERSPECTIVE

KEN WILD AND MARTIN SCICLUNA, DELOITTE & TOUCHE

Accounting for brands has become shorthand for the wider
issue of how we should treat goodwill and intangible assets.
The absence of rules has, arguably, allowed companies too
much flexibility and led to inconsistency of treatment. This
chapter examines the rules that have been proposed over recent
years, and the implications of the more lenient ASB proposals.

The inclusion of intangible assets within a balance sheet occurs in two situations. Firstly, following a corporate acquisition, it is a requirement to allocate the excess of consideration paid over the acquired company's tangible net assets between separate intangible assets such as brands and a residue of goodwill. Secondly, companies wishing to enhance the perceived amount of their net assets may choose to revalue brands which have previously existed, but may not have been carried in the balance sheet. In both cases, brands carried on-balance sheet are generally not depreciated. Commentators have argued that the absence of clear rules has provided UK companies with too much flexibility, and this has led to inconsistencies between companies, and overstated earnings of UK companies.

Proposals for change made by accounting rule setters over the years have generally been directed towards more prudent treatments. The UK Accounting Standards Board (ASB) issued proposals that are more flexible, and are, therefore, expected to be welcomed by UK companies with portfolios of brand assets. At the same time, critics suggest the proposals pay insufficient attention to accounting theory, and risk becoming a charter for creative accounting by the unscrupulous.

THE RULES

The primary source of rules for dealing with brands is the Companies Act 1985. The permitted list of balance sheet items includes 'intangible assets' as the first fixed asset category.

The detailed list which follows includes 'development costs' and 'concessions, patents, licences, trade marks and similar rights and assets'. Although brand names are not listed, they would fall within the group of 'similar rights and assets'. The next question is, what is the amount at which the brand should be stated?

The Act contains two bases of accounting for fixed assets:

– historical-cost rules which apply in all circumstances
– alternative accounting rules which may be superimposed over the historic rules if the directors choose.

Historical-cost rules require that 'assets should initially be recorded at purchase price or production cost'. This rule applies in two circumstances. Firstly, where a brand is bought as a separate asset, it will have a cost that will be capitalised. The situation of a brand being developed 'in-house' does not generally arise since, during the process of development, there is no certainty that the result will have value. Consequently, it is usual practice to write-off all development costs as they are incurred on grounds of prudence. The second situation where a brand is capitalised under the historic-cost rules follows the acquisition of a company which owns brand assets.

Further guidance is provided within the Act, and amplified in an accounting standard, Statement of Standard Accounting Practice (SSAP) 22 'Accounting for goodwill'. This requires the difference between the consideration paid, and the fair value of tangible net assets to be allocated between identifiable intangible assets and goodwill. Identifiable intangibles are described as intangible assets 'which are capable of being disposed of or discharged separately, without disposing of a business of the undertaking'. The list of suggested intangibles includes 'publishing titles, franchise rights and customer lists'. It is not intended to be comprehensive. Product brands are generally considered to be capable of disposal apart from the business. A corporate brand name is unlikely to meet the condition. Although the resulting amount included as an asset is based on a valuation, generally an estimate of replacement cost, it is described as being historic cost since it is an allocation of the total purchase price of the whole company.

Subsequent to the purchase or development of a brand, the directors of a company may choose to adopt alternative accounting rules. While these are widely applied to assets such as property, allowing use of market values, their use for intangibles is restricted to one basis only, that is current cost. The term 'current cost' could be said to imply use of a methodology such as that developed in SSAP 16 'Current cost accounting', ie an annual valuation based on the lower of net replacement cost and recoverable amount. Where applied, the current cost replaces historic cost for all purposes.

CURRENT PRACTICE AND ITS RECENT DEVELOPMENT

In the 1960s, before the advent of UK accounting standards, appearances of intangible assets on a balance sheet were rare, being restricted to those with a separate legal nature and a historical cost, for example, patents. Over the course of the 1970s, a great deal of activity and discussion took place in respect of goodwill, but there was little discussion of intangibles.

This changed in the 1980s, the result of the increased levels of acquisitions and resulting prices paid. Most companies eliminated all goodwill and intangibles directly against reserves. It then became evident that this removal of value paid from the balance sheet was not without its side effects. Companies with significant acquisitions experienced low reserves, breaches of borrowing covenants and resulting poor credit ratings. The inability of the balance sheet to convey meaningful information to shareholders was highlighted in the 1988 Nestlé take-over of Rowntree where the £5bn price was five times the disclosed net assets, and twice the previous market capitalisation of Rowntree.

The relevance of intangible assets, and the need to allow recognition of their existence and value, led, in 1990, to a decision by the London Stock Exchange to allow intangibles to be included within class tests. Throughout this period, the deficiencies that arose with the elimination of goodwill, and the inadequacies of established accounting practice for other intangibles, led a number of companies to seek methods of reflecting these other intangible assets within their balance sheets. Although this debate has been labelled 'the brand name' debate, in view of the role of companies with large brand-name portfolios, this term is perhaps misleading since a far wider group of intangible assets is affected. Companies with brands acquired in take overs adopted an accounting policy which led to the inclusion of the brands as separate assets. Arguably this is required, both by the Companies Act and SSAP 22. For example, Cadbury Schweppes accounting policy states 'Intangibles represent significant owned brands acquired since 1985 valued at historical cost'. Guinness state,

> The fair value of businesses acquired . . . includes brands which are recognised where the brand has a value which is substantial and long-term. Acquired brands are only recognised where title is clear, brand earnings are separately identifiable, the brand could be sold separately from the rest of the business and where the brand achieves earnings in excess of those achieved by unbranded products.

Instances of companies revaluing brands are less frequent. The RHM company adopted a policy of revaluation prior to their acquisition by Tomkins. At the same time, WPP continue to revalue corporate brand names stating,

> Intangible fixed assets comprise certain acquired separable corporate brand names. These are shown at a valuation of the incremental earnings expected to arise from the ownership of brands. The valuations have been based on the present value of notional royalty savings arising from the ownership of those brands and on estimates of profits attributable to brand loyalty. The valuations are subject to annual review.

It is debatable whether this represents a current-cost valuation.

EARLY CALLS FOR REFORM OF UK PRACTICE

While practice was developing, a theoretical debate was progressing. Work performed by various standard-setting bodies within the UK and internationally showed a determination to return to a theory-based approach – generally meaning 'cost less depreciation'. Foremost was a report published in 1989 by the London Business School (LBS), at the request of the Institute of Chartered Accountants in England and Wales (ICAEW), titled 'Accounting for Brands' which, *inter alia* concluded:

- if goodwill were carried in the balance sheet, either amortised or unamortised, the immediate pressure for brand accounting would evaporate
- there are major practical problems in establishing what a brand is worth
- in most cases, the value of a brand is impossible to separate from the rest of the business
- companies that have so far recognised brand values have in fact disclosed little new information about their brands
- at present, there is no general agreement on valuation methods
- to incorporate only brand valuation based on inherently hazardous methodology is not a basis for considered reform.

As a result of this report, proposals for an accounting standard were brought forward which would allow intangible assets to be included on a balance sheet only where:

- historical cost is known – effectively ruling out revaluation of all internally-generated intangibles
- characteristics can be clearly distinguished from goodwill – this was interpreted as restricting capitalisation to intangibles with a separate legal nature such as patents, trade marks and copyrights and excluding intangibles such as brands
- cost can be measured independently of goodwill – generally requiring an active market in a particular type of intangible.

It was further proposed that, once capitalised, all intangibles should be amortised through the profit and loss account over a maximum of 20 years.

The proposal met with a hostile response, with 80 per cent of corporate respondents and 62 per cent of all respondents objecting to this treatment. Recent comment by standards setters now accepts that the reason for this overwhelming opposition was that the approach 'was intuitively wrong and had no economic meaning' (ASB, 1995, Working Paper 'Goodwill and intangible assets'). The hostile response coincided with the formation of a new regulatory body, the ASB, to whom the poisoned chalice of finding a solution was passed.

The first proposals on goodwill and intangibles from the ASB suggested that, following an acquisition, there would be no division between goodwill and intangibles. The entire amount would be described as goodwill and subject to whatever rules were agreed. Although commentators were divided on what that treatment for goodwill should be, they were united in opposition to intangibles being subsumed within goodwill. Reasons stated included a loss of accountability for assets acquired, enforced depreciation of assets that had not lost value, and failure to write down assets at the time when a loss of value actually occurred. Corporate respondents argued that some intangible assets could be critical to their businesses and it was important to account for them separately.

THE CASE FOR INCLUDING BRANDS ON A BALANCE SHEET

In the period following the failure of ASB's proposals, Deloitte & Touche published a study which argued the case for including intangibles on-balance sheet wherever possible. It was argued that separability was the main issue in deciding whether a brand warranted treatment as an asset.

Separability

Separability is not included within the ASB's criteria for recognising assets, but would seem to be a precondition to recognition and valuation. The central test of separability contained in the Companies Act, there termed 'identifiable', is an ability to dispose of the brand while retaining the underlying business of the entity. This test can be approached from two directions:

1. *Is it possible to define the boundaries between the brand and other assets in such a way as to enable it to be disposed of as a discrete asset?*

In the perfect case, it would be possible to identify a legally-separate asset, having an established value in a fluid market, and a distinguishable stream of cash flow or income which is independent of all other assets. However, not only is this unlikely in the case of a brand, it is also unlikely in the case of most tangible assets. For example, an airline company will not be questioned if they record aircraft on their balance sheets as fixed assets. In reality, however, the value to the business of the aircraft is only realised when it is combined with other expertise such as ability of personnel to service and fly the plane, ability of management to obtain access to routes and slots, and ability of sales staff to sell the seats available.

Underlying the capitalisation of the aircraft is the availability of suitable replacements, and the assumption that the asset has an alternative use so that the airline company could, if it wished, sell the aircraft to a third party. However, the fact that many assets are unlikely to be sold does not imply that they could not be sold, as is evidenced in a company liquidation where the liquidator will seek to sell any items for which a buyer can be found. Similarly, the fact that many assets are not the subject of legal documentation does not imply that they could not be made the subject of a sale agreement.

2. *What will remain if the brand is removed from the business?*

Approaching from the other direction, one might examine what is left of the business if the brand is removed, ie whether the business can still function in its chosen field of commerce without the brand. This approach would suggest that a company with a large number of brands could dispose of a single brand without affecting its underlying ability to sell consumer products. By comparison, a company operating under a single corporate trade name that attaches to all its products and services would have difficulty separating

FIGURE 10.1: The spectrum of intangible assets

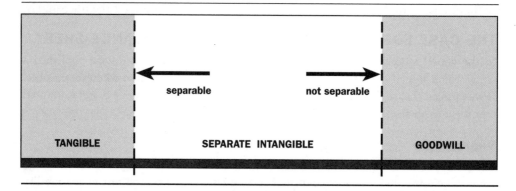

the name from the underlying business. However, the fact that an asset will require replacement if the business is to continue does not alter the 'separableness' of an individual asset, whether tangible or intangible.

Returning to the airline example, to operate an airline requires a tangible asset (an aircraft) and a number of intangible assets (flight slots, service capability and ticket-sales capability). If the airline were deprived of its only aircraft it could not function without replacing the asset. In a similar manner, loss of flight slots would also mean that the airline could not function; but this does not mean that other suitable flight slots could not be acquired (albeit for a different route), nor that the flight slots were not capable of being sold.

One further view is expressed by investment analysts. This argues that a balance sheet provides information about future cash flows. Consequently, any asset based on the capitalisation of part of those cash flows will be disregarded by the analyst. Inclusion of an intangible is, therefore, only justified on the basis that it has an opportunity cost— that is, a market value. On this basis, separability is meaningful where an asset has a valuation which is independent of what it is earning in the activity under analysis. Thus, valuation on a discounted cash flow or profit basis is only relevant if it is a surrogate of market value.

In reality, intangibles fall within a spectrum of 'separableness'. Brands are likely to fall somewhere in the middle of the range. In practice, the reasons put forward against capitalisation as an asset have more to do with reliability of measurement, and less to do with ability to dispose.

Reliability of measurement means that, for a given basis of measurement, different measurers of an item will arrive at amounts that are not materially different. It is affected by the amount of evidence available about two factors: the timing of the benefits inherent in the item in monetary terms; and the size of these benefits.

Expression of an item in monetary terms is more certain where the expected conversion to monetary form occurs in the near future, and thus the impact of the time value of money is small. Conversely, long-term items are inherently more uncertain in amount due to the greater impact of discounting. Uncertainty over the size of benefits relates to both the spread of possible levels of benefit and the chance of any particular level of benefit occurring. Variability of outcome may be reduced by one of three methods:

(a) use of a recent arm's length price
(b) use of a market-based price where a reasonably efficient market exists
(c) grouping together of similar items where the group as a whole can be measured.

Where none of these three apply, an expected value may be used to reflect all possible outcomes. Such assessments of probability may be based on past experience. The uncertainty inherent in the environment in which entities operate means that for many items there will not be complete reliability of measurement and the item will have to be estimated. The use of reasonable estimates is a normal part of the preparation of financial statements and, provided a reasonably reliable estimate can be made of the item, it should be recognised.

The source of brands

It is now appropriate to look at the source of brands in a company. This includes brands acquired separately, those acquired in a business combination, and those internally generated.

Brands acquired separately

Where a brand is acquired singly (that is, as an individual asset), and in an arm's-length transaction, the cost incurred provides clear evidence of reliability of measurement, and a basis for initially recording the brand.

Brands acquired through business combination

Where a brand is acquired as part of a business combination, two boundaries for measurement exist: on the basis that there is unlikely to be negative goodwill (unless there are special and explainable circumstances), the excess of fair value of total consideration over the fair value of tangible net assets provides a fixed figure for 'brands plus goodwill'. If goodwill is zero, the whole amount is the maximum fair value of brands; the minimum amount, clearly, will be zero.

Between these parameters, existing practice for the fair-value process involves the acquiring management determining the intended use of each brand, and thus its value to them. Evidence of published accounts indicates that acquirers generally have little difficulty with this process. In some cases, brands will have been separately negotiated within the purchase price. In other cases, a fair value is usually assessed by one of a number of valuation techniques based on the present value of future incremental cash flows or profits attributable to the brand.

Brands arising through internal generation

Where a brand arises apart from an acquisition, that is by internal generation, the upper and lower boundaries of cost provided in an acquisition situation do not exist, consequently the degree of uncertainty will be greater. To achieve a reliable valuation, either a supportable allocation of cash flows or earnings to the brand must be made, or market value comparisons must be available.

FIGURE 10.2: Routine depreciation of assets

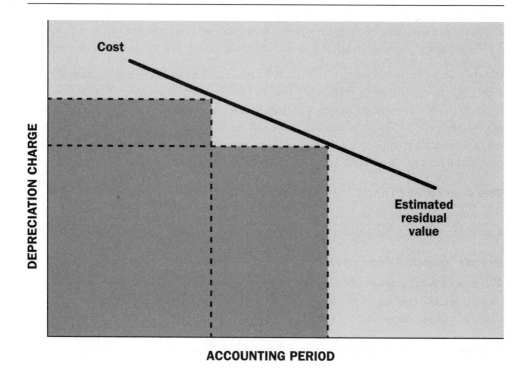

TO DEPRECIATE OR NOT TO DEPRECIATE

The Companies Act contains two requirements:

> *In the case of any fixed asset which has a limited useful economic life, the amount of ... its purchase price or production cost less that estimated residual value shall be reduced by provisions for depreciation calculated to write off that amount systematically over the period of the asset's useful economic life.*
>
> *Provisions for diminution in value shall be made in respect of any fixed asset which has diminished in value if the reduction in its value is expected to be permanent (whether its useful life is limited or not), and the amount to be included in respect of it shall be reduced accordingly.*

The first reference relates to assets that have their service potential consumed through use. The second relates to 'one-off' permanent falls in value due to some event. Routine depreciation is shown graphically in Figure 10.2.

94

Given that the measurement of cost is fixed, the total depreciable amount is dependent on two variables: estimated residual value and estimated useful economic life. Typically, companies will seek to justify that routine depreciation is not needed using one of two justifications:

— the asset (or class of assets) does not have a finite useful life, and thus falls outside the legal requirement for depreciation

— in view of the relative values of cost and estimated residual value, the maintenance of residual value through a programme of asset management, and a long estimated useful life, any depreciation would be immaterial.

Examples of the first justification are found in accounting policies for brands in a quote from Guinness:

> *Amortisation is not provided except where the end of the useful economic life of the acquired brand can be foreseen.*

While the second justification is more common in accounting policies for certain types of property, it favours the policy of Cadbury Schweppes:

> *No amortisation is charged as the annual results reflect significant expenditure in support of these brands and the values are reviewed annually with a view to write down if a permanent diminution arises.*

The willingness to write down for a permanent reduction in value provides a more realistic view of how a brand's value changes. In practice, a brand will be actively managed and supported such that its value will be demonstrably maintained, or even enhanced. It is possible, however, that at some point — perhaps following a period of gradual decline — this support will not be continued. The economic consequences of such a decision will be a rapid loss in value of the intangible, resulting in a consequent fall in its balance sheet carrying amount. This approach has the benefit of allowing a more realistic approach to be reflected in the accounts since it more adequately reflects management performance in relation to intangibles *(see Figure 10.3 on the following page)*.

A WORKABLE SOLUTION

Revised proposals, first issued by the ASB in 1995 as a Working Paper 'Goodwill and intangible assets', and progressed in Financial Reporting Exposure Draft (FRED) 12 "Goodwill and intangible assets", suggest a more workable solution to earlier theoretical models. These allow brands and goodwill to be carried on balance sheet unamortised, provided they are subject to an annual test of their carrying value. Loss of value results in an im-mediate charge to profits.

The ASB's logic flowed from recognition that intangibles fall in a spectrum: some have features that are closer to tangible assets, for example, patents and trade marks; others have

FIGURE 10.3: Changes in the balance sheet value of a brand, before and after the withdrawal of company support

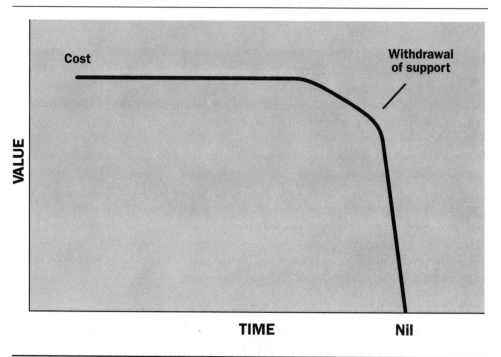

features that are closer to goodwill, for example, a corporate name. Brands fall somewhere in the middle of the spectrum. Where an intangible meets identification and measurement criteria, it may be recognised as a separate asset. This increase in intangibles on the balance sheet has a number of benefits:

- it increases management accountability
- encourages 'intangible husbandry'
- allows greater precision in the allocation of asset lives
- increases the relationship between the profit and loss account charge and economic loss
- reduces the problem of residual goodwill.

FRED 12 sets out the detailed identification and measurement criteria.

ACCOUNTING CONSEQUENCES

If brands are to be allowed on to the balance sheet, there are two consequences which follow. First, it is necessary to ensure that items falling just inside the net of separate assets, or just outside as goodwill, receive a similar treatment. Since the division of 'separable' and 'not separable' is based to an extent on matters of judgement, there is the potential for similar items to be pushed to the most advantageous side of the line.

If different accounting treatment was to be allowed for similar items, there is the risk of 'accounting arbitrage'. It is therefore understandable that ASB has insisted that goodwill be given the same balance sheet treatment as brands, and included on the balance sheet rather than eliminated against reserves.

The second consequence is that where goodwill and brands are assumed to have an indefinite life, there needs to be a reliable mechanism for checking the carrying value at each balance sheet date for permanent reductions in value. The ASB have produced a test known as the 'impairment test'. This is a discounted cash flow calculation based on the smallest income-generating groups for which cash flows can be identified. It is proposed that the full test be applied to all acquisitions at the balance sheet date following acquisition in order to identify over-payment. It would also be applied at each subsequent balance sheet date where an indefinite life, or a life over 20 years, is used.

CONCLUSION

The most obvious area of doubt is whether the impairment tests will be effective, or turn out to be a charter for creative accountants to avoid write-downs. FRED 12 contains three safeguards:

- the use of forecasts formally agreed by management
- a cap on the discount rate that can be used
- rolling verification of estimated cash flows with actual cash flows.

Will there be judgement? Will it be hard to audit? The answer to both questions is 'yes'. However, bad debts and long-term contracts are beset by similar problems. It may be that we need to revisit the impairment tests when we have gained experience and fine tune the detail. In the meantime, we await the signal to start.

11

ACCOUNTING FOR BRANDS: AN INDUSTRY PERSPECTIVE

JANE SIMMS, *MARKETING BUSINESS*

Brand management is now being practised enthusiastically in many companies, and brand valuation has been the catalyst. However, though initially adopted as a purely financial tool, the benefits of brand valuation are generally agreed to go much wider and deeper than a more meaningful balance sheet. This chapter looks at the benefits companies have reaped in terms of more sophisticated brand management, as a result of valuing their brands.

INTANGIBLE ASSETS

It is a truth universally acknowledged that modern business success increasingly depends on intangible assets – and in particular, on brands. More and more, the search for the holy grail of added value leads managers back to the intangible, but very real, assets of their businesses. In market-led businesses the first question is not 'how have unit costs performed?', but 'what has happened to market share?' or 'how have our brands performed?'. Because, for many businesses, brands are often their most important assets and the most important source of competitive advantage. For many business people the success or failure of their brands determines their own future.

Marketers have been preaching the gospel of brand value for long enough. The problem is that they have been unable to quantify it in terms that others in the business – not least the accountants – have been able to relate to, or understand. But, the marketers' (well-documented) lack of accountability and financial nous has been matched by the narrow accountants' view which has prevented them translating the words and enthusiasm and hunches of the marketers into hard financial numbers. The consequence of the gulf in understanding between marketing and finance has been not only a dearth of usable financial management information in the marketing and branding area, but a failure to exploit the potential to drive businesses forward by investing in brands.

The picture is changing, however. Brand management is now being practised enthusiastically – even expertly – in many companies, and brand valuation has been the catalyst. Initially adopted as a purely financial tool, the benefits of brand valuation are generally agreed to go much wider and deeper than a more meaningful balance sheet.

GRAND METROPOLITAN AND RHM

Grand Metropolitan (GrandMet) and RHM (formerly Rank Hovis McDougall and now part of Tomkins PLC) were the first companies to value their brands, in 1988. GrandMet placed a balance-sheet value on the cost of its acquired brands while RHM went one step further and placed a balance sheet value on all its brands, acquired and internally generated. The reason for this was that a clutch of acquisitions, whilst boosting the market capitalisations of both companies, had seriously depleted shareholders' funds because of the accounting requirement to write off the substantial goodwill element involved in the purchases. In 1987, for example, RHM spent some £340m on acquisitions. By the end of the year a market capitalisation of some £1.3bn was supported by shareholders' funds of only £250m. And, had GrandMet written off the goodwill involved in its 1988 purchase of American food business Pillsbury, it would have ended up with negative net assets.

Including brands on the balance sheet provided a clearer picture to investors of the financial strength of the company. More crucially for GrandMet and RHM at the time, their seriously depleted net tangible assets resulting from the goodwill written off on acquisitions, meant that their 'class 1' limit had fallen to such a low level that it meant they would have to go to shareholders for any acquisition or disposal, however small. In theory, had GrandMet wanted to buy a typewriter, it would have needed shareholder approval.

However, having been through the brand valuation exercise, and with a year's experience of having its brands on the balance sheet, RHM realised that it had done the exercise for the wrong reasons. Martin Moorhouse, at the time group chief accountant at RHM, says:

> There is no question that shareholders had a far clearer view of the value of our company. For example, profits may have risen by only 5 per cent, but the value of the brands increased by a far higher factor. And they could now see that. Conversely, had the brands not been valued, we could have lifted profits by 15 per cent – but at the cost of milking the brands, and the shareholders would not have known.
>
> But it was only when we were about to embark on a revaluation a year later that we realised just how much information about our brands we had produced and how much we could learn from that.

As he explains, the company spent 'a fortune' on TV advertising, for example. But though it was well aware of the quantity of spend, the quality – or value for money, or payback – was more difficult to assess. Many brands, as he says, can cope with a three- to six-month cut in advertising spend without suffering any apparent damage. Others cannot. It is difficult to claw back the lost advantage. The benefit of putting brands on the balance sheet forces management constantly to monitor what is happening to their brands:

> *They have to think about the long-term value, which makes them think very hard before taking short-term action which could be seriously damaging. Managers started to concentrate a lot harder on their brands, knowing that they couldn't afford to let anything slip.*

This process also helps the company appraise management performance, adds Moorhouse, who is now head of finance at Yorkshire Bank.

> *Their performance is inextricably linked with the performance of their brands – and brand valuation means there's no hiding from it. Brands are the most valuable assets a company has, and in many ways the most stable – if they are looked after. But they are also the most easy to damage. Putting them on the balance sheet forces management to think about their long-term value.*

Putting brands into the management balance sheet, and regularly revaluing them, enables the manager to see the impact of his decisions, yet remain prudent by writing off all his marketing expenditure with its uncertain return. But Moorhouse believes it is equally important that all brands should be valued on the balance sheet.

> *If one of the most important features of accounts is the ability to compare one business with another, why should those businesses that have grown their brands organically be penalised by showing lower asset values than those which have spent their money on acquiring their brand assets?*

Both routes arrive at the same goal, he argues, and the fact that expenditure in one case was one-off and in the other incurred over a number of years is no reason to treat them differently. Exactly the same methodology can be used, 'and indeed, in my experience', says Moorhouse,

> *It is often easier to value the home-grown brands simply because we know more about them. The assumption that the price you paid for an acquired brand is right, is wrong! Moreover, if a business builds its own factory rather than buying one, we accountants insist that it should be capitalised – why should brands be any different?*

Brand valuation certainly changed management thinking and practice at RHM, claims Moorhouse. Marketers became more accountable, owing to the new focus on the results of what they did. Moreover, employing a valuation method such as Interbrand's, which is unbiased and uses a consistent methodology, provides a bench mark. But, it also serves to impose a discipline and control on the thought processes of all managers – whether marketers, finance people or general management – and forces them down the same lines of thought. Moorhouse points out that these same managers will take other disciplines for granted, eg with regard to property assets, there is never any question that maintenance and insurance are kept up-to-date. With brands there are traditionally no such disciplines.

They also used brand valuation to manage and monitor brand strategy. As Moorhouse recalls:

> *For example, the exercise showed us quite clearly that the direction we were trying to take one particular brand in was wrong, and that we needed to re-track. We had been following this course for a number of years, but the exercise demonstrated that there was actually no financial return. In other situations, we used valuation to test whether developments were bearing fruit. For example, we rigorously tested our 'Hovis White' brand extension. It came out positively, but if it hadn't, we would have canned it.*

Valuing brands also raises their profile, both within the business as well as outside. Many people take the brand for granted, do not understand it, or pay lip-service to it, but brand-valuation techniques provide an insight into what makes the brand tick. Accountants get most excited – they can suddenly understand what the marketers have been banging on about all these years and why the company is investing in these things. As Moorhouse puts it, 'accountants are only counting the score. Brand valuation brings brands into the fold where they can be counted'.

The exercise also opens marketers' eyes, as Moorhouse admits, 'but in my experience, the better the marketer the less frightened they are of being measured, and the greater the opportunity to demonstrate what they have done'.

Since RHM and GrandMet grasped the nettle, a host of other companies has been persuaded of the benefits of brand valuation. It's not just the brand-driven FMCG companies which are doing it, but utilities, publishers, oil and pharmaceutical businesses, among others. Some do it primarily for financial reasons; others do not capitalise their brands at all and use valuation purely for internal purposes. And there is often a specific catalyst.

BP

Take BP, for example. In 1993 it sold a refinery and 500 petrol stations to Tosco in the USA. Tosco had no retail outlet, and therefore no brand presence, and asked if it could use the BP brand and pay a royalty in exchange. Here was an example of a third party putting a significant value on the brand, but the company had no existing internal structured way to assess that value for themselves.

BP was also engaging in more licensing arrangements and joint ventures, eg Eastern Europe and developing Asian countries. A western brand in these countries commands a premium – and BP required a structured methodology to assess and justify this premium. The exercise would also bring home to people developing new areas how they should try to extract value from the brand in terms of new business opportunities.

A third factor in BP's decision to invest more time and effort in brand valuation was to improve internal understanding and appreciation of the brand. Management are more inclined to pay attention to the maintenance and protection of an asset when presented with its true value. Marketers, frequently under pressure about the amount of money being spent on advertising, appreciated that brand valuation would represent a potentially powerful tool which they could use to justify investment in brand development.

BRITISH TELECOM

At British Telecom (BT), which is also in the process of valuing its master brand, competition and the imperative to be more customer-focused is the driving force. According to head of brand and corporate reputation, Simon Ingman:

> Telecom doesn't have marketing at its heart: historically it has been engineering-driven. Companies like Sears and British Airways are more intuitive marketing organisations. The competitive marketplace means that we have had to become more market-focused. Service sector branding is in its infancy and we have some catching up to do. Moving from a utility culture into a customer service organisation represents a major business transformation, and we are using the brand to help that transition.

As Ingman explains, in the increasingly sophisticated telecoms market-place, function is becoming less of a factor. Image – determined by brands and branding – is all important. He thinks it unlikely that the brand will ever be capitalised on the balance sheet, but deems valuation crucial to raising its saliency internally.

> People in this company have historically talked about network development, for instance, rather than brand, image, reputation. Putting a figure on the brand and its component constituents focuses people on it as being a tangible and important asset. You can then start to win their hearts and minds, and ensure that the brand is rooted at the heart of the company.

Better brand management is an inevitable consequence.

> Once people are aware of the importance of the brand, they are forced into examining the consequences of every business decision . . . For instance, how does making customers wait an extra five seconds before their call is answered impact on the brand reputation?

The exercise is already fostering a common currency in BT. Ingman goes on to explain:

> To date the debate about investment levels has been one-sided. The finance man says, 'This makes sound marketing and business sense and will earn us £18m in year one'. And the marketer's response is necessarily subjective. All we can say is, 'it would enhance or dent our reputation'. We have to be able to talk the same language as the finance men and demonstrate the real business contribution proactive brand management and development can make.

MERCK SHARPE & DOHME

Over at Merck Sharpe & Dohme, the UK division of the US pharmaceutical multinational (Merck & Co. Inc.), it was new competition that spurred the company to pay even more attention to valuing its brands two years ago. Competitors launched three new products that were very similar, in terms of efficacy and safety, to Merck's own.

The brands are not capitalised at either a local or central level, but brand valuation has been done informally within marketing – and communicated externally – for some time. Graham Lumsden, marketing director, ascribes MSD's brands' superior performance over its competitors over the past two years to the equity its brands command among farmers and veterinary surgeons as a result of valuation exercises. 'The best of these competitor products only has 6 per cent market share two years on, compared with our 52 per cent', he says. While no monetary value is yet placed on brands, Lumsden believes it is inevitable. It will be the *raison d'être* for advertising and promotional spend. He goes on to say:

> We're already having to be more accountable. Finance is much more rigorous now, and asks us more difficult questions. Which means we have to sit down and do calculations, and as such are making more accurate decisions.

Indeed, he believes marketing will take the initiative over finance when it comes to valuing brands formally.

> If other companies start to take market share from us, our promotional budgets will start to come under more pressure, and we will be forced to demonstrate that our marketing budgets are working. It is in our interests to pre-empt that.

IDV

Chris Banks, director, international marketing at IDV, explains that his company started systematically valuing its brands back in 1993, for brand equity management rather than balance sheet purposes. But while it was adopted primarily to allow the corporate centre to see how its brands were performing, Banks says it soon became clear that marketing benefited equally from the exercise. 'Brand valuation has proved to be an important tool for us to measure trends as opposed to absolute numbers', he says. 'It allows us to determine whether we are building or eroding equity.'

IDV examined three main areas:

- shareholder value drivers (is there evidence of value creation?)
- brand equity measures (market share, market position, relative share price, etc.)
- the customer franchise.

Marketing practice has changed as a consequence, says Banks.

> *We focus on things that matter. We have a clearer and more simple assessment of our brand health and what we need to do to build on it. It helps us understand the balance between shareholder value, brand equity and profit. Not only can we track progress in all three, we can also track a number of measures and monitor trends within them. That allows us to take corrective action or switch the emphasis.*

The IDV company benefits from having as the group chairman George Bull, whose motto is 'brands, brands, brands', a philosophy where building brand equity in world-class brands is one of the principal ways of maximising shareholder value, and an approach where brand equity is a key measure of business performance. But brand valuation has helped refine the brand-building process and help balance short- and long-term interests. Says Banks:

> *We have to measure ourselves not solely on this year's profits, but on whether our brands are in good shape, or not, for the future. We do that by assessing them in a rigorous and consistent and organised way.*

EDUCATION FOR MANAGEMENT

Educating senior managers emerges as a common theme among companies valuing their brands. For example, Phil Taylor, head of marketing information at Allied-Domecq Spirits and Wine, explains that one of the main benefits from valuing his company's brands is 'a greater understanding of brands in a broader context than a single monetary value that doesn't reflect their health'.

Allied embarked on the process five years ago, ostensibly as a marketing exercise. Taylor explains:

> *This exercise has more intrinsic value to the business than purely financial: it represents a reorientation of management focus. It makes you realise that only a small part of the business is fundamentally important to you, and that you shouldn't waste your time fiddling around on the edges. You have to be quite brutal or you dissipate the focus.*

Everyone in the company, from the top down, is now more focused on the brands that drive the business. And while marketing and finance still tend to revert to their base instincts 'when push comes to shove', as Taylor puts it, there is now a healthier balance between cost control and marketing investment.

Andrew Allner, until recently director of financial planning and control at Guinness, and now group finance director at Amersham International, agrees that brand valuation provides a further tool to look at the performance and encourage discussion of trends and value creation through building brands.

Externally, putting brands on the balance sheet demonstrates the very considerable value in premium brands and the focus on investment behind these brands.

Of course, accounting requirements result in Guinness only valuing acquired brands at cost in its balance sheet, resulting in an incomplete picture – and a picture that becomes less useful with the passage of time.

At Cadbury Schweppes, director of financial policy, Peter Cartmel, acknowledges that finance people are excited about brand valuation.

> *In the past brands formed part of this amorphous 'goodwill' that was written off. It might have bothered us temporarily because of the size of the numbers that were disappearing, but then we forgot about it. They can now see that brands represent up to 90 per cent of the value of some of our businesses. That doesn't half focus the mind.*

At SmithKline Beecham, corporate controller Andrew Bonfield says a major benefit of brand valuation is to focus marketers on the bottom line rather than just the top line in brand building. It is an ambition with which Cadbury's brand planning manager, David Lawrence, empathises. He says:

> *Over recent years we have increasingly been driven by short-term volume, and have done more trade promotion than advertising. We are also subject to short-term sales blips. But, we need to ensure we get the right balance between above- and below-the-line and between long- and short-term investment. Putting a value on brands teaches us to assess brand strength in the longer term and build a long-term brand stature. The fact that we are currently so volume-driven means that we are neglecting lots of brand-building activity.*

Despite such testimonies to the benefits of brand valuation, there remain those who stubbornly maintain that brand valuation is largely subjective. Yorkshire Bank's Martin Moorhouse disagrees. 'It is actually significantly less subjective than pension valuation or valuing an oil rig or a gas field – or even property, where we have seen unprecedented fluctuations', he points out.

He also takes issue with those who acknowledge that there might be management benefits in brand valuation but argue such insights should be retained as management information and not extended to financial accounting and hence to the published balance sheet. Moorhouse counters that management accounting systems that produce different results from financial accounting systems are worse than dangerous. 'What is the point of telling the chairman that he has made a management accounting profit when he has to explain a loss to the shareholders?' asks Moorhouse.

> *Many management decisions are based on the impact of various strategies on the financial accounts rather than management figures because it is the financial accounts that communicate performance to the marketplace. Thus if we are to put brand accounting into our management systems and accounts, we must follow this through to the financial accounts.*

But the stewardship function, he says, is equally critical.

> *Putting brands on the balance sheet forces a company to look to their value as well as to profits. It serves as a reminder to management of the value of the assets for which they are responsible.*

CONCLUSION

Moorhouse believes that every country in the world should value brands on their balance sheets. 'It would show up some real comparisons between companies, and would, in particular, show up weak management conducting short-term practices to hide long-term failings', he claims.

While, as he points out, 'financial and balance sheet accounting in Europe have hardly led world practice', he perceives beneath the surface 'real movement on the management side, and the balance sheet will follow. Management practice will determine accounting practice rather than vice versa', he predicts. 'And, at the end of the day I suggest that those companies that are prepared to recognise brands on the balance sheet will be better and stronger for it.'

12

MERGERS AND ACQUISITIONS

EDWARD BUCHAN AND NICHOLAS DAVIES,
CLOSE BROTHERS GROUP LTD
KAREN HACK, INTERBRAND UK

Brands play an important role in take overs and mergers. But the lack of information about brand valuation means that the market could be undervaluing or overvaluing branded businesses. This chapter examines the part brands have played in a number of high profile acquisitions.

It could be stated that merger and acquisition behaviour run in parallel with the cyclical patterns of the economy. When the market is booming, directors begin to look around for possible companies that they could acquire to enlarge their market share, or give them a new market in which to operate. The most active time for corporate finance institutions comes when there is a divergence in the performance of companies in the market, ie companies who are out-performing in the market are keen to acquire companies who are under-performing, on the assumption that there are 'easy' profits to be obtained.

But how do brands fit into this activity? It would be unrealistic to state that before brand valuation, brands were not taken into consideration in the acquisition process. Ever since Heinz stamped their name on Heinz tomato ketchup brands have often played an important role in acquisition behaviour. It is probably safe to say, however, that prior to the increase in understanding of the value of brands, the price of the acquisition would have been set, in the knowledge that a brand was included in the purchase. It was not done by taking the sum of all the net assets, ie including a valuation of the intangibles.

Even today there are probably many acquisitions of brands which are completed without a detailed calculation of the value of brands owned by the acquiree. It is probable, however, that a strategic review of these brands acquired and the value that they might add to the new enlarged company, will be made.

Acquisitions take place through a desire to become global or to exploit undervalued competitors. From a branding perspective, due to the lack of information about brand valuation, the market could be undervaluing and overvaluing branded businesses. This leaves acquirers to make their own assessments as to how the company should be valued.

SMITHKLINE BEECHAM

The pharmaceuticals sector has experienced a variety of brand-related mergers and acquisitions activity in recent years, ranging from deals at the 'micro-level' all the way up to deals at the 'macro-level'. At the micro-level many companies sold off individual brands, while at the opposite end of the size spectrum, the Glaxo-Wellcome and Rhône Poulenc-Fisons deals led to the consolidation of already substantial portfolios of drugs, resulting in wider therapeutic coverage within the new pharmaceutical company. These deals highlighted a number of key issues.

One of the reasons for buying an individual brand is simply to gain market share. This, for example, is what occurred in Colgate-Palmolive's acquisition of American Home Product's Kolynos toothpaste brand for £665.8m in January 1995. Following the deal, Colgate's share of the world toothpaste market rose from 40 per cent to around 50 per cent.

An alternative divestment strategy has also gained prominence in recent years and has risen as a result of the brand-valuation debate. Whereas in the past, companies may have been content simply to let peripheral brands just wither and die, now they seem much more attuned to the fact that non-core brands may have a realisable market value. The reason for this is that these brands, potentially, can be rejuvenated by others who are prepared to manage the brand in a more effective manner, devoting the necessary marketing resources and time. For example, in July 1995 Procter & Gamble sold the rights to the Blue Stratos male toiletries range for £0.6m – even though sales of the Blue Stratos range had fallen from £5m to £1m since 1990.

Another reason for the sale of individual brands has been seen when acquirers and those off-loading have diametrically opposed reasons for their actions. While buyers have usually wanted to improve their brand portfolio and market share, some sellers have had a distinctly defensive motive. There have been attempts to focus on core businesses in an attempt to become global rather than merely international companies as the trend towards globalisation accelerates. SmithKline Beecham (SB) has been an active exponent of this, having disposed of its Quickies and Fresh moist wipes brands, Shloer and PLJ drinks brands, Brylcreem and Badedas toiletry brands, Silvikrin, Bristow and Vosene hair care brands and its Ralgex and Diocalm brands.

One of the more sizeable acquisitions that highlighted the importance of brands in this sector was the successful SB bid for Sterling Winthrop, a world-wide over-the-counter (OTC) medicine manufacturer, for £1.9bn in November 1994. Sterling Health, the consumer health business of Sterling Winthrop, included such brands as Panadol, Solpadeine, Andrews, Bayer Aspirin, Midol Analgesics and Phillips' Milk of Magnesia.

SmithKline Beecham believed that a key strategic rationale for the acquisition lay in the fact that the products would complement its already extensive portfolio of consumer healthcare brands. It stated in its information document that:

> *Sterling Health offered a very high degree of fit ... in terms of geography, brands and categories.*

And went on to claim that:

> *The combination creates a market presence in over 100 countries ... with the*
> *opportunity to develop further strong brand names and formulations from*
> *both companies in more markets and across a broader range of categories.*

Perhaps an indication of SB's growing awareness of the importance of recognising brands can be seen in the fact that it had changed its accounting practice to capitalise the value of acquired brands in the months just prior to the deal. The brands included in the intangible assets at the date of acquisition were £776m and SB's policy is not to amortise them but to review their value annually.

Analysing the rationale for this deal it does seem that SmithKline believed that in order to achieve critical mass in the OTC market it was virtually necessary to acquire an OTC business with established brands in those new markets that it wished to enter. On the back of the acquired brands the acquisition leveraged SB as a key player into the markets of Europe, Latin America, Australia, New Zealand and the rest of the Pacific Rim (excluding Japan). Without this it may not have been a challenge in these markets for many years, if at all.

GRAND METROPOLITAN

Since January 1985 GrandMet has recorded all brands that it has acquired on its balance sheet. In the 1995 accounts it carried around £3.8bn of intangible brand values, having increased this figure during the year by £1.06bn following its acquisition of Pet Inc. in the USA. The announcement of this deal led to a fall in GrandMet's share price of 6.6 per cent, as the market became worried about the net effect on the balance sheet.

GrandMet has been metamorphosed from a 1960s property company which owned a few brands, into a focused international brand business that, today, has a portfolio of household names such as Green Giant, Häagen-Dazs, Burger King, Smirnoff, Old El Paso, Progresso, Baileys and Malibu. On 9 January, 1995 its US subsidiary, Pillsbury, entered into a merger agreement to acquire Pet Inc. for £1.7bn, representing a 19.8 historic-earnings multiple. The deal was completed on 12 May 1995.

The strategic decision to buy Pet, the leading US makers of Mexican food, seemed sound and GrandMet could afford the price tag without any change to its long- and short-term credit ratings. GrandMet set out the rationale for the deal and the importance it placed on acquiring it in the information document sent to its shareholders.

> *The acquisition of Pet is a further step in GrandMet's strategy of*
> *developing its portfolio of leading food and drinks brands with potential*
> *for significant growth. It is a strategic addition to Pillsbury's portfolio of*
> *major US food brands and confirms GrandMet's commitment to grow its*
> *food business. By acquiring Pet, Pillsbury will further consolidate its*
> *position as a leading branded food company in the US.*

However, GrandMet was not content to purchase a portfolio of brands and then just apply the same marketing techniques that Pet had been using. Instead, it intended to try and extract greater value from the brands by managing them in a more effective manner. For example, GrandMet's information document stated that:

> *Pet's leading brands in high growth markets are well suited to benefit from Pillsbury's skills in operations, marketing and overall management.*
>
> *'Pet's largest brand, Old El Paso, will continue to be developed in the $1bn Mexican-food category in the USA, which has grown at a compound rate of 11 per cent per annum over the past five years. Old El Paso leads the category with the number-one market share and over 100 different products. Pillsbury will develop the brand, both in the USA and internationally, expand into new distribution channels, add new products, increase marketing spend and improve its effectiveness.'*

The aggregate of Pet Inc.'s net tangible and intangible assets, even including a brand valuation of £1bn by GrandMet, amounted to £1.3bn, still well below the £1.7bn price paid. What then did the goodwill element of £450m represent, since fair value for the acquired brands was already incorporated? The answer to this may lie partly, in the above paragraph, which shows the outline of a strategy to be undertaken for maximising brand value and also, by implication, shareholder value. If GrandMet believed it could increase brand value by managing Pet Inc.'s brands in a more effective manner then it may be able to justify part of the premium above £1.3bn. However, this is unlikely to tell the whole story.

Possible reasons for payment of a premium to net tangible and intangible assets include:

– a control premium
– synergistic benefits
– cost savings in bringing businesses together
– miscalculation leading to overpayment.

In GrandMet's evaluation of the Pet acquisition it believed that:

> *The combination of Pet and Pillsbury will allow significant cost reductions to facilitate increased investment behind Pet's brands.*

GrandMet's accounting policy of recording as fixed intangible assets significant acquired brands, the value of which is not expected to diminish in the foreseeable future, has the effect of dramatically altering any gearing calculations. Before the Pet deal, net gearing was 60 per cent. But, after stripping out £2.8bn of intangible brand values from previous acquisitions this figure jumped to 268 per cent. Following the deal GrandMet had £3.5bn of shareholders' equity, but reflected in this was £3.8bn of brand values.

GRANADA

More recently, Granada Group launched a hostile £3.3bn bid for Forte, the hotels and catering chain, which was predicated on the reassessment of the company's brands and management. Granada claimed, in its reasons for the offer, that the Forte brands were under-exploited, and that it could extract greater value from them, thereby implying it could generate an increase in shareholder value.

In its defence documents Forte claimed that it had reshaped its operations:

> ... *into distinct, brand-focused businesses ... [and that] Forte's strategy has been to concentrate its hotel portfolio on five clearly defined brands ... [and] its restaurant business on three core brands.*

It also stated that it had valuable intangible assets, namely 'brands, trade marks and other intangibles owned by the company', implying that the Granada bid seriously under-valued the worth of the whole Forte business.

Granada eventually won the day after an acrimonious battle with an improved offer of £3.8bn, promising to revamp Forte's middle and budget-market hotels under the 'Posthouse' and 'Travelodge' names. The restaurant brands, which included Happy Eater and Little Chef, would be rejuvenated.

It is important to note that Forte had already undertaken a thorough brand review, implying that it was already aware that it needed to alter the emphasis of some of its businesses. Unfortunately for Forte, it did not grasp the changing nature of its industry in time and before it had time to implement any of the proposals coming out of its brand review, Granada pre-empted the outcome. The deal highlighted the increasing importance in the hotel and restaurant business of branding and successful marketing.

BAT INDUSTRIES

An interesting example of problems that can be encountered when acquiring brands occurred when BAT bid for American Tobacco; a deal was eventually completed in December 1994 for £673.3m. BAT Industries is an extremely acquisitive group and has been involved in numerous deals over the years. In this particular case, the acquisition was subject to an agreement with the Federal Trade Commission (FTC) in the USA.

The deal arose on the back of a seemingly sustained attack on US cigarette sales, ranging from factors such as the dwindling proportion of adults who smoke, to the threat of large increases in cigarette taxes. This led to a fall in the market value of US cigarette companies, making them more attractive to acquirers. Since BAT already owned Brown and Williamson it stood to benefit, through the acquisition from cost savings that would result by combining the two companies' manufacturing and distribution facilities. These benefits were separate from the strategic benefits cited by BAT in relation to the strengthening of its presence in the key US market where American was the fifth largest US tobacco company. BAT would also gain sole world-wide rights to Lucky Strike and Pall Mall, two international brands that were extremely important to them. Other names acquired were Carlton and Tareyton in the premium segment, with Misty, Montclair,

Private Stock and other private-label brands in the lower-price segment. The BAT also gained the rights to Silk Cut outside Europe.

The FTC was particularly concerned about anti-trust issues since BAT would have a very strong portfolio of established brands in the domestic US market with a market share of 18 per cent, up from 11 per cent. It suggested that it would remove a player from a market that was already highly concentrated, increasing the probability of collusion and higher prices. A settlement was eventually reached and in its 1994 accounts BAT stated that:

> Under the FTC agreement the Group will retain many of the key American Tobacco brands. However, the group is required to sell certain of ATCo's US value brands ... as well as certain ATCo full revenue brands.

The crux of this was that BAT had to divest Montclair, a value-for-money brand, together with a certain number of their minor brands, as well as offering Tareyton, a full-revenue brand, to the acquirer. These sales only applied in the USA and BAT was able to retain its portfolio of brands in the international market-place. It is important to note that in the majority of cases the acquisition of a strong brand portfolio will invariably mean the simultaneous purchase of market share and this is precisely the reason why strong brands are so attractive to purchasers. However, when such acquired brands are integrated into an already substantial brand portfolio, the resultant market share may often exceed permitted levels as determined by a country's anti-trust legislation.

LLOYDS BANK, TSB, CHELTENHAM & GLOUCESTER

In July 1995, Lloyds Bank acquired the Cheltenham & Gloucester (C&G) Building Society. Shortly afterwards in October 1995 it made a further acquisition, the Trustee Savings Bank (TSB).

The financial services industry is an area which, increasingly, is becoming brand-aware. This is evidenced by the rising levels of advertising and sponsorship spent on financial-corporate brands. However, there are still many financial-services companies that would not consider themselves to be branded. One major high-street bank which seems to have realised the value of brands in financial services, and identified areas where its brand is either not large enough nor appropriate for the product, is Lloyds Bank plc.

In 1995 Lloyds energetically entered the house mortgage market by gaining control of C&G and by merging with TSB, which at the time was the ninth largest high-street bank in the UK.

The takeover of C&G was completed at the end of July 1995, when all C&G qualifying account holders received a pay out, as the mutual society became a subsidiary of Lloyds Bank plc. The acquisition was finally struck at £1.8bn which was £0.7bn above the value of the net assets of the business at December 1994. The deal made Lloyds Bank group the third largest bank in the UK with assets of £97bn.

Although the acquisition increased the size of the group it is unlikely that this was the sole reason for making the purchase. The UK's mortgages market is dominated by building societies who have a long history of taking savings at competitive rates to the banks, to provide mortgages. This, however, is beginning to change as building societies are taking advantage of the change in the law, allowing them to convert to banks. They are also prime take-over targets, with established and highly reputable brand names, good locations in high streets and strong balance sheets.

The main high-street banks, over the past five years or so have increased the range of financial products they offer in order to differentiate themselves, gain market share, and offset lower margins from fierce competition. It seems that Lloyds Bank had identified two areas where it felt it could not influence the market, either because the brand did not portray the right message, or it would take too long to build Lloyds into that position.

The C&G plc, as it is now, offers customers C&G-branded mortgage or savings products, and acts as a separate business unit within the enlarged Lloyds Bank group. We can assume that Lloyds decided to maintain the C&G brand to capitalise on its mortgage expertise and brand image. The mortgage market has been very slow throughout the first half of the 1990s and, indeed, into 1996. The deal, however, pushed Lloyds up to fourth in the list of home-loan providers in the UK and made it well positioned to take advantage of an uplift in the market.

Recently, the image of retail banks has been tarnished with tales of enforced bankruptcy on small businesses and eviction of home owners. Using a mortgage brand without these blemishes should help the Lloyds Bank group maintain, or even increase, its share of the market.

Within the same year, Lloyds Bank group also acquired TSB to form Britain's largest retail-banking franchise, having a client base of 14m with £14bn of assets. Analysts at the time of the merger were positive and estimated that this could make Lloyds TSB into Britain's most profitable and efficient bank.

This trend of merging retail banks can be seen across the globe, and is often driven by the opportunity for cost-cutting that can be achieved. Lloyds and TSB have estimated that cost savings will reach £350m a year by 1999. Becoming more economical, however, does not seem to be the primary reason for the merger. The group intends to keep the two brands active, utilising the strengths of both in their existing markets.

There is a commitment to keep the TSB name alive in Scotland, where it has a strong image and network advantage over Lloyds. In England, however, the intention seems to be that Lloyds and TSB branches will co-exist in different regions and for different customers, depending on their relative strength. Keeping the two brands will allow the Lloyds TSB group to offer similar services to different segments of the market.

More and more UK financial-service providers seem to be catching the merger and acquisition fever, with the intention of acquiring established brands in either their own markets or new financial areas. It is likely that cost saving is important to these transactions, but more importantly what value the brand gives.

The question raised, however, is whether using three brands will fit in the long-term strategy for the Lloyds TSB group. Maintaining brands with different price propositions in a market, provided customers are aware that they are run by the same management, may lead to problems and difficulties in the long term.

CONCLUSION

The conclusions from all these transactions are in line with the theory noted in the introduction to this paper, that mergers and acquisitions are generally for globalisation or under-valuation in the market. For national companies, globalisation may mean increasing market share generally and dominance in the local market. Under-valuation, however, may mean identifying cost savings that two companies together may achieve.

The acquisition of brands may also allow a company to acquire a brand which it would either be too risky, too timely, or even too costly, to development internally. Mergers, on the other hand, provide businesses with an opportunity to learn new skills from competitors, or an entirely new industry.

Gradually, as a result of the growing importance and use of brand valuation, and brands being part of acquisitions and mergers, stock markets have been forced to recognise brands as identifiable, separable, valuable assets of companies. Figure 12.1 below demonstrates, using a couple of examples, the difference between the value the market places on a company, ie the market capitalisation, and balance sheet net assets.

FIGURE 12.1: True source of corporate value

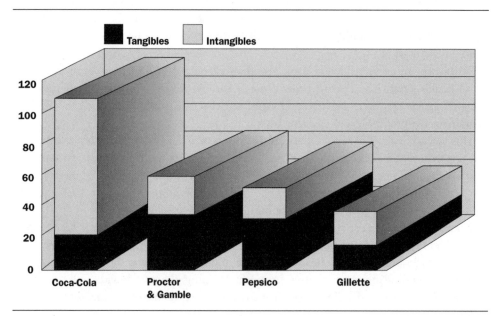

The difference could then represent a rough market estimate of 'intangible' assets, although this would be subject to external factors, such as exchange-rate movements and Government tax policies. The actual proportion of 'intangible' balance which relates to brands will not be known for certain until brands are accounted for in the financial statements of all companies where relevant.

TRADE MARK LICENSING AND
THE ROLE OF BRAND VALUATION

CAROLINE DAVIES, ICI

KYLIE ADCOCK, INTERBRAND UK

*The managerial and fiscal implications of trade mark licensing
are profound, and brand valuation has a key role to play in
adding method and objectivity to an area which has been
plagued by doubt and misunderstanding. This chapter explains
how the creation of structures for brand licensing leads to
better management of brands and trade marks.*

THE COMMERCIAL REALITY OF BRAND VALUE

Regardless of the accountancy profession's debate over balance sheets, the fact remains that the amount being paid to acquire companies with branded goods such as Rowntree Mackintosh, Pillsbury, Bond Brewing and Nabisco, has focused attention on the value of brands and their importance in the net worth of businesses.

Nevertheless, brands do not comprise a significant element of business value and this is now recognised by analysts, shareholders, company boards, bankers and key regulatory authorities (not least the London Stock Exchange and the Monopolies and Mergers Commission). What is more, for many businesses, the brand element is often more important than the tangible assets that, traditionally, have been regarded as the core value of a company. A brief example illustrates this.

The value of the Coca-Cola Corporation, as expressed by its share price in 1996, is approximately $115bn. (This is calculated by multiplying the price per share, which in July 1996 was $46.00, by the number of outstanding shares; such a calculation is usually referred to as the market capitalisation of the company.) A glance at the bottom line of the most recent balance sheet of the Coca-Cola Corporation on 31 December 1995 shows that, in the view of the company's auditors, the Corporation's net book value (the value of its assets *minus* the value of its liabilities) is only $15bn. The market thus believes that there is $100bn of value in the corporation over and above the purely tangible assets which appear on its balance sheet. The main asset of the company that does not appear is its portfolio of trade mark registrations in particular the world-wide rights to the names Coca-Cola and Coke. It is evident that the vast majority of this hidden value can be accounted for by trade marks.

LICENSING OF INTELLECTUAL PROPERTY

One field in which brand valuation and the concept of a brand's value is beginning to have an impact, is the area of trade mark licensing. In recent years there has been a marked increase in the attention given to the licensing of trade marks as well as of other intellectual property such as copyrights, patents and designs.

The notion of a licence is simple: the owner of a piece of property allows another party to make use of that property and in return can expect to receive some form of compensation. The party (individual or company) issuing the licence is called the licenser; the party receiving the licence is called the licensee. Licences need to define a number of elements especially the following:

– the piece of property being licensed, eg the right to use the trade mark Gucci
– the entity to whom the property is being licensed, eg John Smith and Sons Pty Ltd
– the geographic extent of the licence, eg only in Australia
– the commercial extent of the licence, eg only for the manufacture and distribution of polystyrene beer-can holders
– the duration, eg for a period of five years from the date of the licence.

Because of the desire by the owner of the property to safeguard what is being licensed and ensure that the licensee does not undermine its value, licences usually include strict provisions covering quality control for both production and marketing, reporting of performance, collaboration with the licenser and other licensees, and conditions for termination.

Licences will also define in one or more of a variety of ways the manner of calculation and remitting compensation. Figure 13.1 gives some examples.

As can be seen, sometimes the 'royalty' is assessed as a percentage of sales, sometimes as a percentage of gross profit or net profit, sometimes as an amount per litre or per unit or per kilo and sometimes as a fixed amount. Often maximum and minimum amounts are stipulated and, also, the rate may decrease or increase with volume, on a sliding scale.

It is also important to recognise that the amount of a pure royalty may be reduced or eliminated by the use of other means of gaining compensation for the use of the brand: a management fee, an extra contribution to advertising and promotional expenses, the rent on a retail site or the price of a raw material that the licensee is obliged to purchase. For example, agreements between Coca-Cola Corporation and its third-party bottlers or between Body Shop International and its franchisees, do not usually require an explicit payment for the use of the Coke or Body Shop brands. Instead, the licensee will be required to purchase the essential sticky brown concentrate for making a Coke-branded cola, or the finished products for the sale in a Body Shop-branded outlet and will have to buy these at a given price and in certain minimum quantities.

FIGURE 13.1: Examples of royalty charges

5% of the value of all remittances received ('net sales') in relation to products carrying the licensed properties.

5% of the value of all remittances received ('net sales') in relation to products carrying the licensed properties or a minimum of $100,000 pa, whichever is the lower.

20% of the value of the gross contribution received in relation to products carrying the licensed properties, defined as net sales – cost of goods – marketing expenditure.

50% of the value of audited earnings before interest and tax received in relation to products carrying the licensed properties.

50% of the value of audited earnings before interest and tax received in relation to products carrying the licensed properties or $1m whichever is the higher.

$500,000 pa, either in the form of cash or in the form of advertising expenditure, of a manner and type to be agreed with the licenser.

$10 for every gross of product sold.

$15 per hectolitre for the first 10,000 hectolitres of branded product sold; $10 per hectolitre for every hectolitre thereafter.

$2m of branded products to be bought from the licenser every year in equal amounts per quarter at the licenser's annual published price list.

But though the payment for these products may appear to be for a tangible transfer, it is clear that the amount that can be demanded is influenced, as much by the trade mark's rights that go with the product, as by the qualities of the product themselves. It is only by buying these ingredients or these products that the licensee can make use of the brand and so the charge for the use of the brand is hidden within the charge for buying the tangible elements.

TRADE MARK LICENSING

The licensing of technological know-how and patents has been long-established and it is accepted that it is usual for significant royalties to be paid by licensees for the use of such assets. Moreover, the agreements governing such licences are often complex and recognise that the maintenance of the value of the intangible asset is an important task and is the duty of both the licenser and the licensee.

Until recently, however, trade mark licences were not treated as seriously and indeed sometimes were just added in as the icing on the cake of patent/technology licences. For example, when the Japan Victor Company (JVC) was licensing its home-video recorder technology to other Japanese and American companies in the 1970s, they included in the licence (but without charge) the right to use the trade mark VHS. This was indeed a shrewd move since it meant that, as JVC's format for video technology became established as the norm (over that of Philips or Sony), their trade mark VHS became the standard descriptor for the format. In this case, JVC's strategy enabled them to create value in their trade mark as well as in their patented technology. But in many other cases, allowing a patent licensee to use a trade mark as well amounts to giving it away.

The increasing awareness of the value of brands has prompted their owners to wake up to the notion that, although intangible, such properties *do* have significant value and their licensing cannot be regarded as a mere formality. One of the first effects of this is that licence agreements with third parties now pay much more attention to the fact that the property being licensed is valuable. Higher royalty rates are being demanded (and justified) and stricter conditions to ensure that proper use and maintenance of trade marks – both in legal terms and in marketing terms – are put in place.

For example, it has long been established in the area of luxury goods that the licenser (eg Dunhill) has the right to set very strict rules about the design, manufacture and distribution of its licensed goods and may even stipulate specific suppliers of key raw materials. Regular audits, site inspections and blind trials are all part of this approach. It is also now common to find licensees of brands in which 'quality' is less of an issue being subjected to the same strict quality inspections.

While the duty of licensees is not only becoming more onerous, their contribution to, and participation in, the brand is seen as increasing. For example, licensees will often participate with the brand's owner in the development of global advertising campaigns and the design of a visual identity programme. In some organisations – for example, the Body Shop, little distinction is made between the operations that are wholly owned and those that are franchised or licensed. It is only in this way that the integrity, and thus the value of a brand can be safeguarded.

The importance of licensing

Licensing of trade marks is playing a more important role in the activities of multinational companies who own them and actively promote their products and services using them. There are several factors contributing to the increased importance of licensing trade marks.

Global marketing

Companies are now competing in an increasingly global marketing system where the use of a recognised and famous trade mark is invaluable. With the increase in international travel, the flow of advertising literature in magazines and other publications world-wide, and the increase in use of the Internet as an advertising medium, the reputation of a product and its trade mark is not confined to select areas of the world.

Competition

Finance departments now realise that a well-known brand gives them a competitive edge over other companies in the market-place who are selling similar products of similar quality.

New product development

Where a company introduces a new product with new technology to the market-place under a new trade mark and actively promotes the trade mark to establish it in the public mind, once the trade mark becomes well known its owner retains a long-term commercial advantage over competitor companies who eventually introduce similar products into that market-place.

INTERNAL LICENSING

The growth in the awareness and importance of licensing to third parties has made more and more companies aware of the role that internal licensing might play. An internal licence is one in which the licensee is a subsidiary or associate company of the licenser. In such a situation – where the interest in and control of the two parties is common – it might be thought that a trade mark licence was redundant. After all, a wholly-owned subsidiary of Texaco Inc. for example, not only will probably be using the Texaco trade mark, but might well expect to have the *right* to use it. It should not be forgotten, however, that a trade mark, in common with other forms of property, has a defined owner, and within a group of companies the user may not always be the owner. Thus, the trade mark Texaco, is owned in most countries by Texaco Inc., but is used in the UK by Texaco Ltd. Though the UK company is a wholly-owned subsidiary of the American corporation it is a separate legal entity and its use of the mark can only be with the permission (explicit or implicit) of the trade mark owner.

In many cases, the external licensing of trade marks (to third parties) is what has made companies more aware of the need for internal licences. For example, for many years Castlemaine Perkins Pty Limited (an Australian brewer) has licensed its main brand Castlemaine XXXX to a UK brewer (first Allied Breweries Ltd, now Carlsberg Tetley Ltd) who brews and distributes XXXX-branded lager in the UK market. Since its amalgamation into the Lion Nathan group of breweries, Castlemaine Perkins has also seen its brand being brewed by associate companies within the group (eg The Swan Brewery Company Pty Ltd in Western Australia). Since both breweries are wholly owned by the same parent company, Lion Nathan Ltd, a licence between the two breweries might seem excessive, but in fact one has been put in place to formalise the relationship between the two and to ensure that the rights and duties of both trade mark owner and licensee are well understood.

Ironically, the licensing in the UK of XXXX is a good example of internal licensing. Carlsberg Tetley is (at the point of writing) a 50:50 joint venture between Allied Domecq of the UK and Carlsberg of Denmark. It brews a number of brands but it owns none of them. Either (as with XXXX) they are licensed from a third party, or (as with Tetley) they are licensed from the UK partner company, or (as with Carlsberg) they are licensed from the Danish partner company. Though one of the top five brewers in the UK, in a market which is dominated by strong well-established brands, Carlsberg Tetley is in the unique position of not owning any brands itself!

Centralising trade marks

These internal licences – sometimes developed *ad hoc* between associated companies within the same group – are now being made more systematised by the use of central trade mark holding companies. In such a situation, trade mark registrations are transferred from the operating companies that created or acquired them to the parent company itself or to a legal entity that reports directly to the parent and has been given charge of owning the trade marks.

Nestlé is one of the famous examples of this policy of owning most intellectual property centrally (not only trade marks but also patents and copyrights), licensing the right to use them back to subsidiaries and then charging subsidiaries for their use. Thus, for example, even though many of the brands acquired as part of Rowntree were purely British brands, eg Quality Street and After Eight, they are now all owned by the Swiss company and licensed back to the English company. There are specific legal reasons why a multinational company seeks to centralise ownership of the Group's trade marks and licence them to subsidiary companies.

Under most trade mark laws world-wide a trade mark can only be enforced if it is 'in use'. On a world-wide scale, it is probable that 'use' in many countries will be by other companies rather than the trade mark proprietor. To ensure that such 'use' transfers back to the trade mark proprietor, it is necessary to licence the user. Although new trade mark laws in major countries now state that licences do not have to be recorded, for the avoidance of doubt, most trade mark practitioners believe that it is still preferable to have a licence agreement executed by both parties and recorded at the relevant trade mark registry.

A licence agreement clearly states under what terms and conditions the licensee can use the trade mark. This is particularly important in relation to:

- quality control – which ensures that the product is always produced to standards laid down by proprietor and so the reputation of the product and its owner is not tarnished
- correct use – this ensures that the mark is never misused and so becomes vulnerable to cancellation or rectification actions
- termination – this ensures that the licence agreement can be ended by one party subject to certain conditions being carried out, which should prevent unnecessary legal action, to finish a commercial relationship that has become unsatisfactory
- royalties – this ensures that the proprietor receives a set level of payment for use of the mark
- territory – this stipulates the particular countries where a trade mark can be used.

At ICI, as perhaps in most other multinational companies, the international trade marks are owned by only one or two major proprietors world-wide. They are then licensed (as and when required) to users world-wide. This enables the protection, registration and maintenance of these company assets to be managed centrally and ensures that they are properly and consistently maintained. Some trade marks, which are intended for local area use only, can be owned by the local subsidiary company.

The role of internal licensing

Internal licences and especially centrally controlled internal licences, have a number of implications for the good management of trade marks and brands. A few examples follow.

Centralised licences

Centralised internal licences ensure that development of brands is controlled centrally and directed to the benefit of the whole group and not just of a subsidiary.

For example, a European biscuit company owns subsidiaries in both Poland and Finland. The Polish company is very keen to add to its portfolio a brand created by the

Finnish company – it has the capacity to make the product itself but realises that even though it is part of the same Group it has no right to use the Finnish company's brand and needs permission to do so. The Finnish company would be reluctant to grant permission because it feels rationally that such use will undermine its own international strategy and also because it feels irrationally that the brand is so much a part of its heritage that it does not want to see another company producing it.

However, the trade mark now belongs to the parent company, which can, therefore, consider more objectively the cases put by each of the operating companies. It concludes that the overall value of the brand would be maximised if the brand were extended into Poland and is prepared to put in place covenants to protect the Finnish interest. However, there is also a wider Group issue unknown to either the Finnish or Polish subsidiaries, concerning the long-term position of the Polish company within the Group. Serious consideration is being given to divesting the Polish company from the Group within the next 18 months. With that under review it seems safe to delay any possible licensing of the brand until the position is clear.

The maintenance of brand rights – such as the registering and renewing of trade mark registrations, policing, prosecuting infringement and passing-off actions – is co-ordinated and carried out consistently across the world, rather than being left to the interests or abilities of local management.

Some multinationals have found to their embarrassment that the protection of what are considered to be international trade marks, varies markedly from one country to another. In some cases, local management has been too fastidious and has spent an excessive amount registering the mark and pursuing the most unlikely infringement actions. In other cases, local management, intent on being seen to be reducing overheads, has failed to be diligent enough in the registration process and has failed to pursue some winnable actions. A centralised trade mark department is the best way of ensuring that such problems are avoided and that, with advice from local management, an appropriate and consistent policy of trade mark protection is pursued world-wide for international brands.

The licensing of brands, and the charging of brand royalties, rescues brands from the closed world of the marketing department and gives some responsibility to both the financial and legal departments. The brand's position as a valuable asset of the company is crystallised.

Shared brands

International brands, where the marketing may be shared by more than one company within a group or even by more than one division, are centrally co-ordinated to ensure maximum coherence in terms of, eg brand image, product development, and advertising. For example, for a long time Philip Morris has recognised that management of its Marlboro brand cannot be left to the individual companies within the Philip Morris International (PMI) Group but needs to be centrally co-ordinated. The success of PMI in creating an international franchise for Marlboro has now prompted other tobacco companies (eg BAT) to follow this approach and to ensure that autonomy for local companies does not become an obstacle for good international brand management. Centralising ownership of brands – as BAT is doing through its BatMark subsidiary – is one way of ensuring that this happens.

The owner of the trade mark will control how the trade mark is used and promoted regionally and will have final approval for all labels, packs, printed material, advertising and publicity matter, as required by a clause in the licensing agreement. In one licensing exercise which ICI is undertaking in Europe and Scandinavia, the marketing manager and ICI's Group Legal Department will be drawing up a 'Trade Mark User Manual' to give to all licensees which will lay down rules and guide-lines as to how the trade mark will be used, eg in advertising, in accordance with a planned campaign. It is a requirement of the licensing agreement that the licensee will use the trade mark in accordance with this user manual.

Brands can more easily be extended into new areas and licensed to other subsidiaries while firm control is still kept on the integrity of brand equity. For example, after its acquisition from Rowntree, Nestlé recognised that the Aero brand had a franchise in the UK market which was potentially wider than just the aerated chocolate product that Rowntree has used to carry the brand. Recognising developments in the market for dairy desserts in which another Nestlé subsidiary, Chambourcy, operated, Nestlé has now licensed the Aero brand across to Chambourcy and is making a success of this extension which will benefit both subsidiaries and, ultimately, the parent company. Thus, operating companies are made aware that the brands they use are as much a shared resource, and a property of common value as, say, research laboratories, recipes and patents.

Country managers can be made responsible for the local maintenance and development of a global brand. Their contribution to brand value is, after all, a contribution to shareholder value and should be rewarded accordingly.

Internal licences, whether within the home country or overseas, increasingly incorporate the payment of a royalty which reflects the true value of the asset being used rather than just being a nominal amount to 'cover administration'. Making a financial charge for the use of a trade mark (or other intellectual property) focuses the user on the value of the asset and the need both to protect and exploit that value.

The royalties received from licences to overseas subsidiaries can be used to repatriate funds in return for the use of a genuine piece of property. This can have major fiscal implications.

New licences negotiated, both within the Group, with joint-venture partners and outside, can be placed in a context of genuine brand licensing and realistic royalty rates. This gives the opportunity to negotiate much higher returns for the use of brands than has often been the case in the past.

Licensing of products and corporate brands to joint ventures is becoming increasingly more common as an increasing number of companies seek to establish themselves in the emerging commercial regions of the World, eg Asian Pacific, Latin America and the former Eastern Bloc. It is believed that to be commercially successful in such areas, close co-operation is needed with a local company with strong knowledge of the region. Therefore, a new company is formed – a joint venture – between the established multinational company and a local company. The international product brands and possibly the house marks (ie company name and logo) are then licensed to this new joint venture company.

At ICI, the protection, registration and maintenance of the international trade marks, allows for company assets to be managed centrally and ensures that they are intended for local area use only but can be owned by the local subsidiary company. The use of the house marks is governed by a 'Code of Practice for Use of Trade Marks' – reference to which is included in every licence agreement and a copy given to each and every licensee, along with copies of the corporate-identity manuals.

Brand valuation has made a critical contribution in all of these areas both in raising awareness of the concept of brand value and in putting a monetary value to a brand. Insisting that a brand *has* value is one thing; what is important is being able to state what that value is and the best way to make the maintenance and development of it part of company strategy. It also helps to communicate to the outside world that the company takes its brands seriously.

Fiscal advantages of internal licensing

One aspect mentioned previously is the fiscal implication of charging overseas subsidiaries and third-party licensees a proper rental for the use of brands. Our experience is that many companies have yet to realise that the royalty rates they demand are far too small for the value of the trade mark asset being licensed. Increasing the royalty rate demanded not only has managerial benefits but also transfer-pricing advantages.

An example illustrates this. Brand A is being used by FoodCo Japan and FoodCo UK. It was actually developed by FoodCo UK and is used under licence by the Japanese company. However, the Japanese company now makes and distributes all its own A-branded product and relies on FoodCo UK only for rights to use the brand. FoodCo UK charges FoodCo Japan a royalty and there is a subsequent tax saving to the Group. By setting up a trade mark-owning company (FoodMark) the Group is able to benefit from legitimate transfer pricing to improve its tax position. Where the subsidiary is paying tax at approximately 50 per cent and the parent company at 33 per cent, the tax benefit is a net gain of £17 in every £100 of allowed brand royalties.

With such clear commercial benefits, companies are keen to ensure that the licensing arrangement put in place to reflect their management structure also takes advantage of any fiscal benefits available. But when arguments are put forward to the tax authorities to justify increasing royalty rates the licensing company usually lacks the financial robustness of a valuation of the brand as an asset. Instead tax authorities bring the argument back to comparability with other royalty rates and it is the tax authorities themselves who have the best information on what comparable rates are being charged.

This imbalance of power could, it is believed, be greatly improved in two ways:
- by companies taking a more scientific approach to the settling of royalty rates rather than relying on what has been done in the past
- by companies pooling their information on royalty rates so that they are as well informed as the tax authorities with whom they are dealing.

CAUTION OF COMPARABLE TRANSACTION METHODS

It is sometimes argued that it is possible to determine royalty rates in controlled transactions by the use of comparisons with other transactions. However, it is not believed that such an approach would be appropriate in many cases. For this method to work it is necessary to have one or more comparable transactions that can be used as a basis for comparison. These should be transactions in similar circumstances between similar parties and should not have been influenced themselves by any control that one party had over the other. Where the transaction is not directly compatible, an understanding of the transaction is required so that appropriate adjustments can be made to achieve a genuine comparison.

The problem is that it is rare to find situations in which there are comparable transactions that would be suitable for use in such an approach. For the transaction to be comparable it would have to satisfy the following:

- deal with the licensing of a brand to be used in the same or similar product market and in the same or similar territory
- involve the licensing of a brand which has been in existence for the same period of time as the one with which it is being compared
- involve the licensing of the brand to entities that already have well-established brand names themselves
- involve the licensing of a brand with similar general and specific consumer values
- involve a licence of similar duration, with similar terms of renewal, similar restrictions and similar obligations
- be competing in an environment with competitive brands that cover a similar spread of weakness or strength.

From experience, it is rare to find such comparables and royalty rates based on so-called comparables often provide a false basis for comparison. By way of examples a food manufacturer may agree to pay a licence fee of 2 per cent to put the Mickey Mouse brand on a biscuit product (in a low margin, competitive market). But to put the same brand on a T-shirt selling in the same market a higher royalty would be expected. The royalty that should be charged to put the Mickey Mouse brand on a theme park bears little or no relationship to the royalties that may be charged for the use of the brand on food items or on character merchandising.

Similarly, although there may be some comparison with a brand being licensed in a new territory (eg China), it is expected that a royalty for the same brand in a territory where it has been established for many years would be much higher, all else being equal, since its value is more proven and better understood in the latter country. The problem with setting royalty rates by recourse to comparables is that often the so-called comparables are based on peripheral uses of the brand rather than the core of the brand itself and thus give only marginal help in determining an appropriate royalty rate.

CONCLUSION

The managerial and fiscal implications of trade mark licensing are profound and brand valuation has a key role to play in adding method and objectivity to an area which, in the past, has been plagued by doubt and misunderstanding. As companies become increasingly aware of the importance of brands and trade marks they will begin to focus on the better management of these assets. One of the ways of improving such management is the creation of appropriate structures for the internal and external licensing of the brand.

CHAPTER

14

TAX IMPLICATIONS
OF BRAND VALUATION

LUCINDA SPICER AND SUSAN SYMONS, PRICE WATERHOUSE

Brands are part of the capital of a business and, as such,
they can be created, bought, sold, managed and exploited in
the same way as other business assets. From a tax perspective,
however, brands give rise to some special problems. This
chapter considers some of the basic tax issues which arise
from ownership and exploitation of brands, both for the
domestic business and the business which employs its
brands internationally.

The problems arise from both sides of the tax equation. Brands, their value and legal operating environment are often poorly understood by Revenue authorities and the result can be unnecessary challenges and conflicts over judgemental areas, such as capital values and the value of brand-related charges. Even issues such as their location and how they are being used, can give rise to considerable difficulties in an international business.

Added to this, businesses themselves do not always appreciate the full range of tax issues that can arise from the ownership and exploitation of brands, and consequently unexpected tax liabilities may arise or significant tax-planning opportunities be overlooked.

SOME BASIC PRINCIPLES OF TAXATION

Before discussing specific tax issues for brands it is worth noting some basic principles that feature in many tax regimes. In general terms, most business receipts are taxable unless specifically exempted. This is so whether the receipt is of an income nature, eg as a royalty, or of a capital nature, eg a lump sum payment received on sale of a brand and all its associated rights.

On the other hand, business expenditures are not always deductible. Typically, the deduction of costs incurred in acquiring capital assets, such as brands, will not be possible unless provided for by specific rules. These will vary on a country-by-country basis.

There may also be a difficulty in obtaining deductions for related costs, such as legal costs in defending title to a brand, or advertising costs incurred in enhancing its value. Again, this will vary on a country-by-country basis.

It is important to appreciate, however, that a fundamental distinction can be made between brands that have been acquired and brands that have been developed internally. With the former, it may be possible to obtain deductions for the full value (cost) of the brand, whereas for the latter the most that could be achieved would be the deduction of actual costs incurred, which may fall far short of the brand's value.

DOMESTIC TAX IMPLICATIONS OF BRAND VALUATION

The objective for a business should be to obtain tax deductions against income for as many of its expenses as it is legally entitled to, as promptly as possible. Similarly, where there is the sale of a capital asset, a business should aim to maximise deductions against the capital receipt to reduce the taxable gain. Specific local tax rules may sometimes allow deferral of any remaining gain; for example, if the sales proceeds are reinvested.

Tax relief for establishing, developing and protecting a brand

The general principle in most countries is that recurring expenditure relating to a company's trading activity should be tax-deductible as incurred. For brand owners, however, difficulties can arise with:

- expenditure capitalised in a company's accounts
- expenditure on enhancing or building up a company's capital assets, ie its portfolio of brands
- expenditure that can be demonstrated to benefit the business over a number of years
- expenditure which benefits the trade of another related company, often in another country.

The outcome will turn on the facts and what is acceptable to local Revenue authorities. By recognising the issue in advance, however, owners of brands may sometimes be able to structure their arrangements in a way that both achieves their commercial objectives and provides maximum prospect of securing tax deductions. It is unlikely that valuation will become an issue in this area, although capital expenditure on brands may justifiably form a cost basis for the company's brands, in the event of a disposal.

Brand acquisition and tax depreciation

The acquisition of a brand as a separate asset, without the underlying business to which it relates, is relatively infrequent in mergers and acquisitions; however, there may be many situations where it could be divorced from the underlying business and acquired separately by the same purchaser, eg by a different group company.

The legal form and identity of a brand and its associated intellectual property, other intangibles and goodwill then become important, with the objective being to separate the brand and the business without prejudicing the value of either. Naturally, the values ascribed must stand up to scrutiny.

There may be clear tax benefits to the purchaser in doing this, which might include the ability to depreciate the cost of the brand for tax purposes, the prospect of building up profits from exploiting the brand in a favourable tax jurisdiction, or the possibility of reducing transfer duties or value-added taxes on purchase.

Some tax regimes are relatively relaxed about the legal distinction between various forms of intellectual property and may allow tax depreciation if there is a finite life that can be identified or assumed; for example, The Netherlands. Others have rules which distinguish between the legal form of various items of intellectual property; for example, the UK allows no tax depreciation for the acquisition cost of brands, trade marks or designs, whereas patents and know how are eligible.

It is worth remembering, however, that tax depreciation is only useful if there is an income flow to set it against. This might be royalty income charged for use of the brand, or the income of other business operations in the same country.

Disposing of a brand

Revenue authorities are likely to view this as the sale of a capital asset; a significant point as most tax regimes distinguish between trading proceeds and proceeds received on sale of capital assets. As it is unlikely that a brand will be disposed of in isolation, the value attributed to the brand must be carefully appraised. Usually, the disposal proceeds will be compared with any cost basis in the brand to determine if there is a taxable gain. Also, any tax depreciation claimed may be recaptured and taxed.

INTERNATIONAL TAX IMPLICATIONS OF BRAND VALUATION

Businesses increasingly exploit their brands on an international basis, which gives rise to a number of additional tax considerations:

- income flows and assets should ideally be distributed between countries so as to avoid one country paying tax while another has losses
- the effective rate of tax borne should be kept under review
- where there is flexibility in international brand management, expenses should obtain tax relief at the highest rate.

It should be emphasised that the location of business assets, processes and business risk can often be managed between different countries to achieve these objectives quite legitimately, provided the commercial needs allow this. It is here that an appreciation of the value of brands and other intangible property is fundamental to developing a beneficial tax strategy.

The following table sets out corporate tax rates for some major trading nations, including developing markets, to illustrate the background to these principles.

TABLE 14.1: Corporate tax rates for major trading nations and developing markets

Country	%
UK	33.00
Belgium (1)	46.30
Bermuda	–
China	33.00
Czech Republic	39.00
France (2)	33.33
Germany (3)	30/45
Hong Kong	16.50
Japan (4)	37.50
Malaysia	30.00
Russian Federation (5)	35.00
South Africa	35.00
USA (6)	35.00

NOTES

Rates may vary from those shown above due to specific variations, incentives etc. The rates given are those current at 1 January 1996.

(1)   *Includes surcharge. Overall rate can be reduced through advance payments.*
(2)   *There is an additional surtax of 10% of the normal corporation tax before reduction by the avoir fiscal credit and any foreign tax credit.*
(3)   *Higher rate for undistributed profits. Municipal tax additional (up to 20.5%).*
(4)   *Inhabitants tax (up to 20.7% of corporate tax) and enterprise tax (up to 13.2% of income) additional.*
(5)   *Varies by region (35% highest).*
(6)   *Federal tax. State taxes additional.*

Transfer pricing

It is common for the international exploitation of brands to take place within a group of companies. For example, overseas related companies may sell, or sometimes manufacture and sell, branded goods that make use of the group's intellectual property. This provides an opportunity for the group to structure the locations of its brands, and the ownership of the intellectual property comprised in the brands, to achieve the best overall tax result. It also, however, gives rise to possible tax exposures as Revenue authorities are increasingly challenging transfer-pricing between related companies.

The term 'transfer pricing' is a reference to the price at which goods and services are transferred between related companies operating in different countries. A transfer price is related to the underlying value of assets such as brands and intellectual property as well as to more tangible features of goods and services. Revenue authorities are concerned that when goods and services are transferred within the same group there is an opportunity to manipulate prices in order to have profit recognised in the country that benefits the group most. There is a general rule that, for tax purposes, transactions between related companies can be deemed to take place at an arm's-length price, as if the companies had been independent parties.

As a general concept, arm's-length pricing might appear straightforward. In practice, however, it is extremely difficult, particularly for transactions involving intellectual property – such as the sale of a branded product or, a royalty for use of a trade mark. In these situations, there are rarely any comparable transactions with third parties which can be used as a guide to the arm's-length price. In turn, this has meant that the practical application of the general rule has varied and, indeed, in some countries it has been applied in a rather arbitrary fashion.

In an attempt to achieve greater consistency, the OECD has recently issued revised transfer pricing guidelines, which include specific comment on how to determine an arm's-length price for intellectual property. Clearly this is welcome, though many of the problems of practical application are likely to remain.

The OECD sanctions a number of pricing methods, including the so-called 'transaction-based methods' and the 'profit-based methods'. In brief, the transaction-based methods seek to establish an arm's-length price by reference to comparable transactions between independent parties, while the profit-based methods split a transaction, or series of related transactions, into component parts and seek to determine an appropriate profit for each company based on the function it performs.

Branded products present particular difficulties under either method. The problems include:

– determining the value of the intangible assets comprised in the brand
– how they are reflected in the end price
– how this value should be divided between the parties to the transaction.

Transfer-pricing rules apply, not only to sales of products but, eg to royalties for the use of intellectual property and charges for head office services. In principle, the same considerations should apply whether a group chooses to sell its product to an overseas group company at a price inclusive of the rights and services incorporated in the brand or, instead, makes separate royalty or service charges for these items. In practice, however, separate charges have proved more visible and prone to attack.

Also, there may be differences in the domestic tax treatment of royalties compared to an inclusive product price. Typically, withholding tax is applied to royalties but not to an inclusive product price, which has led the OECD to suggest that withholding tax be applied to the notional royalty element of an inclusive product price.

A similar issue exists with Customs Duty. Whether or not a separate royalty payment is added to the product's dutiable value varies from country to country.

To summarise, transfer pricing is a real issue for any business with international brands. With Revenue authorities increasingly active in challenging transfer prices, it is now more important than ever that businesses focus on the value of their brands and how, with other relevant factors, it is incorporated into their transfer pricing.

International structures for brands

In an international context, businesses will wish to maximise tax relief for the costs of developing or acquiring a brand, and to minimise the tax charges on income received from exploiting the brand in different countries. Given the differences in tax rules from one country to another, businesses have sometimes sought to relocate ownership of their brands in a way that improves their overall tax result.

FIGURE 14.1: Structure of trade with an offshore licensing company

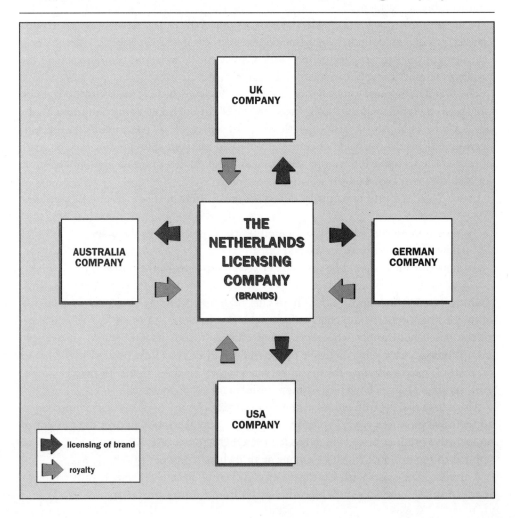

One structure used by some UK-based groups involves the transfer of ownership of their brands, or other intellectual property, to an offshore licensing company. In the context of an acquisition, this is achieved simply by having the intellectual property acquired directly by the licensing company.

The licensing company would be located in a country where the rules for tax depreciation of intellectual property are more favourable than the UK (eg The Netherlands) and licenses the intellectual property for use within the wider group, including the UK. The licensees should receive a tax deduction for their royalty expense, while for the licensing company, the royalty income would largely be matched by depreciation of the intellectual property. The result should be an improvement in the group's overall tax position.

APPENDIX:
THE USE OF OFFSHORE LICENSING TO MAXIMISE TAX BENEFITS

As can be appreciated, many matters of tax, legal and commercial detail will be relevant in determining whether such a structure is feasible and, if so, where the licensing company should be located. Relevant tax issues will include:

– the quantum of any taxable gain on sale of intellectual property to the licensing company
– possible taxation of licensing profits in tax haven locations; some countries tax owners of such 'money box' companies on the profits as they accumulate, eg the UK's 'controlled foreign company' rules could apply here
– level of withholding taxes on royalty flows
– transfer pricing
– the group's existing tax position, country by country.

To summarise, brands and the intellectual property they comprise have assumed increasing importance in international tax planning. Businesses are seeking to structure the ownership and location of their brands in a way that optimises their overall tax position. To achieve this a number of detailed tax, legal and commercial issues must be considered and resolved. As an essential first step, businesses must have a sound understanding of the value of their brands.

CHAPTER

15

BRAND MONETISATION

PHILIP J. ADKINS, J. BOAG & SON

> In reality, brand values are only confirmed when the
> brands or the company owning them are acquired
> through sale or take-over. But a technique called 'brand
> monetisation' has emerged over recent years as one of the
> most radical developments in assessing brand value,
> transcending traditional accounting precepts. This
> chapter illustrates how brand monetisation works,
> using the Walt Disney Company as an example.

While the underlying equity value of a brand and various methodologies to quantify that value for balance sheet purposes have now been widely accepted by international accounting standards boards, realistically these values are only confirmed when the brands or the company owning the brand is acquired through sale or take-over.

Brands may also be given some value as collateral within the framework of debt raised by the company when it provides a charge over all of its assets. However, the true value of brands within this context is dubious since, in any foreclosure scenario, the brand equity would be substantially undermined.

THE CONCEPT OF MONETISATION

Monetisation, both as a technique for raising capital and as an alternative method of brand valuation, transcends traditional accounting precepts and has emerged as a hybrid of debt and equity as well as the ultimate standard of brand value. The essence of brand monetisation is the identity of a discreet cash-flow associated directly with the brand. Most commonly this can be seen in the form of royalties the brand's owner receives through licence agreements. While most licence agreements tend to be less than five years in length, one important determinant in achieving maximum value through monetising is a licence on royalty flow of at least ten years. As seen, the strongest brands can achieve royalty flows of 20, 30 or even 50 years.

The royalty may be associated with merchandise or manufactured goods, proprietary service, or even a technology. However, regardless of the essential differences each of these products has, they share the fundamental values of strong brand identity. This allows the brand to transcend, both the underlying corporation as well as the product, and to generate a cash net-present-value which can be calculated by the discount rate applied against future projected royalty flows.

This proposition requires acceptance of an important assumption. Namely brands which can be monetised must be based on a cash flow which carries the highest implied credit rating in the financial market. This will result in a low discount rate and, in some cases, represent a more attractive investment than afforded by the underlying corporate risk of the brand's owner itself.

THE WALT DISNEY CORPORATION

The best example of a recent transaction which established the framework for monetised brands has been on behalf of The Walt Disney Company.

The Walt Disney Company owns, in the name Disney and its characters, some of the most powerful and recognisable brands in the world today. Yet a close inspection of the balance sheet reveals there is no underlying equity value carried on the accounts. Nor is any amortisation taken against the stable of Disney brands. This may be because it is impossible to pin-point exactly what 'Disney' as a brand represents. However, down the years, The Walt Disney Company through its most famous characters like Mickey Mouse, Donald Duck, and a host of others in their animation pantheon, have acquired an international following of, arguably, near-religious proportions. The essence of these characters has been captured in films and made accessible to the public at their theme-parks, first in the USA and then in Tokyo, Japan when Tokyo Disneyland opened in the early 1980s.

Tokyo Disneyland

Tokyo Disneyland was unique in comparison to the US theme parks in that Disney held no direct ownership interests. They had licensed their characters, technology and management expertise to Oriental Land Corp. through a 50-year licence agreement. In exchange Disney received 5 per cent of the gate admission and 10 per cent of all merchandise, food and beverage sales. In short, their return was attributable directly to the popularity of the brand and the desirability of the 'Disney experience' in the Japanese marketplace.

Company risks

While the park was performing above expectation in its first five years of operation Disney management was concerned about three principal risks which could impact their future returns. These were:

- yen/US$ foreign exchange risks since the payments were all received by Disney in yen

– a major earthquake which could severely damage the park
– the long-term popularity of the park in Japan after the initial novelty wore off and the relative inaccessibility of Japan as an international tourist destination limited potential for new guests to the park.

Disney's solution to eliminating all three was to assign the rights to receive a fixed amount of future royalties to a syndicate of institutional investors. The level of payments to be assigned was based on the most recent annual amount which then was projected to increase in line with inflation (2 per cent pa) for a total period of 20 years. At that time attendance had reached some 11m guests. Theoretically the park had the 'through-put' capacity to entertain as many as 16m guests, assuming no further land was added to the park.

Long-term investment

While the Walt Disney Company had very little debt on its own balance sheet at the time and enjoyed an AA credit rating, its management was loath to borrow in its own name. Investors were, therefore, required to evaluate the risk purely on the strength of the brand, the longevity of the park's assets and the likelihood of a major earthquake destroying the park or temporarily closing it. As Disney required the longest possible term, the only bench-mark rate from which to establish a discount rate was the Japanese Government Bond rate (JGB).

A syndicate of Japanese institutional investors agreed to a rate only marginally above the JGB and agreed to fix it for the entire 20-year life of the transaction. This was equivalent to a rate only available to an AA credit risk. Significantly, any shortfall below the projected royalty stream would be at the sole risk of the investor. However, any surplus above the annual amount was received in its entirety by Disney.

Financing risks

The total net proceeds amounted to Y90 billion (approx. US$ 725 million at the time in 1988). It was clear during syndication of the deal that investors were viewing the credit risk in a highly orthodox manner and it was the strength of the brand which made the opportunity so attractive in the market.

One of the largest participants in the underwriting group was the Long-Term Credit Bank of Japan. When asked why their bank had been so enthusiastic to accept such a long risk at such a narrow spread over the Japanese Government rate, a senior executive remarked:

Micky Mouse is a better risk than the US government.

The transaction itself created a bench-mark in the international capital markets which has never been equalled. It was the longest maturity and the largest size deal at the finest spread ever executed. Accolades in the financial press included 'Deal of the Decade'. Even so, the deal was not fully understood and it was not helped by the description of the transaction in Disney's published accounts.

Characterisation

Disney's auditors were struggling with an accurate characterisation of the deal in accounting terms. Theoretically, Disney had 'sold' future royalties. However, a sale would attract corporate tax in the USA on the entire amount of consideration. Disney argued the transaction was a loan for tax purposes and taxes should be deferred until the time of actual receipt by investors over the 20-year life. However, the non-recourse nature of the deal to Disney made it difficult to establish that the royalty assignment was a true loan and should be characterised as a liability. Disney argued that it was not a liability and was in fact a sale for purposes of their accounts. In the end, Disney's auditors accepted this dual characterisation and attempted to describe the receipt of this large sum of cash with a curious footnote. The accounting world was baffled, the structure was reviewed by the SEC, IRS and FASB emerging issues special task force. After several months of scrutiny it was allowed to stand.

Summary

In essence Disney was able to maximise their inherent brand equity in the Japanese market without actually selling ownership or losing control in any way. The ability to receive the 'up-side' of receipts over the pre-agreed amounts proved fruitful as attendance did in fact steadily climb and hit the 16m mark within three years of opening. At the same time Disney eliminated their down side, by having third parties accept the risk of park attendance declining. Ironically the cost of the transaction was below that at which Disney would have borrowed in their own right. The strength of the brand had created a value paradox.

CONCLUSION

This paradox may be the ultimate standard of brand valuation and achievable only by brands that have achieved universal and permanent value, equal to an almost religious reverence in the marketplace. It presents brand-oriented companies with the ultimate challenge – obtain maximum cash-value for brands without losing ownership or control while not diluting any collateral value by borrowing against the brands as security.

16

BRAND VALUE MANAGER SYSTEM – AS A WORKING TOOL FOR THE BRAND MANAGER

JOHN BJÖRKMAN, FAZER

Because of the limited tenure of most brand managers, continuity in brand management is a rare commodity. State-of-the-art tracking systems can help. This chapter examines how one particular model works in practice.

THE BRAND MANAGER AND THE BRAND MANAGEMENT FUNCTION

The brand manager is often described as the brand's managing director. But, the average tenure of a brand manager in the UK is, on average, around 18 months. How many companies would survive if all managing directors moved on after less than two years at the top?

If companies truly believe in brand management and in the role of the brand manager, then they have to be taken seriously. If companies do not change their practices, in an increasingly competitive market-place, brands will languish and die.

Changing an organisation's philosophy is time-consuming, therefore companies must develop systems to track their brands' performance today, historically and in the future. Even companies which already have tracking systems must ensure that those systems are state-of-the-art, as growing demands on brand managers will put them in the position of being 'mini-MDs' for their brands.

THE BRAND VALUE MANAGER SYSTEM

The brand value manager system (BVMS) is a tracking model developed by Interbrand for brand managers and senior management. Fazer Chocolates is one of the first companies in the world to adopt the model and has used it to develop the strategy of the

FIGURE 16.1: The Main Menu – the user chooses the brand and country which they want to investigate

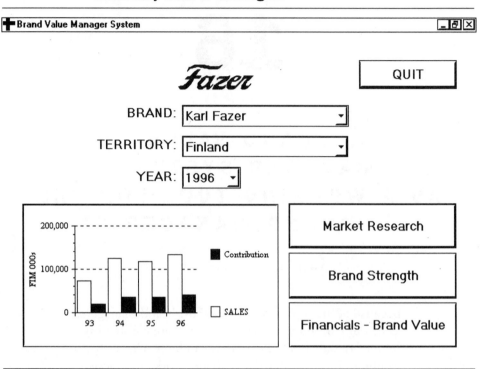

family brand, Karl Fazer *(see Figure 16.1)*. The way the BVMS is used depends on the needs of the user, but essentially it is designed as an everyday tool for brand managers. However, it can also be used by the marketing director to track the performance of individual brand managers, and can provide the managing director with a snapshot of the portfolio performance *(see Figures 16.1–16.3)*.

The BVMS is not a flash in the pan – or something to shove in a drawer and forget about. It should be a valuable tool for every brand manager in companies which take the nurturing of their brands seriously. There are four aspects to the BVMS:

- financial – or brand value
- market research
- portfolio overview
- brand strength *(see Figure 16.1)*.

The first three aspects are the most common. Use of the fourth depends, to a large extent, on what is made of the first three. The BVMS can be used in mergers and acquisitions, for fund-raising, licensing and also for balance sheet purposes. This

FIGURE 16.2: The financial analysis and forecasting screen – giving detailed financial information for the brand in question

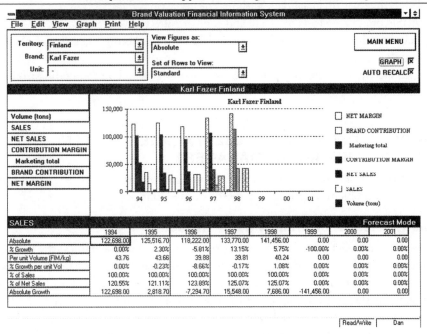

FIGURE 16.3: Analysing 'contract discounts' in more detail – driving assumptions are typed directly into the lower spreadsheet

Karl Fazer Finland

	1994 (Year End)	1995 (Year End)	1996 (Latest Est.)	1997 (Budget)	1998 (Forecast)	1999 (Forecast)	2000 (Forecast)	2001 (Forecast)
Volume (tons)	2,804.0	2,875.0	2,964.5	3,360.0	3,515.0			
SALES	122,698.0	125,516.7	118,222.0	133,770.0	141,456.0			
Contract discounts	4,417.0	4,144.7	4,335.0	4,677.0	4,945.0			
Campaign discounts	16,496.0	17,733.2	18,464.0	22,139.0	23,411.0			
NET SALES	101,785.0	103,638.8	95,423.0	106,954.0	113,100.0			
Direct costs	49,123.0	60,399.9	50,143.7	56,209.0	59,439.0			
Production overheads		8,581.7	9,413.5	10,757.0	11,375.0			
Freights	64.0	115.4	119.0	156.0	165.0			
CONTRIBUTION MARGIN	52,598.0	34,541.7	35,746.8	39,832.0	42,121.0			
Advertising	5,127.0	2,010.7	1,607.0	2,400.0				
Promotion	4,226.3	1,909.2	1,066.0	530.0				
Other marketing expenses	8,403.0	187.2	1,741.0	8,705.0				
Marketing total	17,756.3	4,107.1	4,414.0	11,635.0				
BRAND CONTRIBUTION	34,841.7	30,434.6	31,332.8	28,197.0	42,121.0			
Fixed Costs	17,097.0							
Corporate Fee	859.0	908.0						
Depreciation	1,890.0	4,125.0						
NET MARGIN	14,995.7	25,401.6	31,332.8	28,197.0	42,121.0			

(Advertising + Promotion + Other marketing expenses)

SALES — Forecast Mode

	1994	1995	1996	1997	1998	1999	2000	2001
Absolute	122,698.00	125,516.70	118,222.00	133,770.00	141,456.00	0.00	0.00	0.00
% Growth	0.00%	2.30%	-5.81%	13.15%	5.75%	-100.00%	0.00%	0.00%
Per unit Volume (FIM/kg)	43.76	43.66	39.88	39.81	40.24	0.00	0.00	0.00
% Growth per unit Vol	0.00%	-0.23%	-8.66%	-0.17%	1.08%	0.00%	0.00%	0.00%
% of Sales	100.00%	100.00%	100.00%	100.00%	100.00%	0.00%	0.00%	0.00%
% of Net Sales	120.55%	121.11%	123.89%	125.07%	125.07%	0.00%	0.00%	0.00%
Absolute Growth	122,698.00	2,818.70	-7,294.70	15,548.00	7,686.00	-141,456.00	0.00	0.00

*The financial information used in these examples is fictitious, and for illustration only.

chapter will focus on the use of the BVMS in brand management and for developing brand strategies.

As always when working with models such as the BVMS, it has to be recognised that the outcome or the solution to a given problem does not necessarily tell the whole story. However, in an uncertain world, the BVMS can at least give businesses some guide as to what the future holds. But only if the data is entered correctly.

Skills of the brand manager

As implied above, the life of brand managers is set to get tougher. In theory the brand manager has always been in charge of the brand, but it is the author's opinion that most brand managers have, in practice, considered the brand from a pure marketing perspective – that is, in a limited way. This must no longer be the case. The future brand manager needs to be skilled in finance, product development and market research, as well as in marketing and sales.

To do this, the brand manager needs easily accessible, understandable and processable information. Moreover, information about the financial consequences of marketing actions, and about brand value as a measure of performance of both the brand and the brand manager, is growing in importance.

Tools for the brand manager

To meet the expectations outlined above, the brand manager needs the right set of equipment. These include tools that:

- bring together financial data with marketing actions
- enable brand managers to create and compare alternative plans
- help brand managers to link research data with marketing planning or plans in a simple manner
- give speedy re-casting of pricing, marketing budgets and for responding to changes in other key figures.

HOW DOES THE BRAND VALUE MANAGER SYSTEM WORK FOR THE BRAND MANAGER?

The BVMS creates a framework for the brand manager to work out the best possible solution to a given problem or task, and it speeds up the decision-making process.

1. The financial – or brand value – aspect

The BVMS is an effective way of bringing those supposed arch-enemies, the marketing director and the finance director, together. It gives the brand management a better understanding of financial matters in a more user-friendly way, as well as forcing them to think about the bottom line. Once the brand management has mastered the BVMS they will be in a much better position to enter into a dialogue with the finance department. They are better able to understand the financial consequences of any given marketing actions, to say nothing of being better equipped to question the view of the financial department.

This benefits both sides. The finance people welcome sparring partners who can 'go more than the first round'. Better mutual understanding and respect will be the consequence. The team members will become united, and both the team and the company as a whole will be better equipped to face the challenges.

2. The market research aspect

Market research is a popular tool for assessing a brand's performance and is an effective way of acquiring information to steer future strategy. However, market research is not always managed properly. It often neglects brand-related information and is inadequately co-ordinated. As a consequence, data is gathered by different individuals scattered around the organisation. Even if the data is gathered efficiently, it is not always used properly. It may reside in pockets throughout the organisation, therefore it is time-consuming to unearth the relevant information. It also gets lost.

The BVMS offers a powerful tool to manage market research centrally. The market research aspect of the BVMS functions as the research bank for all the research that has been conducted, not only about the brands but also about eg GDP growth in different markets, consumer price inflation and media-spending levels in a given market for a given medium. It also tracks existing and new products launched into the various markets.

This information can be invaluable in formulating new product-development strategies. As the information is easily accessible it is more likely to be used. The BVMS is structured to allow parallels to be drawn with historical information and to monitor trends. It presents the information in such a way as to facilitate use in the marketing plan. Valuable information that previously would have been left out, purely because of the difficulty of finding it, can now be included – with obvious benefits to decision-making. Cost savings are inevitable.

3. The portfolio overview and documentation aspect

The future involves risks for brands and companies. Brand managers who do not take risks do not move their brands forward. Even intelligent risk-taking involves mistakes, but mistakes should be regarded as intelligent and serious attempts to grow the brand and the company. The BVMS encourages intelligent risk-taking; it makes scenario-making easy, thus helping to minimise risk. As a decision is being taken the BVMS helps the brand manager to monitor the brand's performance in the various markets in an efficient way. Even in sophisticated brand-management organisations a new brand manager will at some stage be appointed, and it is vital that he understands the decisions taken by his predecessors. Decisions must be documented in order to record the brand's history. In the BVMS all decisions can be stored centrally, so contributing to continuity in the brand-building process.

There follow some examples of problems and tasks where the BVMS can be used to build scenarios. The examples are hypothetical and simplified for the purposes of this chapter.

Example 1

A brand's value is declining and resources are being allocated to stem the decline. There are a number of options:

- new product development
- product mix
- pricing *per se*
- discounts
- change advertising strategy.

For the price-cutting alternative the BVMS can help the brand manager to create the following type of scenario:

(a) An elasticity study that shows a 1:1 elasticity has been conducted. A drop in price by 10 per cent is considered as a solution. According to the study sales would go up by 10 per cent. The finance department stipulate that there must also be a cut in the advertising spend. Advertising expenditure is cut from £2m to £1m.

(b) A similar scenario could be built around the changing advertising strategy option. The scenario could include the following assumptions: A study shows that a 10:1 elasticity of advertising and sales is to be assumed in a particular market. Boosting advertising by 75 per cent is considered. This would lead to an increase in sales of 7.5 per cent during the given year.

Example 2

How to devise different, safe as opposed to fast build-up, entry strategies.

(a) For the safe build-up the following scenario is created:
The advertising level is set at £2m. Research tells us that we ought to achieve a volume of 750 tonnes in the first year, with the aim of achieving the year-end target of 1,500 tonnes. The volumes are then expected to rise by 15 per cent with a 10 per cent price increase. The advertising support is set to rise by 5 per cent annually. According to the BVMS this scenario would result in a situation where the brand will be taking a loss for the three first years. The profit after the third year is not more than £140,000. The brand value is estimated to be £7m.

(b) For the fast build-up the following scenario is created:
The advertising level is set at £3m which equals that of the leading advertiser in this particular category. The anticipated volume for the first year is 3,000. After that the volumes are assumed to develop in the same way as in the safe scenario. Advertising support is set to increase at the same rate as in the safe scenario. The conclusions for this scenario would be much more positive. The loss in the first year would be almost £2m; it was less than £1m accord-

ing to the safe scenario. However, the break-even in this scenario would come at the end of the first year, and at the end of the third year the profit will be £2m. The brand value is estimated to be £32m. Without the BVMS this type of scenario would risk failing immediately. It is obvious that the BVMS enables the brand manager and the company as a whole to perform better by giving more trustworthy analyses regarding the future; the long-term solutions will be more profitable as a result.

IMPLEMENTING THE BVMS

Despite the clear advantages of BVMS, the implementation process can be lengthy. The required cultural change does not happen overnight. Staff allocation is a tricky issue in a climate of cost-cutting. The company must be able to see future cost savings from today's investment – not least in the research facilities and financial data necessary to the system. However, in most cases, it is a matter of re-allocating costs from a decentralised to a centralised way of working.

As ever, top management must drive the change. Brand managers, crucial to the process though they are, are too immersed in managing their brands. Senior management must become involved in order to fully understand what can and should be demanded of the brand managers in order to effect the required change.

CHAPTER

17

ALLOCATING
MARKETING RESOURCE

ED BRODY AND HOWARD FINKELBERG,
BBDO MARKETING SCIENCES

The 'Holy Grail' of brand management – how much
should we spend on advertising – is considered here in the
context of work done by BBDO's Marketing Sciences group.
Whilst there are no magical answers, this chapter suggests that
a rational and comprehensive approach to advertising
spending may be better than simply following a 'hunch'.
How this approach can be used to develop concepts
of Brand Value is then discussed.

While there are numerous consultants offering an answer to the question as to how to determine optimal advertising expenditure, it seems that there are just as many saying that it cannot be done. In the meantime, brand owning companies – unable to wait for this much sought after Holy Grail – need to decide each year how much they should be spending in support of their brands. Sometimes they develop sophisticated models for doing this; sometimes they determine spend by trial and error; sometimes they spend simply on the basis that they have always done so and it easier to continue so doing rather than reinvent the process anew.

BBDO, as one of the world's leading advertising agencies, has invested considerable resources in trying to model the impact of spend on branded sales. They have developed models such as NEWS® and AdBank (a registered service mark of BBDO) to examine the correlation between advertising expenditure and increased sales in order to assess optimal levels of expenditure going forwards. Whilst these models inevitably work better in some industries than in others, if used judiciously, they can provide an excellent approach to assessing and modelling on-going spend. By an approach such as this, Mr Micawber's injunction to live within one's means may well be met: "Annual income £20, annual expenditure £19, 19s and 6d – result happiness. Annual income £20, annual expenditure £21 – result misery!"

The following case study illustrates how such a modelling approach can be used to determine the allocation of resources between different countries in an environment of pan-European advertising. Even though there may be arguments about the proper measure of brand value in financial statements, it is widely accepted that if a brand is to secure future revenues and profits it requires appropriate market support. This model shows how determining such support can be done.

As the idea of pan-European and global branding takes hold, existing brands are increasingly being introduced into new markets. This, combined with a the growth of brand extension strategies, has drawn attention to the need to allocate scarce marketing resources across portfolios and markets in an effective way. This chapter summarises the work BBDO has done with several clients to help them solve this problem. With current personal-computer spreadsheets and market modelling, resources can be optimally allocated. This chapter does not discuss whether multinational marketing is appropriate. This is a worthy subject with a rich literature, but it is assumed that this decision has already been made. Our humbler task is to best allocate resources among countries.

GENERAL GUIDELINES

Experience suggests that the approach be guided by four principles. First, there will be substantial differences in the market situation from country to country. Consumers may differ – eg, dry (electric) shaving is preferred in northern Europe but wet (blade) shaving is favoured in southern Europe. The competitive situation can differ – the brand leader in one country can be a secondary brand in another. We must account for this in the model.

Second, all marketing needs can usually not be fully funded; countries and brands compete for resources. Conversely, local companies may not want to invest at the level that the company's headquarters desires. Inputs and calculations must be made clearly visible to managers so that they can consider alternatives and develop a comfort level with the results – this is the planning tool. By allocating, in a formal and consistent manner, one can maximise the outcome and maintain a sense of fairness.

Third, is to minimise the use of qualitative factors. Judgemental or *ad hoc* considerations are unavoidable, but they are the final, not the initial, stage. Judgements are segregated and identified.

Last, is to restrict the amount of information required. A full European analysis can comprise 30 or more countries, but by using simplified mini-models derived from the more detailed proprietary BBDO marketing models – NEWS for new products and AdBank for established products – it is possible to reduce this number. The need is for relative accuracy for allocation, not detailed market-by-market forecasts.

SIMPLE ALLOCATION

Let us start with a simple allocation for a new brand, using only advertising for one year. This makes it easier to understand the process. Later sections show how the allocation model is expanded for established brands, multiple brands and activities. The data represents a synthesis of several products.

Consumer Inputs

The first step is to 'segment the population' into:

- users of client brands (can distinguish several brands)
- users of competitive brands (can distinguish several brands)
- users of alternate forms, eg dry versus canned soup.

These are measured in each country from primary research; the relative proportions can vary substantially.

The 'adoption probabilities' are derived for each segment in each country from consumer research (concept-use test) and our NEWS modelling experience. The 'consumption rate' is readily estimated for each country from prior sales experience.

Financial Inputs

The manufacturer provides the incremental revenue or margin from a newly converted user from each segment by country. Clearly, there is greater value in converting a competitive or non-user than in 'trading up' someone from the existing franchise, though it is often easier to do the latter. The allocation model can consider either revenue or profit maximisation as its objective, as the situation requires.

Table 17.1 summarises these inputs for a 'mini-Europe' consisting of Belgium, Holland, France and Germany.

TABLE 17.1 : Consumer and financial inputs

	Total	Belgium	France	Germany	Holland
Consumer population (m)					
Current customers	17	1	6	8	2
Competitor's customers	19	1	10	7	1
Non-users	20	1	4	14	1
TOTAL	**56**	**3**	**20**	**29**	**4**
Adoption probability					
Current customers	0.14	0.12	0.10	0.18	0.13
Competitor's customers	0.10	0.10	0.08	0.12	0.11
Non-users	0.02	0.03	0.03	0.02	0.02
AVERAGE	**0.08**	**0.08**	**0.08**	**0.09**	**0.10**

TABLE 17.2 : Media inputs

		Belgium	France	Germany	Holland
Cost per GRP		$1,000	$5,000	$7,500	$1,500
Media spill (from/to)					
	Belgium	–	2%	0%	10%
	France	20%	–	0%	0%
	Germany	5%	0%	–	20%
	Holland	30%	0%	1%	–

To read the media spill chart:
Every 100 German GRPs yields an additional 5 Belgian and 20 Dutch GRPs

Media Inputs

Media costs are stated in US dollars for one average 30-second television rating point by country. Rating points represent the percentage of the target audience expected to view a programme; gross rating points (GRPs) are the cumulative rating points for all media vehicles without regard to duplication of audience. The media director is responsible for choosing the appropriate media target and adjusting for national differences and restrictions on television advertising and viewing. Print media are handled comparably.

Advertising in one country may be seen in an adjacent one. This is called 'overspill', and can be substantial. In Exhibit B, Belgium and Holland receive considerable spill from their neighbours. Additionally, pan-European media such as Sky Channel reach many countries but at differing levels.

The model assumes appropriate flighting (such as front-loading for new products, seasonal peaks, etc) across countries. There is no attempt to 'fine tune' the local media plan.

The overall budget is set by the client prior to allocation. We do not try to determine an 'optimal' global budget from the bottom up, as this would require more detailed marketing analyses for each country. However, the model can be used to test a limited number of alternate budgets to help choose the final level.

The inputs are summarised in Table 17.2.

Strategic Considerations

To provide for a variety of media buying and strategic considerations, the model provides for maximum and minimum GRP levels for each country. Competitive presence, share of voice and individual market exposure needs, even organisational or political considerations, may determine spending in one or more countries prior to running the model. The planner can manually override the model results in a country, if necessary. These are acceptable options when done with candour.

TABLE 17.3 : Media allocation

	Total	Belgium	France	Germany	Holland
INITIAL ALLOCATION					
Consumer population (m)	55	3	20	29	4
% of TOTAL	**100**	**5**	**36**	**53**	**7**
Budget allocation (US$m)	**10.0**	0.5	3.6	5.3	0.7
Minimum GRPs		**400**	**400**	**400**	**400**
Maximum GRPs		**1000**	**1000**	**1000**	**1000**
Local GRPs		545	727	703	485
Media Spill		326	11	5	195
Total effective GRPs		**872**	**738**	**708**	**680**
Expected revenue (US$m)	**207.3**	7.5	62.5	124.7	12.6
FINAL ITERATION					
Budget allocation (US$m)	**10.0**	0.4	2.6	6.4	0.6
Local GRPs		400	520	853	400
Media Spill		267	8	4	211
Total effective GRPs		**667**	**528**	**857**	**611**
Expected revenue (US$m)	**214.8**	6.6	59.5	136.5	12.2
% of TOTAL	**100**	**3**	**28**	**64**	**6**

Media Allocation

A multi-step procedure is utilised to assure that a given overall media budget is allocated so as to maximise the objective while satisfying all constraints. In the example, the objective is to maximise expected incremental revenue across all population segments in all countries.

Step One

The first step is the computation of a feasible initial solution, in which the media budget is allocated across countries in proportion to each country's population. The local GRP delivery in each country is calculated and adjusted, subject to minimum and maximum constraints. The overspill coming into each country from every other country is then calculated, yielding the total media weight reaching each country from initial allocation.

Table 17.3 reveals that Belgium received about 40 per cent of its media weight from spill, while France and Germany received very little.

Step two

The total effective media weight in each country, local plus spill-in, and the adoption probabilities are input to a mini-version of the NEWS model which accounts for the non-linear (diminishing returns) effect of advertising expenditure on sales.

In Table 17.3, while Germany accounts for half of the provisional advertising expenditure it provides 60% of the incremental revenue. This suggests that an allocation based on population is sub-optimal.

Step three

A 'method of steepest ascent' procedure is then utilised to exchange:

(i) an increase in budget allocation in the country yielding the greatest increase in total expected revenues for
(ii) a corresponding decrease in allocation in the country yielding the smallest decrease in expected revenues, without violating minimum or maximum constraints.

This procedure is repeated until the marginal improvement becomes insignificant.

In Table 17.3, local spending in both Belgium and Holland could be reduced to the minimum level (taking advantage of considerable overspill), with Germany getting the bulk of the allocation. Because the model was able to reallocate resources to where they have greatest impact, the expected overall revenue was US$7.5 m higher (+3.5 per cent) than allocating solely on the size of the market, without any increase in advertising budget.

Note that revenues are now reduced from France, Belgium and Holland, but that this is outweighed by the increased revenue from Germany for a total European gain. The reward structure for local managers must equitably reflect this.

EXPANDED ALLOCATION MODELS

After the first year, the approach described in the illustration is modified to include the effect of retaining the previous year's users while adding new ones. For mature brands, advertising elasticities are computed from historical data using a simplified version of the AdBank methodology to estimate marginal sales. In most other respects, the allocation procedure is similar.

In most of the applications, resources must be allocated, not only between countries but also between brands and elements of the marketing mix – eg advertising, consumer promotion, trade support. The modelling process must now reflect the fact that different brands are at different stages of the product life-cycle and could have markedly different objectives. The new brand is building awareness and trial, the slightly older brand is building market share, while the well-established brand is trying to maximise its cash flow. The model must also reflect halo and cannibalisation effects if we have several brands in a category.

In some cases, the allocation across brands is extended over several years, such as to

TABLE 17.4 : Multi-brand allocation model

	Total	Belgium	France	Germany	Holland
INITIAL ALLOCATION					
Actual 1995 sales revenues (m)					
Brand A	700	50	230	350	70
Brand B	225	20	75	100	30
TOTAL	**925**	**70**	**305**	**450**	**100**
FINAL ALLOCATION					
1996 budget allocation (US$m)					
Advertising - Brand A	13.0	0.7	4.0	7.6	0.7
Advertising - Brand B	5.0	0.3	1.4	3.0	0.3
TOTAL ADVERTISING	**18.0**	**1.0**	**5.4**	**10.6**	**1.0**
Trade support - Brand A	12.9	1.0	3.8	6.9	1.2
Trade support - Brand B	4.1	0.4	1.2	2.0	0.5
TOTAL TRADE SUPPORT	**17.0**	**1.4**	**5.0**	**8.9**	**1.7**
Total marketing budget	**35.0**	2.4	10.4	19.5	2.7
Change from initial plan	0%	-9%	-10%	+15%	-29%
Expected 1996 revenue (US$m)	**980**	70	290	515	105
Change from initial plan	+2%	-7%	-3%	+8%	-5%

investigate whether investment spending in a technically new product will pay back over the entire line.

Table 17.4 shows specimen model results from a case with two brands and two activities per country. As many as four concurrent brands for several years have been considered.

At this stage, the input data demands become substantial. We are currently developing a version of the model that will draw on our extensive modelling experience – more than 200 brands in many product categories – to enable us to estimate model parameters from relatively few historical observations by accessing our database.

COMPARISON AND VALIDATION

A test of the model for one of BBDO's clients showed that potential profit was 5 per cent higher using the model's allocation than was achieved allocating the media budget purely on a population basis.

When the model was applied, the overall unit sales forecast for 17 European countries, not corrected for *post facto* knowledge or actual budget, was within 7.5 per cent of the Nielson measurement, although some countries did show higher variance.

ADVERTISING MODELLING AND BRAND VALUATION

As shown above, models such as those used by BBDO can be very effective in determining the return on advertising and in setting the optimal proportion of advertising expenditure across a portfolio or across a region. Such models, however, concentrate solely on the return on advertising expenditure that is achieved within the period in question: by spending US$10m more in Year 1 in the most effective way we can increase sales in Year 1 by US$31.8m. Brand Value can then play an additional role by putting this analysis into a wider context.

The impact of advertising expenditure on Brand Value is principally threefold: it will increase costs, it should increase sales, and it should increase Brand Strength.

The positive impact of increased advertising on Brand Value can be seen in the case study described in this chapter. In Year 1, sales increase by $31.8 million and produce a Gross Margin of $15.9 million whilst costs increase by only $10 million. A result that would make Mr Micawber more than happy and means that the investment justifies itself purely on that one comparison alone.

However, although the investment here can be justified without considering any further return, in reality good brand investment will have an impact beyond the year in which it is made. It will improve preference for the brand for some years to come while the cumulative outcome of brand support year-on-year is to create a multiplier effect which leverages the effect of annual expenditure. This can be demonstrated by including the concept of Brand Value.

Increases or improvements in brand advertising – or indeed any other kind of advertising support – will enhance not only Brand Revenues but also Brand Strength. A well-supported brand will enjoy higher Brand Strength and thereby lower its risk. Using the Interbrand model set out in Chapter 7, the Brand Strength Score would increase under the attribute 'Support' and also potentially under the attributes 'Leadership' and 'Stability'. Thus, by improving advertising, the brand would have a higher Brand Strength Score and consequently a lower risk rate and a higher value – even if everything else remained the same.

Applying this approach to marketing resource allocation has some interesting implications. Firstly, increased advertising expenditure can be justified not only because it increases returns in the short term but also because it increases brand strength and therefore brand value. Secondly, increased advertising expenditure may be justifiable even when it does not increase returns in the short term. It may be instead that it increases returns in the longer term and that this, combined with the increase in brand strength, can demonstrate a higher brand value.

A certain brand investment strategy might knowingly decrease returns in the short term by increasing advertising costs by more than the expected level of increase in gross margin. The result of this would never be contemplated on a pure brand return analysis. However, it would be justified if we looked to the longer term returns on the project. This is precisely the sort of analysis that companies do every day when they introduce brands into new markets or extend them into new activities. They know that the returns will not come immediately but they accept that this is a risk worth taking, given the returns expected in the longer term.

The same approach can be taken when looking at established brands. The assumption usually is that returns on established brands must be made immediately and that otherwise they cannot be justified. This ignores the impact that advertising and other forms of marketing investment have on reducing the risk of future earnings. High spend today on a brand under pressure from own-label competition may not pay for itself straightaway but may ensure that the brand is less likely to be under similar pressure from own-label competition in the future (this is what Nescafé continues to do). High spend today on a market which is currently showing low growth may be justified by establishing the brand early on in the market's development thus ensuring that the brand is stronger when the market begins to grow more rapidly (as evidenced by Microsoft in the software market).

Example's of this were found in many markets through the recession. Those brands that advertised fared better than those that used price cutting to enable them to reach volume targets. Had these scenarios been assessed purely on the basis of sales or earnings the two approaches would have seemed equally acceptable – as long as we meet our forecasts it does not matter what we do. But in fact it is clear that the strategy that enables the brand to meet forecasts and to ensure on-going investment is the better one. The Brand Value measure alongside the Brand Return measure would have ensured that the better strategy was identified and pursued.

By adding the dimension of Brand Strength alongside the question of short term Brand Earnings, models for determining return on advertising can be made even more applicable and can show the longer term benefit of marketing expenditure.

CONCLUSION

For as long as brand owners advertise they will be seeking ways of justifying expenditure – to themselves, to the finance director and to the advertising agency. The models developed, such as the one shown above, already provide a very strong case for a more sophisticated and thoughtful approach to determining levels of marketing expenditure. Looking only at short term return runs the risk of investment decisions being based purely on immediate benefit. A portfolio of brands should be like an investment portfolio or even like a good garden – whilst there needs to be trees to bear fruit in the near future, there should also be those that are planted and nurtured for their longer term potential. And this might mean reallocating resources away from the short term investments and onto those for the longer term.

Brand Value and the principles that it embodies are ways of ensuring that the allocation of marketing resources follows just such a strategy.

EXPERT EVIDENCE
AND BRAND VALUATION

JEREMY PHILLIPS,
INTELLECTUAL PROPERTY CONSULTANT

The growing attention paid to brands over the past decade has forced businesses and lawyers to look afresh at the role of the legally-protected brand. Phenomena such as placing brands on the balance sheet, the facility to raise money on the security of trade marks, the sale of marks independent from the business and the purchase of companies for their brands rather than their physical assets all provide good reasons for seeking expert advice on how much a brand is worth. This chapter looks at when expert evidence should be sought and how the expert witness should conduct himself.

The amalgam of law and science which underlies the work of the expert witness is an imperfect binary system, presently marred by culture conflicts, by ambition and by self-delusion.[1]

The expert witness in brand valuation matters is no different to any other expert witness. He is forced to expose his reputation and to lay bare his expertise and the rules which govern it within the hostile environment of a judicial system which admits the validity of no laws but its own. He is, however, placed at a great disadvantage by the proximity of his own area of expertise to the perimeters of judicial familiarity with brand-based concepts. Few judges are intimately acquainted with the coefficient of expansion of polymeric materials or the chemical composition of antihistamine metabolites. Most, however, given the opportunity, will wax lyrical over their

---

[1] SMITH, DEREK (1993) 'BEING AN EFFECTIVE EXPERT WITNESS', THAMES PUBLISHING

favourite port or choice of car. While judges may not state explicitly that they prefer their own impressions to the evidence submitted to the court, they are all members of the same public which brand-related advertising addresses and which makes its own brand-based market choices.

This chapter, however, is not concerned with judges' purchasing habits. It will ask why brand valuation expert evidence should ever be sought and will then address two issues:

(a) by what rules should an expert witness conduct himself in general?
(b) do these rules have any special degree of significance to the brand valuation specialist?

BRAND EVIDENCE – WHO NEEDS IT?

A swift review of trade mark case law reveals little trace of any interest in brand valuation, either in theory or in practice. Courts have discharged their functions in adjudicating upon the validity of trade marks, prohibiting their unauthorised use and calculating the amount of damages recovered by trade mark owners, to the apparent satisfaction of the business world. In doing so, the judiciary have been able to discharge their judicial functions untroubled by the burden of unsolicited knowledge concerning the relationship of marks to brands and the mathematical techniques for converting theoretical market models into precise financial quantifications.

However, in law as in love, a review of the past provides no clear prescription for the future. Since the mid-1980s there have emerged three distinct, but not unrelated, phenomena. These have forced businesses and their lawyers to look afresh at the role of the legally protected brand. They are:

(a) the controversial placement of brands on balance sheets
(b) the emergent facility for raising money on the security of trade marks
(c) the sale of marks apart from the business to which they were attached and the purchase of companies for their brands rather than for their physical assets.

These phenomena provide three good reasons for seeking expert advice in answering the simple question, 'how much is this brand worth?'.

The recent conspicuous demand for advice on a brand's value has not been reflected by reports of litigated legal disputes on the subject. For this reason, some members of the legal professions are sceptical of the value of the exercise. As an assessment of the value of an intangible, good brand valuation inevitably involves a level of conjecture and supposition. Different techniques have been devised for the calculation of a brand's valuation and the relative values reached by different valuation methodologies. These relative values may bear no similarity at all to each other. Consequently sceptics have been quick to dismiss brand valuation as witchcraft and quackery. Their scepticism has not been eradicated by the doubts and tensions manifested by the accountancy profession in its reflections over the adoption of proper standards for the reporting of brand values within a company's balance sheets.

Much of this scepticism is misplaced. For example, methodologies developed in the USA are likely to differ from those developed in the UK where accounting conventions, the writing-off of assets, tax considerations and take-over mechanisms, dictate that different valuation procedures should be evolved. British brand-valuation experts, however, have not done as much as they could have done in order to displace that scepticism. This stemmed, initially, from an understandable, but now arguably misplaced, desire to preserve the secrecy of their valuation procedures. Some would substitute 'mystique' for 'secrecy'.

A further point should be noted. Brand valuation experts are not the same as market survey experts. Brand valuation experts draw their professional expertise from the world of accounting and finance. They seek to place a market value upon a brand. Market survey specialists do not inhabit that world. They are drawn from the disciplines of psychology and sociology and seek to measure and explain consumer responses to developments within the market-place.

Over recent years market survey evidence has been subjected to the rigours of the most severe judicial criticism. This has reached the situation where there is no point in conducting a market survey unless an expert's survey brief has been drafted from the starting-point of a commitment to comply fully with the legal guidance given, as to relevance and admissibility. This may not be seen by brand valuers as a matter of relevance to them but it would be wrong to ignore it. Psychologically speaking, judges in trade mark cases have developed a heightened awareness of the risk of methodological deficiencies in expert evidence. This does not mean that they will reject such evidence. It indicates, however, that they will not view uncritically the basis upon which brand valuation evidence has been brought, where that evidence is itself the subject of attack in court.

THE 'MAGNIFICENT SEVEN'

As recently as February 1993 the Commercial Court considered the role of the expert witness and laid down seven key guidelines on the duties and responsibilities of expert witnesses. These guidelines, laid down by Mr Justice Cresswell in *The Ikarian Reefer* [1993] FSR 563, are not intended to be exhaustive. They may be supplemented or refined in the light of individual situations in which expert evidence is required. Although *The Ikarian Reefer* was a marine insurance case, it appears that its guidance is intended to influence practice in other areas of law as well.

The seven guidelines are expressed concisely in the law reports. Each is listed in this chapter together with observations which seek to relate them to the general area of brand valuation.

1. Expert evidence presented to the court should be, and should be seen to be, the independent product of the expert uninfluenced as to form or content by the exigencies of litigation.

The test here is whether the brand valuation evidence would be the same, regardless of which party was seeking to introduce it, a test which can only be passed if the expert can refer his conclusions to a consistent and objectively definable methodology. In the case of brand valuation, there are different approaches which may be employed, based, for example, on the criteria of historical development, acquisition costs, current market value or market share. The expert should state clearly which test he has applied and, if necessary, give reasons. If he has applied a different test previously when submitting expert evidence, he should be prepared to explain the basis upon which he has declined to employ the previously used approach.

2. An expert witness should provide independent assistance to the court by way of objective, unbiased opinion in relation to matters within his expertise. An expert witness in the High Court should never assume the role of an advocate.

In one recent intellectual property case involving copyright, one of the experts submitting evidence to the court had rashly gone into print, expressing his view that expert evidence could be partisan. This proposition was vigorously rejected by the court, which considered such expert evidence worthless. The role of expert witness as advocate is less of a problem, since barristers in High Court proceedings jealously guard the right to control the presentation of their client's case. Also brand valuation experts have not, hitherto, had so much experience of court proceedings as to give them the confidence and the inclination to act beyond their brief. In the less formal atmosphere of arbitrations, however, the roles of the two sets of counsel and their respective experts are sometimes less clearly defined and time can be saved by letting one expert question the other directly.

3. An expert witness should state the facts or assumptions upon which his opinion is based. He should not omit the consideration of material facts which could detract from his concluded opinion.

This is really two guidelines rolled into one. Certainly, in a field as publicly visible as brands, it is scarcely feasible for an expert to ignore, for example, such 'extraneous' matters as the effect of product recalls, competition from supermarket lookalikes or imports of 'grey goods' which legitimately bear the same brand name. As to the statement of facts or assumptions upon which the expert opinion is based, the expert witness should not be embarrassed to spell these out in the simplest terms and to repeat them as often as is necessary if it will enable others to follow the evidence more clearly. He will almost certainly be more familiar with the facts and with his assumptions than will those to whom his report is addressed.

4. An expert witness should make it clear when a particular question or issue falls outside his expertise.

Obviously a brand valuation expert would be unwise to be drawn into speculating on a trade mark's validity. Depending upon his expertise and the availability of relevant information, he may well be equally unwise to pass an opinion as to whether a price paid for the acquisition of a brand is reasonable. If a valuation seeks to appraise the worth of a brand internationally, the expert may have made assumptions relating to legal provisions and requirements in other countries. If this is the case, it is better to say so clearly than to have the same admissions teased out of him in the course of examination by a hostile barrister who may be seeking to undermine his credibility.

5. If an opinion is not properly researched because he considers that insufficient data is available, then this must be stated with an indication that the opinion is no more than a provisional one. In cases where an expert witness, who has prepared a report, could not assert that the report contained the truth, the whole truth and nothing but the truth without some qualification, that qualification should be stated in the report.

When the report is being prepared, information may be lacking because:

(a) there is insufficient time to obtain it
(b) the party seeking to introduce the expert evidence has not made it available
(c) the other party has not made it available.

In each case its absence should be noted and may well be remedied, by discovery (if appropriate) or by other means, before the brand valuer is called into the witness box.

6. If, after exchange of reports, an expert witness changes his view on a material matter having read the other side's expert's report or for any other reason, such change of view should be communicated (through legal representatives) to the other side without delay and when appropriate to the court.

This will be relevant where one side's report contains material facts which may require the other side's expert to recalculate his figures or amend his conclusions. Divergence between opposing sets of brand valuation evidence is most likely to result from each expert's initial choice of valuation methodology. In such cases there is little likelihood of one expert being influenced by the contents of the opposing expert's report.

7. Where expert evidence refers to photographs, plans, calculations, analyses, measurements, survey reports or other similar documents, these must be provided to the opposite party at the same time as the exchange of reports.

This should be done as a matter of routine, even where the calculations have been provided by, or are based upon, data supplied by the other party.

BRANDS ARE DIFFERENT

What further points should brand valuation experts bear in mind when preparing or presenting their expert evidence? In this brief chapter an exhaustive review of pitfalls and how to avoid them is impossible, but at least experts can be put on 'red alert' as to problems which careful planning and forethought can reduce or avoid.

In particular, there is a terminological gulf which separates the disciplines of law and brand valuation, not to mention brand valuation experts themselves. Lawyers talk of trade marks, which may be registered or otherwise and which operate within known and predictable parameters. They may indiscriminately use the word 'mark' to indicate a registered trade mark or an unregistered mark and they may use the word 'brand' either as an occasional synonym for 'mark' or in a casual, colloquial sense.

Brand valuers use 'brand' in a more precise and defined sense, though they may define 'brand' differently. It will include the bundle of definable characteristics which enable the public to differentiate one product from another. It may, or may not, include those characteristics which cause the public to prefer that product. It may also include elements which are protected by copyright and design rights, or factors which are related to a product or service but which are extraneous to it. For example, is the fact that Gucci handbags are only sold in the UK in up-market retail outlets such as Harrods part of the bundle of features which defines the Gucci brand? If so, is it also part of the bundle of features which defines the Harrods service brand, assuming that services are 'brands' in the same way as products? The brand valuation expert will know in his own mind exactly what he means by 'brand', but it is not enough merely to know one's own mind if one is being paid to deliver expert evidence. The message is that if one does not define one's terms, convey clearly to lawyers and litigants what those definitions are and remind them as often as they forget, one runs the risk of being misunderstood, or of not being understood at all.

CONCLUSION

Guidelines exist for the creation and presentation of expert evidence. They *are not* there to undermine the expert or to inconvenience the party which relies upon him. They *are* there to reinforce the commitment of the legal system to affirming the primacy of a value which, unlike brands, is absolute: the value of justice before the law. By complying with these guidelines, brand valuation experts also affirm this higher value.

PART THREE

CONCLUSIONS

ACCOUNTABILITY OF
BRAND MANAGEMENT

STEVE CUTHBERT,
THE CHARTERED INSTITUTE OF MARKETING

Marketers must be tired of being told that their profession is
going through a mid-life crisis! Despite significant strides towards
giving marketing a new, more meaningful *raison d'être*, they have
only themselves to blame. Systems to measure the effect of
marketing expenditure lag woefully behind modern management
practice. Ironically, it is measures from the finance profession –
the 'bean counters' whom marketers have always loved to hate –
that are forcing marketing to justify its existence. The exercise,
however, could well prove to be marketers' salvation.

A plethora of surveys over recent years has shown marketing to be sadly lacking. In
1994 the consultancy, Coopers & Lybrand, found that while marketing directors were,
on the whole, happy with their performance, their managing directors were less than
enthusiastic about marketing's contribution to corporate health. A survey conducted by
The Leo Burnett Brand Consultancy and Arthur Andersen, two years later, indicated
that more than 50 per cent of finance directors believe the marketing function has not
been properly accountable for a whole decade. In a further study conducted in 1995 by
Total Research and Interbrand, only 61 per cent of finance directors believed marketing had become more accountable over the past ten years, and just 40 per cent believed
marketers understood the value of brands any better than they did in the mid-1980s.

When it is considered that, according to the Advertising Association, EU countries collectively spent £37bn on advertising in 1996 (and the expenditure on marketing as a whole was more than three times that figure), it is not surprising that
marketing is in the firing line. Ways to measure it effectiveness are, consequently,
being urgently sought.

CURRENT SITUATION

It is tempting for marketers to dismiss criticism of their performance as a lack of understanding by accountants of their creative role. But they do so at their peril. Marketers have lost much of the corporate high ground in terms of a perceived lack of accountability. Thus, they cannot afford to let themselves be marginalised any longer. Marketers are the first to complain when their budgets are plundered when times get tough. But, until they can justify why they need their budgets and demonstrate a definite link between marketing expenditure and profit, they will continue to be taken advantage of.

Marketing escaped relatively unscathed from the rigorous analysis and re-engineering suffered by many corporate departments in the early 1990s. But the legacy of recession is a new climate of accountability, which means giving value for money. Marketing is not immune from these demands. The finance director will be less than impressed by jargon describing 'reach' or 'levels of awareness' from the marketing director when the latter is asked what contribution his department has made to the bottom line!

During the 1980s a rather casual approach to accountability did not seem to matter. Growth was good and new sectors – financial services, IT and retailing – were adopting marketing techniques. Brand managers presided over powerful fiefdoms while chief executives delegated to young ambitious marketers. Concomitantly, budgets and departmental head counts rose. Support services, such as advertising agencies, were the happy beneficiaries of marketing largesse.

These halcyon days are over, and it is generally acknowledged that marketing has been too remote, for too long, from the nerve centre of the organisation. It has failed to pick up on major trends in its sphere of operations. These involve:

- global competition
- new technology
- the service revolution
- confident powerful buyers
- the need for innovation.

Thus, it is not surprising that many marketing departments are being examined, analysed and turned inside out. Words such as 'measurement' and 'accountability' are starting to be applied to marketing, which has for too long been regarded as something of a budgeting black hole.

Value of brands

It is a happy coincidence – and a useful catalyst – that the financial community has begun to take such an interest in the value of brands. The 'brands on the balance sheet' debate has been instrumental in forcing many people in the company – investors, analysts, accountants, followed by general managers and marketers – to focus on those assets which constitute the true worth of many businesses. What began as a narrow balance-sheet exercise has developed into techniques that allow companies to effectively manage their major assets – their brands.

The renewed emphasis on brands has forced marketing to take a long hard look at itself and challenge many of its long-held and fundamental tenets. For example:

- who is the brand manager?
- has conventional brand management delivered?
- should conventional product branding be replaced by corporate branding?
- should there be a marketing department at all?

Enlightened marketing departments are in painful transition towards radically re-engineered and reconstituted functions.

STRUCTURAL ISSUES

The role of marketing

One of the most basic issues marketers are having to wrestle with is: Marketing (with a capital M) or marketing (with a small m)? Should Marketing be a discrete function, with a hierarchy of people reporting in to a marketing director? Or should it be a philosophy, a *modus operandi*, that permeates the entire organisation, so that everyone thinks 'marketing' in everything they do?

Management consultants McKinsey are strong advocates of the latter option. They recommend breaking down functional 'silos' within organisations and replacing them with cross-functional teams. It is a compelling argument. The longer marketing, finance, distribution and human resources and production sit in their ivory towers, the longer the futile struggle of each for predominance, and the longer the needs of the customer are neglected. Everyone in the organisation should be financially literate, argue McKinsey, and should understand people and the marketing strategy. This knowledge should all be directed at a 'customer needs first' orientation. If one starts with customer satisfaction and works backwards, the argument is that the company will be more profitable and successful in the long term than if it persists with the traditional 'strait-jacket' approach.

In such a structure the ultimate brand manager should be the chief executive who leads and drives the philosophy of customer orientation. He becomes the corporate brand champion. The chief executive, however, clearly does not abrogate responsibility for marketing and customer service. In many cases each 'function', eg marketing, finance and human resources, needs its own dedicated champion. This is because of the need to provide a technical infrastructure for the management of its respective disciplines. Each brand – whether product or company – needs a custodian, who manages its interests and development across what is often a growing number of different markets and countries. But the idea is to avoid the 'marketing – that's not my job' syndrome.

Relationships
Corporate brand v. product brand

There is the complex relationship between the corporate brand and the product brand to consider. As Alan Mitchell has said in *Marketing Business*:

> *Any conceivable calculation of marketing weight or importance, whether it is by advertising or total marketing spend, or the turnover and profits generated by the brands in question, would reveal the corporate brand to be the centre of modern marketing gravity.*

While the words of marketing still tend to revolve round the fast moving consumer goods (FMCG) brand, more and more FMCG companies are following organisations such as Heinz, Kellogg and Cadbury down the road of umbrella branding and corporate endorsement.

Nevertheless, most published thinking, analysis and research assumes otherwise. Firms such as Nielsen, IRI and OHAL have developed sophisticated econometric models using scanning data to track the effects of promotions, pricing changes and advertising campaigns. But the corporate brander has no equivalent tools at his disposal.

There are some signs that this vacuum is being filled – not least by two studies conducted by The Chartered Institute of Marketing. The first, in 1995, by researchers at Bradford University Management School, examined the correlation between marketing and profitability in manufacturing industry. The second, by London Business School, looked at the return on marketing expenditure in financial services companies. The Marketing Council is building on this knowledge with research from the London Business School (LBS) showing a positive link between marketing orientation and business performance.

Corporate branding, with its emphasis on the pervading corporate ideology which is expressed in everything the company does and which creates an unmistakable corporate identity, represents another potential threat to the traditional marketing department. According to James Collins and Jerry Porras, in their book *Built to Last,* the continual stream of great products and services from some companies, eg 3M, American Express, IBM and Motorola, stems from the companies being outstanding organisations, not the other way round.

Likewise, Chris Macrae of the World Class Branding Network, argues in his book, *Brand Chartering*, that global umbrella and corporate brands have moved beyond the deliverance of 'unique selling points'. They have become 'unique organising purposes' that reach back into the company, influencing its values, its priorities, style of work and the structure of the business itself.

Implicit in such arguments are uncomfortable questions about the exact status of marketing personnel. Who will lead which troops in the battle of the corporate brands? How are they to be organised? As yet, these increasingly important questions remain tantalisingly open, but marketers have a perfect opportunity to seize the high ground.

Unique organisation proposition

Stan Maklan of the ForeFront Consultancy, and Cranfield School of Management's Simon Knox, are two proponents of the theory that conventional brand management has outlived its usefulness. They draw attention to the gap that has arisen between product brand value and customer value. Traditional product branding no longer adds sufficient customer value, they argue, because it is generally a standardised offer which is the result of a functional management hierarchy not structured to be sufficiently broad or responsive to satisfy modern customer demands.

Maklan and Knox suggest a new management tool, the 'unique organisation proposition' (UOP), to bridge this gap. The UOP will integrate a company's core business processes into a visible set of credentials that adds customer value through the supply chain. The metaphor for the UOP is that of a cable sheath which holds, directs and provides a consistent purpose to the individual 'wires' of business processes. The sheath is the visible embodiment of the organisation's reputation, network of relationships and portfolio of its products and customers.

In this view of the world, marketing's task is to design and build a cable sheath that represents the organisation's UOP in a compelling manner to the organisation's stakeholders. In so doing it allows companies to build powerful and branded value chains that deliver superior customer value while differentiating the company's offering. The UOP allows the company to return to competition and pricing based on value added.

The activities that develop and sustain the UOP are very different from the conventional product branding practices that it replaces. Designing the UOP means integrating the core business processes, which Maklan and Knox define as supply partnership, asset management, resource transformation, customer development, and marketing planning. Marketing, with its traditional focus on understanding customers' purchasing motivations and competitive threats, is well-placed to lead UOP management. However, marketers must lay aside their traditional product brand engineering tools, advertising and promotion, in order to focus on the major issue of what creates customer value. This is necessary if they are to regain their role at the heart of the value-adding process.

Global marketing

Another issue currently taxing marketers is the concept of global marketing versus strong local brands. Perhaps the best analysis of this problem again comes from Alan Mitchell (*Marketing Business*, September 1995). He suggests that, while competition may be forcing many companies to 'go global', not all companies need global brands; world-class branding is not necessarily the same thing as global branding. Mitchell urges marketers to remember that, for the vast majority of the population, life is a very local affair – and they want it to remain so.

ACCOUNTABILITY

It is these structural issues that companies must resolve before they can move towards defining and developing appropriate and robust measures of accountability. Few, if any, are of the opinion that one measure of accountability is sufficient on its own. The primary techniques used to measure the effectiveness of marketing expenditure have not changed for many years. They are:

- market share analysis
- ad tracking
- consumer satisfaction surveys
- adstock modelling
- measures of consumer brand equity
- econometric modelling.

Important though these are, they do not explicitly link marketing investment to profit. What's more, marketing directors feel that these evaluation measures are inadequate. For example, it is agreed that no technique is totally accurate, and it is also difficult to agree on criteria for evaluation.

Continuous model budgeting

In the search for a solution the Leo Burnett Brand Consultancy and Arthur Andersen have, together, come up with an approach to marketing accountability based on cross-functional teams and 'continuous model budgeting'. These teams, including marketing and finance, will understand financial and marketing goals within overall corporate objectives. From this standpoint they will develop a mutual and shared understanding of current brand performance, including the relationship between sales and profitability. This mutuality will, hopefully, result in agreement on alternative strategies. Key financial issues which they will address include:

- identifying the basis for the allocation of overheads
- the timing of revenue and expenditure
- potential capacity constraints
- the forecasting period and/or the risk factor which should be applied to forecast profit streams of the alternative strategies.

The continuous model budgeting includes key financial and market data from an evaluation model which has been successfully used on a number of well-known brands to explain previous activity and to predict future brand performance.

This approach will allow the development of what Leo Burnett and Andersens call 'brand portfolio management'. They believe that this will help marketing management discuss investment options on an equal basis with their finance colleagues. Continuous budgeting provides a tool to show the impact of investment decisions on future profitability, thereby helping marketing to participate meaningfully in decisions on marketing investment. It is a process which involves modelling key variables, including price, distribution, advertising spend and consumer perceptions of relative worth over the medium- to long-term and helps management to forecast the profit impact of different investment decisions. As Andersens partner, Howard Barrett, suggests:

To be able to corral marketing and finance together over such a model would avoid the slow death by a thousand cuts that is suffered by so many marketing budgets: finance would be jointly accountable with marketing for achieving consistent brand earnings over the medium-term.

Information-age accounting

While marketers complain that their companies information systems do not provide the information needed to manage a marketing strategy effectively, Barrett warns that accountants, who are busily re-inventing their own profession, also have designs on marketing information. Information-age accounting is designed to move the accounting function from being a passive recorder of historic data to providing a forward-looking and holistic view of the business.

Information-age accounting seeks to integrate knowledge from across the entire company in a systemic fashion. It draws heavily on computer simulation, scenario planning and strategic gaming to test alternative strategies and develop creative approaches to implementation. It also seeks to identify the contribution of teams, processes, divisions and the total company. A key feature is process understanding, measurement and charting of patterns of behaviour that enable problem diagnosis. The principles represent a positive opportunity for marketing to work jointly with finance to create a shared understanding of the profit-creation process.

CONCLUSIONS

According to research conducted by the Leo Burnett Brand Consultancy and Arthur Andersen, marketing and finance directors agree that profit contribution, volume, market share and shareholder value creation are the key aspects of performance on which marketers should be measured. However, a third of finance directors believe there are no procedures in place to measure the effectiveness of marketing expenditure, and 84 per cent of finance directors are only partially satisfied that the effectiveness of marketing activity is being properly evaluated. The message that comes across loud and clear, is that marketing needs to become smarter in systematically quantifying the effect of its activities and of marketing expenditure.

If marketing is to be truly pro-active it needs to convince senior management that it is indeed accountable. It has to do so in order to participate meaningfully in debates about brand investment and to contribute to the complex process of managing trade-offs in expenditure between, for example, discount levels versus consumer pricing and media allocations.

Systems being developed to track brand equities will form the reference point for consistent brand valuations and the source from which key data will be extracted for the annual report. They will become a vital part of good corporate governance and transparent reporting of marketing performance. They will also contribute to raising the profile of marketing in the boardroom. If marketing tackles its mid-life crisis, and takes the initiative, it can only be a matter of time before the marketing director takes his place beside the finance director and the chief executive in the investor-relations line-up.

The speed at which he does so is largely in his hands. As John Murphy of Interbrand observed in his foreword to the second edition of *Brand Valuation*,

> *The stringency of accounting procedures is bringing together marketing and brand management, areas which in the past have relied to a large extent mainly upon intuition. These new analytical tools seem certain to have a profound and long-lasting impact.*

Whether marketing directors truly have the appetite to be judged and rewarded according to such tools remains to be seen. According to Interbrand's Tom Blackett, 'perhaps the most random of the management disciplines will at last be brought to book'.

20

BRAND VALUATION: TODAY AND TOMORROW

JEREMY SAMPSON, INTERBRAND AFRICA

Writing a chapter at the end of a book, with contributions by a dazzling array of highly knowledgeable experts, is akin to speaking at the end of a two-day conference. There is a need to review the common threads, attempt to focus on the key issues and create a platform on which to base the future vision.

Some have defined the brand and branding and explained how the brand benefits the manufacturer, the retailer and the consumer. Others have talked about valuing brands as a common day occurrence, as indeed it is in some countries, forgetting that in others it is a rarity. This debate could not have taken place before 1980. Indeed, while Rupert Murdoch first put his mast-head valuations on to the balance sheet of Australia's News Group in 1984, and the UK's Rank Hovis McDougall (RHM) did the same in 1988, there has been much activity. Yet today in the UK very few companies put brands on their balance sheets. Of all Interbrand's valuation work, little more than 15 per cent is for balance sheet purposes. If brand valuations are to be published regularly in the annual financial statements, a fresh valuation must be carried out each year. After all, any valuation is based on an appraisal of all the facts as they are *now*, not yesterday or tomorrow. In the case of RHM, the result was that the value of the brands went down each year, so reinforcing the warning that brands are not a licence to print money.

In the boardrooms of top companies it is usual to find that most, if not all, directors have a financial background. Therefore it is hardly surprising to find that, for much of the twentieth century, the majority of a company's assets have been tangible, ie property, plant and equipment, stock, investments and cash. The statement made by John Stuart, a former chairman of Quaker that: 'if this business were to be split up, I would be glad to take the brands, trade marks and goodwill and you could have

FIGURE 20.1: A 'Continuum'

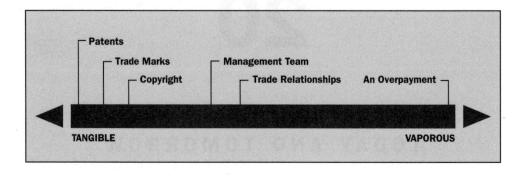

Patents
Trade Marks   Management Team
Copyright   Trade Relationships   An Overpayment

TANGIBLE   VAPOROUS

all the bricks and mortar and I would fare better than you', still meets with blank looks. Yet, there is a growing acceptance among the marketing-based companies that Stuart was correct.

Today, intangible assets are made up of:

- copyrights, licences and patents
- technical expertise and know-how
- management teams, skills and competencies
- trade marks and brands (including mastheads)
- recipes and formulae
- trade agreements.

These are often far more valuable than the 'tangibles', with trade marks and brands the most valuable of all. In fact, in merger and acquisition (M&A) activity, the percentage of the bid price made up by the intangibles was 20 per cent in the Eighties. Ten years on, some brand-rich companies were quoting a figure of over 70 per cent. This reflects the price that some companies were prepared to pay for corporate growth, future success and ongoing profitability.

WHY VALUE BRANDS?

The methodology now accepted as the best internationally, was developed by Interbrand in London, starting in the early 1980s. Interbrand has now valued over 1,500 leading brands, in more than 25 countries, to an aggregate total value exceeding $50bn. Apart from providing a unique analytical tool for putting a financial value on a brand, it is also relatively easy to measure its strength and potential, thus providing crucial data, critical to marketing investments and strategic brand decisions.

Brands are, therefore, valued for a wide variety of reasons, recognising that different people have different needs:

- chief executives, wanting to unlock shareholder value, buy or sell brands as the result of changes in strategy or to increase the accountability for these valuable assets
- bankers, wanting to establish a fair value for brands as part of their security
- brand managers, wanting to develop and extend the equity of their brands
- advertising agencies, wishing to demonstrate that a reduction in ad-spend can reduce the value of the brand
- marketing directors, wanting to improve the management of their brand portfolios
- accountants, wanting to recognise these most valuable assets on balance sheets
- finance directors, wanting to communicate the value of their brands to investors and shareholders
- finance directors, establishing royalty rates for brands used by third parties in joint ventures
- marketing directors, assessing the potential impact of key investment decisions such as resource allocation, disposal identification and portfolio management.

THE EMERGING CORPORATE BRAND

Given the background outlined above, it is easy to fall into the trap of thinking that brands revolve around products and services alone. Such an outlook ignores what is probably becoming the most potent brand of all, the corporate brand.

The corporate brand is increasingly being given international priority. There is a growing awareness that companies have a value way above the tangible value of their assets, provided they have created the added-value aspect by creating and building brands and projecting their own image.

A recent edition of *Fortune* magazine put it another way when it said that, "in the next few years reputation will only grow in value as an asset". Corporate reputation can mean the difference in raising funds, recruiting the top graduates, keeping the best staff and persuading people to buy your products at a premium. It is surely common sense that, if the corporate is not perceived favourably, it is put at a huge disadvantage. In rating the USA's most admired companies, *Fortune* makes it clear that companies cannot live by numbers alone and that 'intangibles', such as the ability to attract and keep talented people, are taking on greater importance.

Arguably two of the most successfully marketed companies in recent years are Microsoft of the USA headed by the inimitable Bill Gates, and Virgin of the UK with the up-front Richard Branson. Virtues such as obsession and passion spring to mind, and all marketing emanates from a co-ordinated structure, with the leaders totally involved.

Currently, the marketing shift in emphasis is to the corporate brand, something in which both Virgin and Microsoft were ahead of the game. This view was put forward by the UK magazine *Marketing* recently when 'talking about the emerging power brands'. A vital factor common to the list of rising stars is that they have shifted emphasis from product to corporate brands. The leverage power of the corporate identity is under-utilised by many companies, concentrating instead on the individual strengths of brands within the company. The Virgin company has exploited the strength of its corporate brand to the full. In an era where strategic management of the corporate brand is key, marketing literacy at the top has never been so important. Companies facing up to the challenges of the next millennium realise that it is the marketer who will achieve the breakthrough.

ACCOUNTANT V. MARKETER

Added to the valuation debate is the diametrically opposed culture of the accountant, who writes everything off as quickly as is legally possible, and the culture of the marketer. The latter's function is to build brands in every way possible. However, an interesting change occurred in June 1996, with the UK Accounting Standards Board issuing an exposure draft on accounting for goodwill and intangible assets. In essence it proposes:

– that intangible assets (including brands) be recognised *separately* from purchased goodwill
– that intangible assets believed to have indefinitely long lives (such as brands) *do not need to be depreciated*
– that the values of intangible assets *must* be reviewed for impairment at year end, based on economic value.

From the above it would appear that the ASB now supports the view that:

– brands are separable assets
– the value of a brand does not necessarily decline in a straight line over a predetermined period and indeed may not decline at all
– companies need to monitor regularly that a brand value has not declined.

It is not surprising that, as a result of this clash of cultures, accountants and marketers do not always sit together easily. This situation is exacerbated by the increasing perception of the potency of the corporate brand, highlighting the inadequacy of some company chiefs and their internal structures to handle this new opportunity. Another cause of friction is the culture of the financial world to be accountable and deal in tangibles, whereas the marketers – whose budgets are now big – often appear unaccountable because they are dealing in image and other intangibles.

Increasingly it can be argued that companies, reporting on a quarterly or half-yearly basis to shareholders (especially institutions whose concern is short- to medium-term gain), are under great pressure. The institutions have immense power and, if not satisfied, will use it. Compare this with the marketer, who has to be consistently and persistently nurturing his brands over years and even decades, steadily developing them rather than lurching about.

In the past some companies deliberately chose not to declare their parentage of brands, but this is changing. Certainly the recognition by Ernest Sanders, when at Guinness, of the underlying value of Distillers with its treasure chest of brands in the mid-1980s, and the subsequent hostile and extremely bitter takeover battle helped to change attitudes. Two recent examples of companies arguing that their share prices did not truly reflect the value of their brands were LIG, owner of global condom brand-leader Durex, and the Pearson Group, owner of: Lazards *Financial Times*, Penguin Books and Madam Tussaud's. It is perhaps the debate about releasing the value of segments of companies, commonly termed un-bundling, of searching for hidden value and the need to add value; and, if someone can add more value than you, sell it. It is a debate that is set to become increasingly noisy.

The annual report is increasingly seen as a sort of sanitised financial gobbledegook, with many of the key indicators heavily camouflaged and net asset value (NAV) being totally irrelevant to ruling share prices. Currently, many African mining houses trade at a discount of up to 20 per cent to the declared NAV, while a company such as Coca-Cola, owning the world's most valuable brand at $56bn, trades at a 1400 per cent premium to the declared NAV. The lack of reference to some of the key drivers of corporate success, 'the intangibles', prompted the following comment from Fortune:

> *Leaving the most important assets off the balance sheet, and counting money spent on them as immediate expenses, gives readers of financial reports – including company executives – a distorted picture of how a company makes money.*

The potency of leveraging the corporate brand is still in its infancy. Certainly in investor-relations terms, the notion that brand leaders can ensure better-than-average results to their owners, is gaining in recognition. In other words, buying shares in companies owning top brands can be highly beneficial to investors. Over a decade Gillette's stock averaged an annual return of a stunning 30 per cent, while Procter & Gamble's return averaged a little under 20 per cent and it has just reported its 41st year of continuous year-on-year financial growth.

As *Marketing* magazine stated in an editorial:

> *If investment in brands is cut the effects will take time to appear – but appear they will, weakening brands fatally just as increasing consumer demand means that stronger brands can prosper. It's like being on a roller-coaster and cutting the power whenever you come to an uphill section. Momentum may carry you forward for a while, but eventually you'll stall.*
>
> *Marketing then, needs investment, and more so in bad times than in good. But it's no good whingeing. Marketers will simply have to present their case more effectively, convincing both their own internal money men and outside investors that what they do, far from being peripheral, is vital to the long-term success of a business.*

This is a task which will never be finished, for every year a new generation of graduate accountants and would-be merchant bankers arrives on the scene and is trained to rate companies by asset value or dividend.

Thus marketers will have to use the jargon of the accountants to present their case. This is not easy when they often have a jaundiced perspective of that catch-all phrase 'goodwill'. But, for the first time, a device is available that can span the differing cultures, the ability to value and monitor brands that will be acceptable to both accountant and marketer.

FUTURE TRENDS

At present a range of trends is emerging that will impact to varying degrees on brands:

1. Chief executives are being exposed increasingly to the heat of accountability, and if both they and their companies' share price are not performing to satisfaction, institutions will demand or indeed take what they deem as suitable action be taken.
2. Major US manufacturers and owners of top brands, facing a mature domestic market and in some cases the erosion of their brands by private label, are exporting those brands to emerging markets. These brands are tried and tested, everything is in place and all that is required is to take them global. When it is considered that by the year 2000, 50 per cent of the US population will be over 55, in Europe population growth is static or even negative, while in Africa and the Far East population is increasing dramatically; in South Africa 50 per cent of the population will be under the age of 18, which means that the marketing opportunities are fascinating.
3. Companies are realising the need to adjust from a financial to a total marketing culture. The days of cost cutting are gone, cost controls become a given, and the new mood recognises that key to future competitiveness is in providing consumer value, and this comes from marketing.

The Marketing Council view

John Stubbs, chief executive of the Marketing Council states, "in an increasingly competitive world companies can only succeed against foreign competition through innovation and differentiation – marketing again". Recent research by the 'Council' among stock brokers and investment managers indicates that:

- 96 per cent consider the survival of companies to be dependent on marketing
- 75 per cent concur with the statement, "there is a need for the whole company to understand marketing and not just one department"
- 41 per cent think business competitiveness is driven by marketing.

TABLE 20.1: Some present valuation activity concerning major brands

			AMOUNT	YEAR
(a) INVESTOR RELATIONS				
• Pearson Group/UK				
– *Financial Times*			£585m	
– *Penguin Books*			£600m	1996
– *Madam Tussaud's*			£345m	
– Lazards			£255m	

			AMOUNT	YEAR
(b) M&A ACTIVITY				
• IBM		Lotus	$3.5bn	1995
• Novell		Wordperfect	$1.42bn	1995
• Quaker	taking over	Snapple	$1.70bn	1994
• Time Life	taking over	Warner	$12.84bn	1995
• AT&T	taking over	NCR	$7.53bn	1995
• Glaxo	taking over	Wellcome	£9.1bn	1996
• Chase Manhattan	merge with	Chemical Bank	$10bn	1996
• Gillette	taking over	Duracell	$7bn	1996
• Lloyds Bank	taking over	TSB	$5.1bn	1996
• Granada	taking over	Forte	$3.4bn	1996

			AMOUNT	YEAR
(c) BRANDS				
• L'Oréal	buying	Maybelline	£660m	1995
• Mastercard	buying	Access	£100m	1995
• Heinz	buying	Farleys (Boots)	£94m (NAV £20.7m)	1994
• SmithKline Beacham	buying	Sterling Health (Kodak)	$3bn	1994
• Unilever	buying	Colman's Mustard (RK&Co)	£147m	1995
• Bass	buying	Robinsons Barley (Unilever)	£103m	1994

NB: The largest recorded deal, done in 1988, remains the $25bn paid by Kohlberg Kravis Roberts for R.J.R. Nabisco (NAVx2)

Marketing budgets

Management increasingly asks where, what are often large, marketing budgets were used and to what effect. It is no longer good enough to reiterate Leverhulme's 50 : 50 advertising principle.

Corporate brand's power

Those that continue to talk about products and product life cycles are failing to realise that by making products into brands you can mitigate or even avoid 'life cycles'. With over 70 per cent of the top brands in the USA and UK having been first introduced some forty years ago, the message must be to remain persistent and consistent. Oscar Wilde's view that "the refuge of the uncreative is consistency" is not entirely relevant here, although one must always maintain a point of difference, continually review and if necessary update the appearance of the identity and all visual elements, and never relinquish ownership of the brand to a third party. The 'halo effect' of a company built up to be a strong corporate brand, with its name and trade marks registered and protected globally, raises the barriers significantly to entry for newcomers. Today, creating a new global name that can work and be registered in all locations is highly complicated, time consuming and expensive. Difficult to achieve it may be but, it is still possible if placed in the right hands.

Concluding remarks

In conclusion, it should be remembered that brand valuation was only first used in the early Eighties and is still little more than 15 years old and, while gaining in recognition and credibility, remains a concept that causes unease to many. But then, anything new has the same effect.

Given the opportunity that brand valuation brings to management, to start quantifying previously nebulous 'black holes' termed the 'marketing budget', the concept is creating increasing interest, and to some is already a 'tool' which they could not do without. Certainly with the increasing awareness of brands and their value, many companies that until now have remained faithful to products and services, are coming to realise that the future for commodities is strictly limited, and with this will come a surge of branding activity.

The multinational companies with global brands will continue to adjust their core activities. New labels will be created for 'transformation dynamics' and 're-engineering'. There will, inevitably, if growth is to continue be a realignment of global brands and a move to universal brand centricity.

The founder of Interbrand, John Murphy is very clear about the future:

> *The major trend is to treat brands as 'things' which are buyable, sellable, memorable, mortgageable, licensable etc. etc., not as insubstantial puffs of Scotch mist which are somehow 'there' but can never be.*

APPENDIX

DRAFT FINANCIAL REPORTING STANDARD: GOODWILL AND INTANGIBLE ASSETS

ACCOUNTING STANDARDS BOARD (UK)
JUNE 1996

- [Draft] Financial Reporting Standard • is set out
in paragraphs 1–101.

- The Statement of Standard Accounting Practice set out in
paragraphs 4–59 should be read in the context of the Objective as
stated in paragraph 1 and the definitions set out in paragraphs 2 and
3 and also of the Foreword to Accounting Standards and the
Statement of Principles for Financial Reporting currently in issue.

- The Explanation set out in paragraphs 60–101 shall be regarded as
part of the Statement of Standard Accounting Practice in so far as it
assists in interpreting that statement.

- Appendix III 'The Development of the FRED' reviews
considerations and arguments that were thought significant by
members of the Board in reaching the conclusions on the [draft] FRS.

*This draft is issued by the Accounting Standards Board for comment. It should be noted that
the draft may be modified in the light of comment received before being issued in final form.*

CONTENTS

PREFACE

Financial Reporting Exposure Draft (FRED) 12 addresses the accounting for goodwill and intangible assets. Its proposals are based on those included in a Working Paper 'Goodwill and Intangible Assets', published by the Accounting Standards Board in June 1995 and discussed at a public hearing in September and October 1995. The Board received support for the overall approach proposed in the Working Paper from the majority of those commenting on it.

No major changes have been made to this approach. However, certain details have been amended in the light of suggestions made by respondents. The FRED also deals with matters not covered by the Working Paper, such as disclosure requirements and the accounting for negative goodwill. The Board would welcome comments on any aspect of the FRED.

The development of the proposed approach

Accounting for goodwill has been a contentious issue in the UK for many years. SSAP 22 'Accounting for goodwill' has been criticised for a number of reasons. First, it permits a choice of accounting treatments. Its preferred treatment, used for the vast majority of acquisitions, requires purchased goodwill to be eliminated immediately against reserves. This treatment has been criticised for giving the impression that the acquirer's net worth has been depleted or even eliminated and for causing the financial statements to overstate the rates of return achieved on acquired investments. The problem of equity depletion has encouraged companies to reduce amounts attributed to purchased goodwill by separately valuing brands and similar intangible assets as identifiable assets on the balance sheet. Given that such intangible assets are very similar in nature to goodwill, it is often considered inappropriate for the two to be accounted for so differently. Furthermore, inconsistencies exist in the manner in which the elimination of goodwill against reserves is presented. Most companies currently eliminate goodwill against the profit and loss reserve, showing the cumulative amount written off in a note to the accounts. Others set up a separate goodwill reserve. Finally, it is of note that SSAP 22's preferred treatment is not one that is accepted internationally, either in present practice or as a possible future development.

However, no alternative approach has gained universal acceptance. Each possible approach leads to inconsistencies with other aspects of financial reporting and each attracts criticism. Against this background, the Board has sought to develop an approach that provides meaningful information to users of financial statements while also being considered to be workable and acceptable by those preparing financial statements.

The Board started by exploring a number of options in a Discussion Paper issued in 1993. It then undertook extensive consultation with industry, the profession and the investment community before arriving at what it believed to be a meaningful and workable approach. This approach requires goodwill and intangible assets to be capitalised and either amortised over their useful economic lives or, where their useful economic lives are indefinite, reviewed for impairment each period. The rationale underlying this approach is explained in Appendix III 'The Development of the FRED'.

The proposed approach was field-tested by a number of major companies and published in a Working Paper 'Goodwill and Intangible Assets' in June 1995.

Many interested parties responded to the Working Paper proposals, a number also choosing to present their views at the subsequent public hearing. A wide range of views was presented and Board members appreciated the contributions made. The proposals attracted the broad support of the majority of those responding to the Working Paper. In the light of the arguments presented at the hearing, the FRED has been developed without changing the basic approach proposed in the Working Paper.

Changes made to the Working Paper proposals

The Working Paper presented outlined proposals for the accounting for goodwill and intangible assets. In the drafting of the FRED, certain requirements have been added or refined. The Board has sought to minimise the extent of additional detail and, in particular, has not made the proposals for impairment reviews any more detailed or prescriptive than those included in the Working Paper.

New proposals added to the FRED concern:

- *the presentation of positive goodwill*—which the FRED proposes should be shown amongst the assets of the reporting entity, rather than as a negative balance amongst reserves. Most of those commenting on the two options put forward in the Working Paper believed that presentation amongst the assets better reflects the nature of goodwill. The presentation has no effect on any other requirements proposed by the FRED.
- *the treatment of negative goodwill*—which the FRED proposes should be recognised within the same heading on the balance sheet as positive goodwill and written back in the statement of total recognised gains and losses as it reduces.
- *disclosure requirements*—these were not discussed in detail in the Working Paper.

In the light of comments made by those responding to the Working Paper and those presenting their views at the public hearing, a number of minor changes have been made to the Working Paper proposals. These are explained in paragraphs 47–52 of Appendix III 'The Development of the FRED'.

Alternative view

One Board member favours an alternative approach to that proposed in this FRED. Under the alternative approach, goodwill would be deducted immediately from shareholders' equity. In this respect, the approach would be similar to the preferred accounting treatment presently permitted by SSAP 22, but the deduction would be by way of establishing a goodwill reserve within shareholders' equity. While the business continued to be held, the goodwill would be treated as a quasi-asset, not amortised but reviewed for permanent impairment. This would be achieved using high-level impairment indicators to identify possible impairment and using the full impairment reviews outlined in the FRED only for that goodwill whose value was in doubt. Intangible assets would undergo the same impairment reviews as goodwill.

The Board member who favours this approach believes that it places greater emphasis on the nature of goodwill, recognising that it is neither an asset nor an immediate loss in value; he further argues that it recognises stewardship, eliminates current options and places greater emphasis on the needs of users.

The rationale for this approach is explained in Appendix IV 'Alternative View'. The reason why the remaining Board members do not support this approach is explained in paragraphs 53–58 of Appendix III 'The Development of the FRED'.

Particular issues on which comments are invited

The Board would welcome comments on any aspect of the FRED. Respondents' views are especially sought on the matters set out below. It would be helpful if respondents could support comments with reasons and, where applicable, preferred alternatives.

1. Do you accept the basic approach proposed, ie that purchased goodwill and intangible assets should be capitalised and subjected either to systematic amortisation over a limited period or to an annual impairment review? If you do not accept the basic approach proposed, what approaches would you accept, and why?
2. Do you support the rebuttable presumption that acquired businesses and intangible assets have useful economic lives that do not exceed 20 years?
3. Are there any other events or changes in circumstances indicating a possible impairment that you believe should be added to the list given in paragraph 80 of the Explanation?
4. Do you believe that the procedures set out for performing impairment reviews are meaningful and workable? In particular:
   (a) do you believe that it is possible to continue to trace and measure purchased goodwill after the acquisition date?

(b) do you believe that it is appropriate that individual income-generating units may be combined for the purposes of assessing the recoverability of the goodwill, as proposed in paragraph 28?

(c) are there any ways in which the procedures could be improved?

5. Do you support the proposed accounting for negative goodwill, as set out in paragraphs 38–40 of the Statement of Standard Accounting Practice and 95–99 of the Explanation? In particular, in view of the arguments given in paragraph 45 of Appendix III 'The Development of the FRED', do you agree that the FRS should require goodwill to be written back in the statement of total recognised gains and losses (rather than the profit and loss account) unless the investment has been sold?

6. Do you believe that the proposed disclosure requirements are sufficient and necessary? In particular:

(a) do you support the proposal to require disclosure of the bases on which intangible assets are fair valued on initial recognition?

(b) should such disclosure be required in the notes to the accounts or encouraged in the operating and financial review?

(c) it is proposed that the carrying values of intangible assets should be disclosed by class. No further disclosure is proposed. Do you believe that further disclosures (for example by segment or of major individual assets or groups of assets) should be required in the notes or encouraged in the operating and financial review?

7. Do you think that the transitional arrangements are appropriate?

8. Do you prefer the alternative approach outlined in Appendix IV (whereby goodwill is deducted from shareholders' equity and subject to high-level impairment reviews but not amortisation)? If so, why?

SUMMARY

General

(a)   [Draft] Financial Reporting Standard • sets out the principles of accounting for goodwill and intangible assets. Its objective is to ensure that goodwill and intangible assets are capitalised only when they can be measured reliably at the time of initial recognition and that they are charged in the profit and loss account as far as possible in the periods in which they are depleted.

The nature of goodwill and intangible assets

(b)   The accounting requirements for goodwill reflect the view that goodwill arising on an acquisition is neither an asset like other assets nor an immediate loss in value. Rather, it forms the bridge between the cost of an investment shown as an asset in the acquirer's own financial statements and the values attributed to the acquired assets and liabilities in the consolidated financial statements. Although purchased goodwill is not in itself an asset, its inclusion amongst the assets of the reporting entity, rather than as a deduction from shareholders' equity, recognises that goodwill is part of a larger asset, the investment, for which management remains accountable.

(c)   An intangible asset may meet the definition of an asset when access to the future economic benefits that it represents is controlled by the reporting entity, either through legal protection or physical custody. However, intangible assets fall into a spectrum ranging from those that can readily be identified and measured separately from goodwill to those that are essentially very similar to goodwill. The basic principles set out for initial recognition, amortisation and impairment of intangible assets are therefore closely aligned with those set out for goodwill.

Initial recognition

(d)   The values of goodwill and intangible assets can be measured sufficiently reliably for initial recognition only when established through purchase or, in the case of an intangible asset, when evidenced by the existence of a readily ascertainable market value. Hence, purchased goodwill and intangible assets should be capitalised as assets but internally generated goodwill should not be recognised and internally developed intangible assets should be recognised only where they have a readily ascertainable market value.

Amortisation

(e)   The proposed approach seeks to charge goodwill to the profit and loss account only to the extent that the carrying value of the goodwill is not supported by the current value of the goodwill within the acquired business. Systematic amortisation is a practical means of recognising the reduction in value of goodwill that has a limited useful economic life. It is also a means of ensuring that where goodwill is not capable of continued measurement (so that impairment reviews cannot reasonably be performed each year), its depletion is recognised over a prudent, but not unrealistically short, period.

(f)   Reflecting the view of goodwill as the bridge between the value of an acquired business in the entity's own financial statements and the values of its net identifiable assets shown in the consolidated financial statements, the useful economic life of purchased goodwill is the period over which the value of an acquired business is expected to exceed the values of its identifiable assets and liabilities.

(g)   There is a rebuttable presumption that the useful economic lives of purchased goodwill and intangible assets are limited and do not exceed 20 years from the date of acquisition. However, there may be valid grounds for rebutting that presumption and treating the useful economic life as greater than 20 years, or even indefinite.

(h)   The requirements for amortisation depend on the nature of the goodwill or intangible asset:
- where it is believed to have a useful economic life of 20 years or less, it should be amortised over the estimated useful economic life.

- where it is believed to have a useful economic life of more than 20 years, but its value is not significant or is not expected to be capable of continued measurement in future, it should be amortised over a deemed useful economic life of 20 years from the date of acquisition.
- where it is believed to have a useful economic life of more than 20 years and its value is significant and expected to be capable of continued measurement in future, it should be amortised over the estimated useful economic life or, if this is indefinite, not amortised at all. Annual impairment reviews should be performed in addition to, or instead of, amortisation.

(i) Companies legislation requires goodwill to be amortised over a limited period. Hence, where the financial statements of a company include goodwill that is not amortised, they should explain that the departure from this specific requirement is necessary for the overriding purpose of providing a true and fair view, also detailing the reasons for and the effect of the departure.

Impairment reviews

(j) An asset is regarded as impaired if its recoverable amount (the higher of net realisable value and value in use) falls below its carrying value. Impairment reviews should be performed to ensure that goodwill and intangible assets are not carried at above their recoverable amounts. Where goodwill and intangible assets are amortised over a period that does not exceed 20 years, impairment reviews need be performed only at the end of the first full financial year following the initial recognition of the goodwill or intangible asset and, thereafter, if subsequent events or changes in circumstances indicate that its carrying value might not be recoverable in full. Where goodwill and intangible assets are not amortised, or are amortised over a period exceeding 20 years, impairment reviews should be performed each period.

(k) Where an intangible asset has a readily ascertainable market value, the recoverable amount may be taken to be that market value (less any disposal costs). Otherwise, the recoverable amount should be estimated by calculating the present value of the future cash flows expected to be generated by the goodwill or intangible asset.

Revaluations and restoration of past losses

(l) Intangible assets with readily ascertainable market values may be revalued by reference to these market values.

(m) The reversal of a past impairment loss may be recognised only if it can clearly and demonstrably be attributed to the unforeseen reversal of the external event that caused the recognition of the original impairment loss. Past impairment losses may not be restored when the restoration in value is generated internally.

Negative goodwill

(n) Negative goodwill, which is expected to arise rarely, should be recognised adjacent to positive goodwill on the balance sheet. It should subsequently be written back as the difference between the value of the investment and the values of the net assets diminishes. For example, where negative goodwill arises because of an expectation of future losses, it might be written back as these losses are incurred. The write-back of negative goodwill should be recognised in the statement of total recognised gains and losses, unless the investment to which it relates has been sold.

Disclosures

(o) There are few disclosure requirements other than those normally required for any type of fixed asset. Significant additional disclosure requirements include requirements to explain:
- the bases of valuation of intangible assets
- the grounds for believing a useful economic life to exceed 20 years or to be indefinite
- the reason for recognising an impairment loss or the reversal of an impairment loss.

[DRAFT] FINANCIAL REPORTING STANDARD

OBJECTIVE

1.   The objective of this [draft] FRS is to ensure that:
     (a) goodwill and intangible assets are capitalised only when their values can be measured reliably at the time of initial recognition;
     (b) capitalised goodwill and intangible assets are charged in the profit and loss account as far as possible in the periods in which they are depleted; and
     (c) sufficient information is disclosed in the financial statements to enable users to determine the impact of goodwill and intangible assets on the financial position and performance of the reporting entity.

DEFINITIONS

2.   The following definitions shall apply in the [draft] FRS and in particular in the Statement of Standard Accounting Practice set out in paragraphs 4–59.

Class of intangible assets:-
A group of intangible assets that have a similar nature or function in the business of the entity.

Identifiable assets and liabilities:-
The assets and liabilities of an entity that are capable of being disposed of or settled separately, without disposing of a business of the entity.

Impairment:-
A reduction in the recoverable amount of an asset below its carrying value.

Income-generating unit:-
A group of assets, liabilities and associated goodwill that generates income that is largely independent of other income streams of the reporting entity. The assets and liabilities include those directly involved in generating the income and an appropriate portion of those used to generate more than one income stream.

Intangible assets:-
Non-monetary fixed assets that do not have physical substance but are identifiable and are controlled by the entity through legal rights or physical custody.

Net realisable value:-
The amount at which an asset could be disposed of, less any disposal costs.

Purchased goodwill:-
The difference between the fair value of the consideration paid for an acquired entity and the aggregate of the fair values of that entity's identifiable assets and liabilities. Positive goodwill arises when the fair value of the consideration paid exceeds the aggregate fair va.ues of the identifiable assets and liabilities. Negative goodwill arises when the aggregate fair values of the identifiable assets and liabilities of the entity exceed the fair value of the consideration paid.

Readily ascertainable market value:-
The value of an intangible asset that is established by reference to a market where:
(a) the asset belongs to a homogeneous population of assets that are equivalent in all material respects; and
(b) an active market, evidenced by frequent transactions, exists for that population of assets.

Recoverable amount:-
The higher of net realisable value and value in use.

Residual value:-
The net realisable value of an asset at the end of its useful economic life. Residual values are based on prices at the date of acquisition (or revaluation) of the asset and do not take account of expected future price changes.

Useful economic life:-
The useful economic life of an intangible asset is the period over which the entity expects to derive economic benefit from that asset. The useful economic life of purchased goodwill is the period over which the value of the underlying business is expected to exceed the values of its identifiable net assets.

Value in use:-
The present value of the future cash flows obtainable as a result of an asset's continued use, including those resulting from its ultimate disposal.

3   **References to companies legislation mean:**
(a) in Great Britain, the Companies Act 1985;
(b) in Northern Ireland, the Companies (Northern Ireland) Order 1986; and
(c) in the Republic of Ireland, the Companies (Amendment) Act 1986 and the European Communities (Companies: Group Accounts) Regulations 1992.

STATEMENT OF STANDARD ACCOUNTING PRACTICE

Scope

4   [Draft] FRS • applies to all financial statements that are intended to give a true and fair view of a reporting entity's financial position and profit or loss (or income and expenditure) for a period. Although the [draft] FRS is framed in terms of the acquisition of a subsidiary undertaking by a parent company that prepares consolidated accounts, it also applies when an individual reporting entity acquires a business other than a subsidiary undertaking.

5   The requirements of the [draft] FRS apply to all intangible assets with the exception of:
(a) oil and gas exploration and development costs;
(b) research and development costs, which are accounted for in accordance with SSAP 13; and
(c) any other intangible assets that fall within the scope of another accounting standard.

Initial recognition and measurement

Goodwill

6   Positive purchased goodwill should be capitalised and classified as an asset on the balance sheet. Negative purchased goodwill should be recognised and separately disclosed on the face of the balance sheet, immediately below the goodwill heading.

7   Internally generated goodwill should not be recognised.

Intangible assets

8   An intangible asset purchased separately from a business should be capitalised at its cost.

9   An intangible asset acquired as part of the acquisition of a business should be recognised separately from goodwill if its value can be measured reliably on initial recognition. It should initially be recorded at its fair value, subject to the constraint that, unless the asset has a readily ascertainable market value, the fair value should be limited to an amount that does not create or increase any negative goodwill arising on the acquisition.

10   If its value cannot be measured reliably, an intangible asset purchased as part of the acquisition of a business should be subsumed within the amount of the purchase price attributed to goodwill.

11   An internally developed intangible asset may be recognised only if it has a readily ascertainable market value.

Amortisation of positive goodwill and intangible assets

Determining useful economic lives

12   There is a rebuttable presumption that the useful economic lives of purchased goodwill and intangible assets are limited and do not exceed 20 years. This presumption may be rebutted only if there are valid and disclosed grounds, based on the nature of the underlying investment, for believing the useful economic life to be a longer period or indefinite. A useful economic life may be considered to be indefinite only if it is expected to exceed 20 years.

13   Where access to the economic benefits associated with an intangible asset is achieved through legal rights that have been granted for a finite period, the economic life of the asset may extend beyond that period only if, and to the extent that, the legal rights are renewable and renewal is assured. The amount of the asset that is treated as having the longer useful economic life should exclude those costs that will recur each time the legal right is renewed.

Requirement for amortisation

14   Where the useful economic life of goodwill or an intangible asset is believed to be 20 years or less, the carrying value should be amortised in the profit and loss account on a systematic basis over the estimated useful economic life.

15   Where the useful economic life of goodwill or an intangible asset is believed to exceed 20 years but the value of the goodwill or intangible asset is not significant or is not expected to be capable of continued measurement in future (so that annual impairment reviews would not be feasible), the carrying value should be amortised in the profit and loss account on a systematic basis over a deemed useful economic life of 20 years from the date of acquisition.

16   Where the useful economic life of goodwill or an intangible asset is believed to exceed 20 years and the value of the goodwill or intangible asset is significant and expected to be capable of continued measurement in future (so that annual impairment reviews will be feasible):

(a) if the useful economic life can be estimated, the carrying value of the goodwill or intangible asset should be amortised in the profit and loss account on a systematic basis over the estimated useful economic life;

(b) if the useful economic life is indefinite, the goodwill or intangible asset should not be amortised. The goodwill or intangible asset should also be reviewed for impairment each period. The requirements for impairment reviews are specified below.

Residual value

17   In amortising an intangible asset, a residual value may be assumed only if such residual value can be measured reliably. No residual value may be assumed for goodwill.

Method of amortisation

18   The method of amortisation should be chosen to reflect the expected pattern of depletion of the goodwill or intangible asset. A straight-line method should be chosen unless another method can be demonstrated to be more appropriate.

Review of useful economic lives

19   The useful economic lives of goodwill and intangible assets should be reviewed at the end of each reporting period and revised if necessary. Where a useful economic life is revised, the carrying value of the goodwill or intangible asset at the start of the period in which the revision is made should be amortised over the revised remaining useful economic life. If the effect of the revision is to increase the useful economic life to more than 20 years from the date of acquisition, the additional requirements of this [draft] FRS that apply to goodwill and intangible assets with useful economic lives in excess of 20 years become applicable.

Impairment of positive goodwill and intangible assets

Recognition of an impairment loss

20   Goodwill and intangible assets that are amortised over a finite period not exceeding 20 years from the date of acquisition should be reviewed for impairment only:

(a) at the end of the first full financial year following the acquisition; and

(b) in subsequent periods if previously unforeseen events or changes in circumstances indicate that the carrying values may not be recoverable.

21   Goodwill and intangible assets that are amortised over a period exceeding 20 years from the date of acquisition or are not amortised should be reviewed for impairment at the end of each reporting period following initial recognition.

22   The impairment review should comprise a comparison of the carrying value of the goodwill or intangible asset with its recoverable amount (the higher of net realisable value, if known, and value in use). To the extent that the carrying value exceeds the recoverable amount, the asset is impaired and should be written down.

23   Unless the impairment arises on a previously revalued intangible asset, the loss should be charged in the profit and loss account. If the impairment arises on a previously revalued intangible asset and the original revaluation gain was recognised in the statement of total recognised gains and losses, the impairment loss should also be recognised in the statement of total recognised gains and losses until the carrying value of the asset reaches its depreciated historical cost. Any further impairment should be recognised in the profit and loss account.

24   Where an intangible asset has a readily ascertainable market value, it may be assumed that the recoverable amount of that intangible asset is its market value less any disposal costs. Alternatively, the value in use may also be calculated and taken to be the recoverable amount if it is greater than the market value less disposal costs.

25   Following the recognition of an impairment loss on goodwill or an intangible asset, the remaining useful economic life should be reviewed and revised if necessary. The revised carrying value should be amortised over the revised estimate of the useful economic life.

Impairment calculated by reference to value in use

26   An impairment review performed by reference to value in use should be performed at the level of income-generating units, identified as explained in paragraphs 27 and 28 below. The carrying value of each income-generating unit containing the goodwill or intangible asset under review should be compared with the present value of the expected future cash flows of that unit.

27   Income-generating units should be identified by dividing the total income of the entity into as many largely independent income streams as is reasonably practicable. Each of the identifiable assets and liabilities of the entity, excluding interest-bearing debt, dividends payable and other items relating wholly to financing, should be attributed to (or apportioned between) one (or more) income-generating unit(s).

28   Capitalised goodwill should be attributed to (or apportioned between) income-generating units or groups of similar units: individual units identified to monitor the recoverability of intangible assets may be combined with other units to assess the recovery of the related goodwill if they were acquired as part of the same investment and are involved in similar parts of the business.

29   The expected future cash flows of the entity, including tax payments and central overheads but excluding cash flows relating to financing, should be forecast on the basis of reasonable and supportable assumptions and projections. Short-term forecasts and projections should be consistent with the most up-to-date budgets and plans that have been approved formally by management. Longer-term projections should assume a steady or declining growth rate that does not exceed the long-term average growth rate for the country or countries in which the business operates.[1] Only in exceptional and disclosed circumstances should the short-term forecasts and projections cover a period of more than five years.

30   The expected future cash flows should be attributed to (or apportioned between) income-generating units. The present value of the income-generating unit under review should be calculated by discounting the expected future cash flows of the unit. The discount rate used should be an estimate of the rate that the market would expect on an equally risky investment. It should be calculated on an after-tax basis.

31   The carrying values of the income-generating units under review should be calculated as:

---

[1] THE PRESENT UK 40-YEAR AVERAGE GROWTH IN GROSS DOMESTIC PRODUCT, EXPRESSED IN REAL TERMS, IS 2.5 PER CENT.

(a) the net of the carrying values of the assets, liabilities and goodwill allocated to the unit; plus

(b) where any asset within the unit has a net realisable value significantly in excess of its carrying value, an adjustment to increase the carrying value of that asset to its net realisable value. The adjustment is required to ensure that the impairment of one asset is not concealed by the fact that another is held at less than its net realisable value.

32 To the extent that the carrying value of the income-generating unit exceeds its value in use, the unit is impaired. In the absence of an obvious impairment of specific assets within the unit, the impairment should be allocated:

(a) first, to any goodwill in the unit;

(b) thereafter, to any capitalised intangible asset in the unit; and

(c) finally, to the tangible assets in the unit, on a pro rata or more appropriate basis.

In this allocation, which aims to write down the assets with the most subjective valuations first, no intangible asset with a readily ascertainable market value should be written down below its net realisable value. Similarly, no tangible asset with a net realisable value that can be measured reliably should be written down below its net realisable value.

33 Where an acquired business is merged with an existing business such that an income-generating unit contains both purchased and (unrecognised) internally generated goodwill:

(a) the value of the internally generated goodwill at the date of merging the businesses should be estimated and added to the carrying value of the income-generating unit for the purposes of performing impairment reviews;

(b) any impairment arising on merging the businesses should be apportioned solely to the purchased goodwill;

(c) subsequent impairments should be apportioned on a pro rata basis between the purchased and (notional) internally generated goodwill; and

(d) only the impairments apportioned to the purchased goodwill (and, if necessary, to any intangible or tangible assets) should be charged in the profit and loss account.

34 In the periods following an impairment review, the actual cash flows achieved should be compared with those forecast. If the actual cash flows are so much less than those forecast that use of the actual cash flows could have required recognition of an impairment in previous periods, the original impairment calculations should be re-performed using the actual cash flows. Any impairment identified should be recognised in the current period unless, in exceptional and disclosed circumstances, recognition is considered not to be warranted.

Revaluations and restoration of past losses

35 Where an intangible asset has a readily ascertainable market value, the asset may be revalued to its market value. If one intangible asset is revalued, all other capitalised intangible assets of the same class should be revalued. Once an intangible asset has been revalued, further revaluations should be performed sufficiently often to ensure that the carrying value does not differ materially from the market value at the balance sheet date.

36 Where an external event caused the recognition of an impairment loss in previous periods, and subsequent external events clearly and demonstrably reverse the effects of that event in a way that was not foreseen in the original impairment calculations, any resulting reversal of the impairment loss that increases the recoverable amount of the goodwill or intangible asset above its current carrying value should be recognised in the current period.

37 Except as permitted and required by paragraphs 35 and 36 above, goodwill and intangible assets should not be revalued, either to increase the carrying value above original cost or to reverse prior period losses arising from impairment or amortisation.

Negative goodwill

38   Negative goodwill arising on the acquisition of a business should be written back in the periods following the acquisition as the difference between the value of the investment and the values of its identified net assets diminishes.

39   The write-back should be recognised in the statement of total recognised gains and losses, rather than the profit and loss account, unless the investment to which the negative goodwill relates has been sold. If the investment has been sold, the gain should be recognised in the profit and loss account to the extent that it has not previously been recognised in the statement of total recognised gains and losses.

40   Purchased goodwill (positive or negative) should not be divided into positive and negative components.

Disclosures

Recognition and measurement

41   The financial statements should disclose the accounting policy for goodwill and intangible assets and a description of the method used to value intangible assets.

42   The following information should be disclosed separately for positive goodwill, negative goodwill and each class of intangible asset capitalised on the balance sheet:
(a) the cost or revalued amount at the beginning of the financial period and at the balance sheet date;
(b) the cumulative amount of provisions for amortisation or impairment at the beginning of the financial period and at the balance sheet date;
(c) a reconciliation of the movements, separately disclosing additions, disposals, revaluations, transfers, amortisation, impairment losses, reversals of past impairment losses and amounts of negative goodwill written back in the financial period; and
(d) the net carrying value at the balance sheet date.

43   Movements in goodwill and each class of intangible asset resulting from acquisitions in the period should be shown separately for each acquisition, where material.

44   The following should be disclosed in respect of each material disposal of a previously acquired business, business segment or intangible asset:
(a) the profit or loss on disposal; and
(b) the carrying value of attributable goodwill and intangible assets.

Amortisation

45   The financial statements should disclose the methods and periods of amortisation of goodwill and intangible assets and the reasons for choosing those periods.

46   Where a method of amortisation other than the straight-line method is selected, the financial statements should explain why the method selected is more appropriate.

47   Where an amortisation period is shortened or extended following a review of the remaining useful economic lives of goodwill and intangible assets, the reason should be disclosed.

48   Where goodwill or an intangible asset is amortised over a period that exceeds 20 years from the date of acquisition or is not amortised, the grounds for rebutting the 20-year presumption should be explained.

49   Where goodwill is not amortised, the financial statements of companies should state that they depart from the specific requirement of the relevant companies legislation to amortise good-

will over a finite period[2] for the overriding purpose of giving a true and fair view. Details of the departure, the reasons for it and its effect should be given.

Impairment

50 Where an impairment loss is recognised in the financial period, the financial statements should disclose the reason for the impairment.

51 Where an impairment loss recognised in a previous period is reversed in the current period, the financial statements should disclose the reason for the reversal of the impairment. The explanation should be consistent with the explanation given when the impairment was first recognised.

52 Where an impairment loss would have been recognised in a previous period had the forecasts of future cash flows been more accurate and, for exceptional reasons, the loss is still not recognised in the current period, these reasons should be explained.

53 Where, in exceptional circumstances, the cash flow forecasts and projections incorporating growth rates in excess of the long-term average for the country concerned cover a period of more than five years, the financial statements should disclose:
- the length of the longer period
- the growth rates assumed
- the reason why the long-term growth rate is not expected to be achieved within a five-year period.

Revaluation

54 Where a class of assets has been revalued, the financial statements should disclose:
    (a) the year in which the assets were separately valued, the separate values and the bases of valuation; and
    (b) the original cost (or fair values) of the assets and the amount of any provision for amortisation that would have been recognised if the assets had been valued at their original cost.

55 Where any asset has been revalued during the year, the name and qualifications of the person who performed the valuation should be disclosed.

Date from which effective and transitional arrangements

56 The accounting practices set out in the [draft] FRS should be regarded as standard in respect of goodwill and intangible assets first accounted for in financial statements relating to accounting periods beginning on or after ['effective date' to be inserted after exposure]. Earlier adoption is encouraged but not required.

57 Where goodwill and intangible assets purchased in periods beginning before [effective date] are capitalised within an asset heading on the balance sheet, the accounting practices set out in the [draft] FRS should be regarded as standard in respect of such goodwill and intangible assets for accounting periods beginning on or after that date.[3]

58 Where goodwill purchased in periods beginning before [effective date] was eliminated against (or, in the case of negative goodwill, added to) reserves on acquisition as a matter of accounting policy and is not subsequently capitalised in accordance with the accounting practices set out in the [draft] FRS:
    (a) the financial statements should disclose:

---

[2] SEE PARAGRAPH 6 OF APPENDIX I 'NOTE ON LEGAL REQUIREMENTS'.

    (i)   the accounting policy followed in respect of that goodwill; and

    (ii) the cumulative amounts of positive goodwill eliminated against reserves and negative goodwill added to reserves, net of any goodwill attributable to businesses disposed of before the balance sheet date.[3]

(b) in the reporting period in which the business with which the goodwill was acquired is disposed of or closed:

    (i)   the amount included in the profit or loss account in respect of the profit or loss on disposal or closure should include attributable goodwill to the extent that it has not previously been shown as a charge to the profit and loss account; and

    (ii) the financial statements should disclose as a component of the profit or loss on disposal or closure the attributable amount of goodwill so included.

Where it is genuinely impractical or impossible to ascertain the goodwill attributable to a business that was acquired before 1 January 1989, this should be stated and the reasons given.

Withdrawal of SSAP 22 and UITF Abstract 3

59   The [draft] FRS supersedes SSAP 22 'Accounting for goodwill' and UITF Abstract 3 'Treatment of goodwill on disposal of a business' [following its publication in final form].

---

[3] In Great Britain and Northern Ireland, under paragraph 16 of Schedule 4A to the Companies Act 1985 and the Companies (Northern Ireland) Order 1986 respectively, disclosure of amounts pertaining to an overseas business need not be given if it would be seriously prejudicial to the business and agreement has been obtained from the Secretary of State. For acquisitions before 23 December 1989 (in Northern Ireland, 1 April 1990), disclosure need not be made if the information necessary to calculate the amount with material accuracy is unavailable or cannot be obtained without unreasonable expense or delay. The exclusion of such amounts and the grounds for the exclusion should be stated.

EXPLANATION

Definitions

Intangible asset

60   The definition of an intangible asset includes the requirement that the asset is identifiable, ie it can be disposed of separately without disposing of a business of the entity. If an asset can be disposed of only as part of the revenue-earning activity to which it contributes, it is considered to be indistinguishable from the goodwill relating to that activity and is accounted for as such.

61   The definition of an asset given in the draft Statement of Principles for Financial Reporting requires that access to future economic benefits is controlled by the reporting entity.[4] 'Control' in this context means the ability to obtain the economic benefits and to restrict the access of others. In the context of an intangible asset, control is normally secured legally: a franchise or licence grants the entity access to the benefits for a fixed period; a patent or trade mark restricts the access of others.

62   In the absence of legal rights, it is more difficult to demonstrate control. However, control may be obtained through physical custody. This could be the case where, for example, technical or intellectual knowledge arising from development activity is maintained secretly.

63   Where it is expected that future benefits will flow to the entity, but these benefits are not controlled through legal rights or physical custody, the entity does not have sufficient control over the benefits to recognise an intangible asset. For example, an entity may have a portfolio of clients or a team of skilled staff. There may be an expectation that the clients within the portfolio will continue to seek professional services from the entity, or that the team of staff will continue to make their expert skills available to the entity. However, in the absence of legal or physical custody of the clients or staff, the entity has insufficient control over the expected future benefits to recognise them as assets.

64   Each legal right does not necessarily represent a separate intangible asset: a single product is likely to have only one intangible asset associated with it unless there are two or more processes involved in the income-generation that are essentially independent of each other. Processes should be regarded as independent if their fair values on acquisition can be measured separately, if the cash flows each generates can be measured separately and if they could be disposed of separately. For example, a specific drug could have several legal rights associated with it: there could be a patent securing unique rights to manufacture the drug, a trade mark securing the brand name and copyright protection of the packaging used in distributing the drug. If the manufacturing and distribution processes could be valued and sold separately, then the manufacturing rights would constitute a separate intangible asset. However, it is unlikely that the distribution process could be further divided; the trade mark and the packaging copyright would each form part of the same intangible asset.

Class of intangible assets

65   A 'class' of intangible assets is defined as a group of intangible assets that have a similar nature or function in the business of the entity. Licences, quotas, patents, copyrights, franchises and trade marks are examples of groups that may be treated as separate classes. Further subdivision may be appropriate, for example where different types of licence have different functions within the business. Intangible assets that are used within different segments of the business may be treated as separate classes of intangible asset.

---

[4] EXPOSURE DRAFT 'STATEMENT OF PRINCIPLES FOR FINANCIAL REPORTING', PARAGRAPHS 3.5–3.10 AND 3.16–3.18.

Readily ascertainable market value

66   An intangible asset is considered to have a readily ascertainable market value only if it belongs to a homogeneous population of assets that are equivalent in all material respects and if an active market has established a market value for these assets. Intangible assets that meet those conditions might include certain operating licences, franchises and quotas. Examples might include cable television operating licences, import quotas and EU milk quotas.

67   Other intangible assets are by their nature unique: although there may be similar assets, they are not equivalent in all material respects. It follows that such assets do not have readily ascertainable market values. Examples of such assets include brands, publishing titles and patented drugs.

Initial recognition and measurement

Intangible assets purchased with a business

68   FRS 7 'Fair Values in Acquisition Accounting' requires that where an intangible asset is recognised, its fair value should be based on its replacement cost. FRS 7 goes on to explain that the replacement cost will normally be the asset's estimated market value but that it may be estimated by other methods.[5]

69   As explained in paragraph 67 above, it is not possible to determine a market value for unique intangible assets such as brands and publishing titles. Replacement cost may be equally difficult to estimate directly. However, certain entities that are regularly involved in the purchase and sale of unique intangible assets have developed techniques for estimating their values indirectly and these may be used for initial recognition of such assets. Techniques used can be based, for instance, on 'indicators of value'—such as multiples of turnover—or on estimating the present value of the royalties that would be payable to license the asset from a third party.

Amortisation of positive goodwill and intangible assets

Determining useful economic lives

70   The useful economic lives of goodwill and intangible assets will usually be uncertain. This uncertainty does not in itself form grounds for treating a useful economic life as indefinite. Where, for example, the useful economic life of goodwill or an intangible asset is not expected to exceed 20 years, the [draft] FRS requires an estimate of the useful economic life to be made.

71   Similarly, whilst uncertainty forms grounds for estimating the useful economic life on a prudent basis, it does not form grounds for choosing a life that is unrealistically short.

72   If purchased goodwill includes intangible assets that have not been recognised separately because they cannot be measured reliably, then the useful economic lives of these intangible assets will have a bearing on that of the goodwill as a whole.

73   There may be both economic and legal factors influencing the useful economic life of an intangible asset: economic factors determine the period over which it is expected that future economic benefits will arise; legal factors may restrict the period over which the entity continues to control access to these benefits. The useful economic life of an asset is the shorter of the period over which it is expected that the future benefits will arise and that over which it is expected that the entity will control the benefits.

74   It follows that where a legal right securing access to an intangible asset has been granted for a finite period, as may be the case with a patent or licence, the useful economic life assigned to

---

[5] FRS 7 'Fair Values in Acquisition Accounting', paragraph 10.

the asset cannot in general exceed that finite period. It would be appropriate to assign a longer useful economic life only if, and to the extent that, the legal right is renewable and renewal is assured. Renewal may be regarded as being assured if:

(a) the value of the intangible asset does not reduce as the initial expiry date approaches, or reduces only by an amount reflecting the cost of renewal of the underlying legal right;

(b) there is evidence, possibly based on past experience, that the legal rights will be renewed; and

(c) where the entity is required to abide by any conditions under the terms of the legal right and breach of these conditions may prevent renewal, there is no evidence that any of these conditions have been or will be breached.

75 It follows that, where legal rights are essential to the benefits arising from the use of an intangible asset, the asset may be regarded as having an indefinite life only if such legal rights can remain in force for an indefinite period exceeding 20 years, or are renewable over such a period with each renewal process being assured.

Goodwill and intangible assets that are not capable of continued measurement

76 If the value of goodwill or an intangible asset is not expected to be capable of continued measurement in future, it will not be possible to perform impairment reviews. The [draft] FRS requires such goodwill or intangible assets to be amortised over a maximum period of 20 years. Goodwill and intangible assets will not be capable of continued measurement if the cost of such measurement is considered to be unjustifiably high. This may be the case when, for example:

• acquired businesses are merged with existing businesses to such an extent that the goodwill associated with the acquired businesses cannot readily be tracked thereafter

• the management information systems used by the entity cannot identify and allocate cash flows at a detailed income-generating unit level.

Residual value

77 In practice, the residual value of an intangible asset is often insignificant. It is likely that the residual value of an intangible asset will be significant and capable of being measured reliably only when:

(a) there is a legal or contractual right to receive a certain sum at the end of the period of use of the intangible asset; or

(b) there is a readily ascertainable market value for the residual asset.

Method of amortisation

78 The pattern of depletion of intangible assets will normally be relatively uncertain and occur with the passing of time. Hence, a straight-line method of amortisation will normally be the most appropriate. However, there may be circumstances, for instance where a licence entitles the holder to produce a finite quantity of a product, where another method is more appropriate. It is unlikely that there will be circumstances in which there is justification and evidence to support a method of amortisation for goodwill that is less conservative than straight-line.

79 A method of amortisation that aims to produce a constant rate of return on the carrying value of an investment is not one that aims to reflect the pattern of depletion of goodwill. Hence, interest methods, such as the 'reverse sum of digits' method, are not appropriate methods of amortising goodwill.

Impairment of positive goodwill and intangible assets

Goodwill and intangible assets amortised over a period of no more than 20 years

80   The [draft] FRS requires impairment reviews to be performed whenever previously unforeseen events and changes in circumstances indicate that the carrying value of a business's goodwill and intangible assets may not be recoverable. Examples of such events and changes in circumstances include:
- a current period operating loss or net cash outflow from operating activities, combined with either past operating losses or net cash outflows from operating activities or an expectation of continuing operating losses or net cash outflows from operating activities
- a significant adverse change in either the business or the market in which the goodwill or intangible asset is involved, such as the entrance of a major competitor
- a significant adverse change in the legal or other regulatory environment in which the business operates
- a significant adverse change in any 'indicator of value' used to measure the fair value of an intangible asset on acquisition
- a commitment by management to undertake a significant reorganisation
- a major loss of key employees.

81   If any such events or changes in circumstances are identified, an impairment review is performed. A review of the useful economic lives of the assets affected might also be appropriate: even if the assets are not impaired, their remaining useful economic lives may have changed as a result of the events or changes in circumstances.

First year impairment reviews

82   If an impairment is identified at the time of the first year review, this impairment reflects:
(a) an overpayment;
(b) an event that occurred between the acquisition and the first year review; or
(c) depletion of the acquired goodwill or intangible asset between the acquisition and the first year review that exceeds the amount recognised through amortisation.

The [draft] FRS requires that the reason for recognition of such an impairment is explained. A review of amortisation methods and rates may also be appropriate.

83   The requirements of the [draft] FRS are such that the recognition of an impairment loss must be justified in the same way as the absence of an impairment loss, ie by reference to expected future cash flows. In particular, a belief that the value of goodwill will not be capable of continued measurement in future does not justify writing off the balance at the time of the first year impairment review: it should be possible to perform the first year impairment review by updating investment appraisal calculations. The remaining carrying value would then be amortised over a period not exceeding 20 years.

Annual impairment reviews

84   Where goodwill or intangible assets are not amortised, or are amortised over a period in excess of 20 years from the date of acquisition, impairment reviews are necessary at the end of every period. However, after the first period the reviews need only be updated. If expectations of future cash flows and discount rates have not changed significantly, then the updating procedure will be relatively quick to perform. If there have been no adverse changes in the key assumptions and variables, or if there was previously substantial leeway between the carrying value and estimated value in use, it may even be possible to ascertain immediately that an income-generating unit is not impaired.

Identifying income-generating units

85   The value in use of an asset is the present value of the future cash flows obtainable as a result of the asset's continued use, including those resulting from its ultimate disposal. In practice, it is not normally possible to estimate the value in use of a single intangible asset or goodwill balance: it is groups of assets and liabilities together with their associated goodwill that generate cash flows. Hence value in use is estimated in total for groups of assets and liabilities. These groups are referred to as income-generating units.

86   To perform impairment reviews as accurately as possible:
  • the groups of assets and liabilities that are considered together should be as small as possible, but
  • the income stream underlying the future cash flows of one group should be largely independent of other income streams of the entity and should be capable of being monitored separately.

Income-generating units are therefore identified by dividing the total income of the business into as many largely independent income streams as is reasonably practicable in the light of the information available to management.

87   In general terms, the income streams identified are likely to follow the way in which management monitors the different lines of business of the entity. Unique intangible assets, such as brands and mastheads, are generally seen to generate income independently of each other and are usually monitored separately. Hence they can often be used to identify income-generating units. Other income streams may be identified by reference to major products or services.

88   Income-generating units are defined by allocating the assets and liabilities of the reporting entity, excluding interest-bearing debt, dividends payable and other items relating wholly to financing, to the identified income streams. Certain assets and liabilities that are directly involved in the production and distribution of individual products may be attributed directly to one unit. Others, such as head office assets and working capital, may have to be apportioned across the units on a logical and systematic basis. The resulting income-generating units will be complete and non-overlapping, so that the sum of the carrying values of the units equals the carrying value of the net assets (excluding financing items) of the entity as a whole.

89   Goodwill is allocated to income-generating units in the same way as are the assets and liabilities of the entity. However, where several similar income-generating units (such as branded products) are acquired together in one investment, these units may be combined to assess the recoverability of the goodwill. The income-generating units are then reviewed individually for the purposes of assessing the recoverability of any capitalised intangible assets.

Discount rates

90   The present value of the future cash flows is estimated by discounting the expected cash flows at the rate of return that the market would expect on an equally risky investment. The hurdle rate used by the entity to make investment decisions may be useful in estimating that rate. The entity's current post-tax weighted average cost of capital may also be used to estimate an appropriate discount rate, since it represents the return that the market expects from the reporting entity as a whole. If the weighted average cost of capital of the reporting entity is used to estimate the discount rate:
  • the entity's overall weighted average cost of capital will be adjusted to reflect any risk factors specific to the unit under consideration.
  • where the cash flow forecasts assume a real growth rate that exceeds the long-term average growth rate for more than five years, it is likely that the discount rate will be increased to reflect a higher level of risk.

- the discount rates applied to individual income-generating units will always be estimated such that, were they to be calculated for every unit, the weighted average discount rate would equal the entity's overall weighted average cost of capital.

Acquired businesses merged with existing operations

91   An acquired business may be merged with an existing operation of the reporting entity in such a way that a single income-generating unit includes the assets and liabilities of both the acquired and the existing businesses. This combined income-generating unit contains both acquired and internally generated goodwill and any future impairment needs to be apportioned between the two. This can be done by notionally adjusting the carrying value of the income-generating unit to recognise a notional carrying value for the internally generated goodwill of the existing operation at the date of merging the two businesses.

92   The notional carrying value of the internally generated goodwill is estimated by deducting the fair values of the assets within the existing income-generating unit from its estimated value in use before combining the businesses.

93   Because the calculation of the internally generated goodwill takes account of any impairment of the existing business at the time of merging it with the acquired business, any initial impairment in the combined income-generating unit will, by definition, relate to the acquired business. Any subsequent impairment cannot be attributed directly to either the acquired or the existing businesses and is therefore apportioned between the acquired and internally generated goodwill pro rata to their current carrying values.

Revaluations and restoration of past losses

94   An impairment review may identify that an impairment loss recognised in a prior period has reversed in the current period. In general, such reversals will be the result of the internal generation of goodwill or intangible asset value. The [draft] FRS does not permit such restorations to be reflected in the financial statements. However, where the original impairment was caused by an external event and reverses because the external event reverses in a way that was not foreseen when the original impairment calculations were performed, then the [draft] FRS requires the resulting restoration to be reflected in the financial statements.

Negative goodwill

95   The apparent existence of negative purchased goodwill may indicate that the fair values assigned to assets have been overstated or that liabilities, such as provisions for onerous contracts, have been omitted. It is therefore important that the fair values assigned to assets and liabilities are checked carefully before negative goodwill is recognised.

96   The [draft] FRS requires negative goodwill to be written back in the statement of total recognised gains and losses as the difference between the value of the investment and the values of its identified net assets diminishes. The time and manner in which the difference will diminish will depend on the nature of the circumstances giving rise to the negative goodwill.

97   Negative goodwill may result from a 'bargain purchase', perhaps as a result of a forced or liquidation sale. Where this is the case, the acquirer has made an instant gain and the negative goodwill should be written back immediately.

98   Negative goodwill may result from the fact that allowance for a reorganisation has been built into the price paid for a business. As the reorganisation costs are incurred, the difference between the values of the assets and the value of the investment as a whole reduces and the negative goodwill reduces. A similar example is negative goodwill that arises because an

expectation of short-term operating losses is built into the price paid for the business. As these losses materialise, the net assets of the business reduce in value, thus reversing the negative goodwill.

99 There may be circumstances in which the negative goodwill does not reduce in line with initial expectations. For example, it may be the case that, despite a reorganisation, an acquired business's performance does not improve in line with initial expectations. In such circumstances, the value of the business as a whole will not increase by the amount of the reorganisation costs and the negative goodwill will not be eliminated. In such circumstances, and to the extent that the value of the business remains less than the values of the acquired assets, the negative goodwill is not written back.

Disclosures

Disclosure of true and fair override

100 Companies legislation requires goodwill that is treated as an asset to be amortised systematically over a finite period. Where a company's financial statements depart from the specific requirements of companies legislation for the overriding purpose of providing a true and fair view, they are required to disclose particulars of the departure, the reasons for it and its effect.[6] UITF Abstract 7 'True and fair view override disclosures' gives guidance on the interpretation of this statutory requirement. This guidance encompasses the disclosures necessary when it is not possible to quantify the effect of the departure, as will be the case when goodwill is not amortised.

Transitional arrangements

101 The transitional arrangements reflect the Board's belief that it would not be reasonable in all circumstances to require restatement of goodwill acquired and eliminated against reserves in prior periods.

---

[6] SEE PARAGRAPHS 6 AND 20 OF APPENDIX I 'NOTE ON LEGAL REQUIREMENTS'.

APPENDIX I
NOTE ON LEGAL REQUIREMENTS

GREAT BRITAIN

1   In Great Britain, the statutory requirements on accounting for goodwill and intangible assets are set out in the Companies Act 1985. The main requirements that are directly relevant to goodwill and intangible assets and the requirements of this [draft] FRS are set out in Schedules 4 and 4A and are summarised below.

2   Schedule 4 to the Companies Act 1985 does not apply to banking and insurance companies and groups. Requirements equivalent to those of Schedule 4 are contained in Schedule 9 (for banking companies and groups) and in Schedule 9A (for insurance companies and groups).

Goodwill

3   The acquisition method of accounting and the calculation of goodwill are described by paragraph 9(4) and (5) of Schedule 4A. The interest of the parent company and its subsidiaries in the adjusted capital and reserves of an acquired subsidiary undertaking should be offset against the acquisition cost. The resulting amount if positive should be treated as goodwill, and if negative as a negative consolidation difference.

4   The balance sheet formats in Schedule 4 require purchased goodwill, to the extent that it has not been written off, to be included under the heading of intangible fixed assets, and shown separately from other intangible assets. Note (3) to the formats states that amounts representing goodwill shall be included only to the extent that the goodwill was acquired for valuable consideration.

5   Paragraph 5 of Schedule 4 states that amounts in respect of items representing assets may not be set off against amounts in respect of items representing liabilities. For this reason, the [draft] FRS requires negative goodwill to be shown separately from positive goodwill on the face of the balance sheet.

6   Paragraph 21 of Schedule 4 requires that, where goodwill is treated as an asset, it shall be depreciated systematically over a period chosen by the directors. The period chosen shall not exceed the useful economic life of the goodwill. The period chosen and the reason for choosing that period should be disclosed in a note. (No residual value is permitted for goodwill.)

7   Paragraph 31(1) of Schedule 4 prohibits the revaluation of goodwill.

8   Paragraph 14 of Schedule 4A requires the notes to the accounts to state the cumulative amount of goodwill resulting from acquisitions in that and earlier financial years that has been written off. That figure should be net of any goodwill attributable to subsidiary undertakings or businesses disposed of before the balance sheet date. Paragraph 16 of Schedule 4A states that disclosure of amounts pertaining to an overseas business need not be given if it would be seriously prejudicial to the group's business and agreement has been obtained from the Secretary of State. Further, for acquisitions before 23 December 1989, disclosure need not be made if the information necessary to calculate the amount with material accuracy is unavailable or cannot be obtained without unreasonable expense or delay (paragraph 9 of Schedule 2 to the Companies Act 1989 (Commencement No. 4 and Transitional and Saving Provisions) Order 1990). The exclusion of such amounts and the grounds for the exclusion should be stated.

Intangible assets

9   Paragraph 9(2) of Schedule 4A requires, under the acquisition method of accounting, the identifiable assets and liabilities of an acquired undertaking to be included in the consolidated balance sheet at their fair values as at the date of acquisition. It defines 'identifiable' as capable of being disposed of or discharged separately, without disposing of a business of the undertaking.

10   The following headings for intangible assets are set out in the balance sheet formats in Schedule 4:

B   Fixed assets
I   Intangible assets
  1. Development costs
  2. Concessions, patents, licences, trade marks and similar rights and assets
  3. Goodwill
  4. Payments on account.

11   Note (2) on the balance sheet formats permits amounts in respect of assets to be included in a company's balance sheet under the heading of concessions, patents, licences, trade marks and similar rights and assets only if either (a) the assets were acquired for valuable consideration and are not required to be shown under goodwill; or (b) the assets in question were created by the company itself.

12   Paragraph 18 requires that, where a fixed asset has a limited useful economic life, the purchase price or production cost less any residual value is reduced by provisions for depreciation calculated to write off that amount systematically over the period of the asset's useful economic life.

13   Paragraph 31(1) permits intangible assets, other than goodwill, to be included at their current cost. Where an intangible asset is valued at its current cost, the depreciation rules are to be applied by substituting the most recently determined value for the purchase price or production cost (paragraph 32(1)).

Provisions for diminution in value

14   Paragraph 19(2) of Schedule 4 requires provisions for diminution in value to be made in respect of any fixed asset that has diminished in value if the reduction in its value is expected to be permanent. The amount to be included in respect of the asset shall be reduced accordingly. Any provisions that are not shown in the profit and loss account shall be disclosed (either separately or in aggregate) in a note to the accounts.

15   Paragraph 19(3) of Schedule 4 requires that where the reasons for which a provision was made have ceased to apply to any extent, the provision is written back to the extent that it is no longer necessary. Where any amounts written back are not shown in the profit and loss account, they shall be disclosed (either separately or in aggregate) in a note to the accounts.

Amortisation and other amounts written off fixed assets

16   The formats set out in Schedule 4 prescribe the headings under which depreciation and other amounts written off tangible and intangible fixed assets are to be included in the profit and loss account. Under Formats 1 and 3, such amounts are to be included in cost of sales, distribution costs and administrative expenses. Under Formats 2 and 4, such amounts are to be shown as a separate heading.

Disclosure requirements

17   Disclosure of the accounting policies adopted by a company (including the policies regarding the depreciation and diminution in value of assets) is required by paragraph 36 of Schedule 4.

18   Paragraph 42 of Schedule 4 details the disclosures required of the movement on goodwill and intangible asset balances. The same level of detail is required as for other fixed assets.

19   Paragraphs 33 and 43 of Schedule 4 prescribe additional information to be given for any assets that have been revalued. This includes comparable amounts determined according to the historical cost accounting rules and details of the basis and date of the valuation and the qualifications of the valuer.

True and fair override

20   Sections 226(3) and 227(4) require the individual and group accounts of a company to comply with the provisions of Schedules 4 and 4A respectiveiy. If, in exceptional circumstances, compliance with any of the provisions is inconsistent with the requirement to give a true and fair view, sections 226(5) and 227(6) require the directors to depart from those provisions to the extent necessary to give a true and fair view. Particulars of any such departure, the reasons for it and its effect are to be given in a note to the accounts.

NORTHERN IRELAND

21   The statutory requirements in Northern Ireland are set out in the Companies (Northern Ireland) Order 1986. They are similar to those in Great Britain. Most of the references cited above have parallel references in the Companies (Northern Ireland) Order 1986. The only exceptions are that:

(a) the requirements of sections 226 and 227 of the Companies Act 1985 are found in Articles 234 and 235 of the Companies (Northern Ireland) Order 1986; and

(b) the transitional arrangements permitted by paragraph 9 of Schedule 2 to the Companies Act 1989 (Commencement No. 4 and Transitional and Saving Provisions) Order 1990 are found in paragraph 9 of the Companies (1990 Order) (Commencement No. 1) Order (Northern Ireland) 1990. They apply to acquisitions made before 1 April 1990.

Great Britain

- Section 226 of the Companies Act 1985

- Sections 227(4) and 227(6) of the Companies Act 1985

- Paragraph 5 of Schedule 4 to the Companies Act 1985
- Schedule 4 to the Companies Act 1985:
  - notes (2) and (3) on the formats
  - paragraph 18
  - paragraph 19(2) and(3)
  - paragraph 21
  - paragraphs 31(1) and 32(1)
  - paragraphs 33 and 36
  - paragraphs 42 and 43

- Schedule 4A to the Companies Act 1985:
  - paragraph 9 (2), (4) and (5)
  - paragraphs 14 and 16

Republic of Ireland

- Section 3(1) of the Companies (Amendment) Act 1986

- Regulations 15(1) and 14(4) of the European Communities (Companies: Group Accounts) Regulations 1992

- Section 4(11) of the Companies (Amendment) Act 1986

- The Schedule to the Companies (Amendment) Act 1986:
  - notes (1) and (2) on the formats
  - paragraph 6
  - paragraph 7(1) and (2)
  - paragraph 9
  - paragraphs 19(1) and 20(1)
  - paragraphs 21 and 24
  - paragraphs 29 and 30

- European Communities (Companies: Group Accounts) Regulations 1992:
  - Regulation 19 (2), (4), (5) and (6)
  - no corresponding references

REPUBLIC OF IRELAND

22   The statutory requirements in the Republic of Ireland that correspond to those listed above for Great Britain are shown in the following table.

23   There are no transitional provisions in the Republic of Ireland that correspond to those given in paragraph 9 of Schedule 2 to the Companies Act 1989 (Commencement No. 4 and Transitional and Saving Provisions) Order 1990.

APPENDIX II
COMPLIANCE WITH
INTERNATIONAL ACCOUNTING
STANDARDS

The accounting for goodwill is addressed in International Accounting Standard (IAS) 22 'Business Combinations'. The objective of IAS 22 is to write off goodwill over the estimated useful economic life of the original purchased goodwill. The difference between this approach and the approach adopted in the [draft] FRS gives rise to a number of differences in the detailed requirements. IAS 22 requires that:

(a) purchased goodwill should be amortised over its estimated useful economic life in all circumstances.

(b) the amortisation period should not exceed five years unless a longer period, not exceeding 20 years from the date of acquisition, can be justified.

(c) the unamortised balance of goodwill should be reviewed at each balance sheet date and, to the extent that it is not expected to be recoverable, it should be written down. The write-down may not subsequently be reversed.

(d) one of two treatments should be adopted for negative goodwill. The benchmark treatment requires the fair values of the non-monetary assets acquired to be reduced proportionately until the negative goodwill is eliminated. The permitted alternative treatment requires negative goodwill to be shown as deferred income in the balance sheet and released to the profit and loss account on a systematic basis over a period that does not exceed five years, unless a longer period not exceeding 20 years can be justified.

[The International Accounting Standards Committee is developing an IAS that addresses the accounting for intangible assets. Up-to-date details to be inserted following exposure.]

APPENDIX III
THE DEVELOPMENT
OF THE FRED

THE NEED FOR A REVIEW

1   The accounting for goodwill is currently governed by SSAP 22. The SSAP permits a choice of two approaches to accounting for purchased goodwill. The preferred approach is immediate elimination against reserves. The permitted alternative approach is capitalisation as an asset, with subsequent write-off by systematic amortisation through the profit and loss account. SSAP 22 prohibits the recognition of internally generated goodwill.

2   In the late 1980s, the Board's predecessor body, the Accounting Standards Committee, started a project to replace SSAP 22. On its inception, the Board decided to continue this project. The decision was taken for a number of reasons. First, the Board took the view that there was a need to restrict the accounting for goodwill to a single method. Secondly, it believed that with the growing practice of separating intangible assets from goodwill, there was a need to codify best practice regarding the accounting for intangible assets. The similarities between goodwill and certain types of intangible assets acquired with a business made it appropriate to review the two together. Finally, the Board recognised that SSAP 22's preferred method of accounting for goodwill, whereby it is eliminated immediately against reserves, attracted criticism and was becoming less accepted internationally. (IAS 22, the latest International Accounting Standard on accounting for business combinations, now prohibits SSAP 22's preferred approach.)

ISSUES FACED

3   It is generally accepted that internally generated goodwill, although of value, is not an asset that should be recognised by a reporting entity: it is not a right to future economic benefits that are controlled by the entity and can be reliably measured. The costs of generating goodwill internally are therefore charged in the profit and loss account as they are incurred and the benefits recognised when they subsequently materialise in the form of profits.

4   In contrast, purchased goodwill arises from a distinct transaction that must be accounted for. However, no single method is universally accepted as being the correct one.

5   The vast majority of reporting entities in the UK choose to adopt the preferred approach in SSAP 22 and eliminate purchased goodwill against reserves on the date of acquisition. The conceptual rationale for this approach is that it provides for consistency of treatment between purchased and internally generated goodwill, since neither is capitalised as an asset on the balance sheet. However, the approach has been criticised for several reasons:

- immediate elimination of goodwill implies a loss in value and is inconsistent with the accounting for other components of the purchase price that are recognised as assets and liabilities.
- the problem of equity depletion has encouraged companies to reduce amounts attributed to purchased goodwill by separately valuing brands and similar intangible assets. Given that such intangible assets are very similar in nature to goodwill, it is often considered inappropriate for the two to be accounted for so differently.
- by not capitalising the full cost of an investment, the financial statements overstate the return on that investment.
- although there is consistency in the balance sheet treatment of purchased and internally generated goodwill, there is no consistency in the profit and loss account treatment: the costs that can be

attributed to building up internally generated goodwill are offset against profits in the profit and loss account whereas the costs of acquired goodwill are not charged against profits in this way unless the acquired business is sold.

- this inconsistency serves to make companies that grow by acquisition appear more profitable than those that grow organically.

6   The alternative approach to accounting for purchased goodwill, permitted by SSAP 22 and widely adopted internationally, is to capitalise it and amortise it on a systematic basis over a finite period. This approach is based on the rationale that purchased goodwill has a value at the time of recognition but that this value diminishes over time as the purchased goodwill is gradually replaced by internally generated goodwill.

7   This approach does not receive widespread support in the UK. In 1990, the Accounting Standards Committee issued Exposure Drafts ED 47 'Accounting for goodwill' and ED 52 'Accounting for intangible assets'. These Exposure Drafts proposed that purchased goodwill and intangible assets should be capitalised and amortised systematically over their estimated useful economic lives, which in general should not exceed 20 years and in no circumstance could exceed 40 years. Opposition to the proposals was strong: 93 per cent of corporate respondents and 73 per cent of all respondents opposed ED 47; 80 per cent of corporate respondents and 62 per cent of all respondents opposed ED 52.

8   Those opposing the proposals argued primarily that, where large sums are spent on maintaining and developing the value of an acquired business, a requirement to amortise a significant part of the investment over an arbitrary period had no economic meaning. Many of these respondents agreed with the concept of capitalising goodwill but thought that it should subsequently be written down only if and to the extent that the carrying value of the goodwill was not supported by the current value of goodwill in the acquired business.

THE BASIC APPROACH TO ACCOUNTING FOR GOODWILL

9   The Board recognised when it started its review that goodwill is considered by some to be an accounting anomaly. As illustrated above, each method of accounting for goodwill results in inconsistencies with other aspects of financial reporting. Preferences for one method or another tend to be determined by the conceptual and practical issues deemed to be the most important in the light of each individual's particular experience.

10   Hence, rather than develop proposals immediately, the Board issued a Discussion Paper that explored a number of options.[7] Its aim was to gauge overall opinion on various aspects of accounting for goodwill. Six possible methods were discussed:
1. Capitalisation and amortisation over a finite period.
2. Capitalisation and annual impairment reviews.
3. A combination of methods 1 and 2, with method 2 being used only in the special circumstances where goodwill has an indefinite life believed to exceed 20 years.
4. Immediate elimination against reserves.
5. Immediate elimination to a separate goodwill write-off reserve.
6. Transfer to a separate goodwill write-off reserve, with annual reviews of recoverability and any impairments being charged to the profit and loss account.

11   Methods 2, 3 and 6 represent a departure from traditional methods of accounting for goodwill. They seek to recognise the cost of goodwill as a loss only to the extent that the value of goodwill within the acquired business has reduced below the carrying value of the purchased goodwill.

12   No overall consensus emerged in the responses to the Discussion Paper. The method that individually achieved greatest support was method 4 – immediate transfer to a separate write-off

---

[7] DISCUSSION PAPER 'GOODWILL AND INTANGIBLE ASSETS', DECEMBER 1993.

reserve. However, more respondents favoured one of the capitalisation methods than favoured one of the elimination methods. Given the arguments made by respondents, and in the light of both the direction being taken internationally and the previous opposition to ED 47's proposals for compulsory amortisation, the Board decided to develop proposals based on method 3 – capitalisation with a combination of amortisation for goodwill with a finite life and annual impairment reviews for goodwill with an indefinite life expected to exceed 20 years.

13 In developing the chosen approach, the Board conducted extensive consultations with preparers, users and auditors of financial statements, in particular addressing concerns that the procedures proposed for impairment reviews were too complicated. The simplified proposals formed the basis of the Working Paper issued in June 1995 for subsequent debate at a public hearing.

14 The proposals received broad support from the majority of those responding to the Working Paper. They form the basis of the proposals for accounting for goodwill in the FRED. Commentators made a number of suggestions on how the proposals could be improved. As a result of these suggestions, the Board has made changes to the detail of the proposals. These changes and the rationales underlying the specific requirements proposed in the FRED are explained later in this appendix.

THE BASIC APPROACH TO ACCOUNTING FOR INTANGIBLE ASSETS

15 Intangible assets fall into a spectrum ranging from those that can readily be identified and measured separately from goodwill to those that are essentially very similar to goodwill. Companies legislation permits intangible assets to be recognised separately from goodwill only where they are capable of being disposed of separately from a business of the reporting entity.[8]

16 In its Discussion Paper, the Board expressed a view that certain intangible assets such as brands and publishing titles cannot be disposed of separately from a business and that, furthermore, there is no generally accepted method of valuing such intangible assets. Given this, and given that the dividing line between goodwill and intangible assets can be unclear, the Board proposed in the Discussion Paper that intangible assets acquired as part of the acquisition of a business should be subsumed within the value attributed to goodwill.

17 This proposal met with strong opposition. Corporate respondents stressed that intangible assets could be critical to their businesses and that it was important to account for them separately.

18 The Board accepted these arguments and in its subsequent Working Paper proposed that intangible assets could be recognised separately from goodwill if they met the legal and conceptual requirements for separability and could be measured reliably on initial recognition. However, to prevent the results of the reporting entity being shown in a more or less favourable light merely by classifying expenditure as an intangible asset rather than goodwill, or vice versa, it proposed that the accounting for intangible assets should be aligned with that for goodwill.

19 This proposal was accepted by most respondents to the Working Paper and has formed the basis of the accounting for intangible assets in the FRED.

THE RATIONALE FOR THE DETAILED PROPOSALS OF THE FRED

Conceptual basis

20 The proposed approach outlined in the Working Paper and now developed in the FRED seeks to charge goodwill in the profit and loss account only to the extent that the carrying value of the goodwill is not supported by the current value of the goodwill within the acquired business. It is this concept, along with basic principles relating to the recognition and measurement of assets, that has formed the basis of the detailed proposals of this FRED. Legal

---

[8] SEE PARAGRAPH 9 OF APPENDIX I 'NOTE ON LEGAL REQUIREMENTS'.

considerations and the desirability of aligning the accounting treatment of goodwill and intangible assets have also been taken into consideration.

21   The following paragraphs explain how these principles underlie the detailed proposals of this FRED.

Capitalisation of goodwill as an asset

22   The proposed approach recognises that purchased goodwill is neither an identifiable asset like other assets nor an immediate loss in value. It represents the balance of the purchase consideration that is recognised neither as an identifiable asset nor as a liability in the consolidated financial statements. Essentially, it forms a bridge between the cost of the investment shown as an asset in the acquirer's individual financial statements and the identifiable assets and liabilities recognised in the consolidated financial statements of the combined entities. Although purchased goodwill is not in itself an asset, its inclusion amongst the assets of the reporting entity, rather than as a deduction from shareholders' equity, recognises that goodwill is part of a larger asset, the investment, for which management remains accountable.

Presentation of negative goodwill adjacent to positive goodwill

23   Just as positive goodwill is not viewed as an asset, negative goodwill is not viewed as a liability. It too represents the bridge between the consolidated financial statements and the investment shown as an asset in the acquirer's own financial statements. Accordingly, it is recognised next to positive goodwill. Separate disclosure of positive and negative goodwill on the face of the balance sheet is necessary to comply with companies legislation.[9]

Capitalisation of intangible assets

24   The draft Statement of Principles states that an asset should be recognised only if it can be measured as a monetary amount with sufficient reliability.[10]

25   Clearly, where an intangible asset is purchased separately from a business, its cost provides a reliable measure of the value of the asset. Similarly, where an intangible asset has a readily ascertainable market value, that value provides a reliable measure of the value of the asset. In other circumstances, the measurement of the value of an intangible asset is subject to a significant degree of uncertainty. However, where an intangible asset is purchased as part of the acquisition of a business, a natural ceiling exists for the amount that may be capitalised in respect of purchased intangible assets. This ceiling is the difference between the total purchase consideration and the aggregate of the fair values assigned to the other assets and liabilities of the acquired entity.

26   It is the existence of this natural ceiling that differentiates the reliability with which purchased intangible assets can be measured from the reliability with which internally developed intangible assets can be measured. Hence, the Board believes that without the natural ceiling established by the existence of a purchase price, the value of an internally developed intangible asset can be measured sufficiently reliably for recognition only if the asset has a readily ascertainable market value.

27   Given this reliance on the natural ceiling, the Board also believes that, in the absence of a readily ascertainable market value, it would be inappropriate to assign to an intangible asset a fair value that has the effect of creating or increasing any negative goodwill arising on the acquisition of a business.

Amortisation of goodwill

28   The proposed approach seeks to charge goodwill in the profit and loss account only to the extent that the carrying value of the goodwill is not supported by the current value of the goodwill within the acquired business. Systematic amortisation is a practical means of recog-

---

[9] SEE PARAGRAPH 5 OF APPENDIX I 'NOTE ON LEGAL REQUIREMENTS'.

[10] EXPOSURE DRAFT 'STATEMENT OF PRINCIPLES FOR FINANCIAL REPORTING', PARAGRAPH 4.6

nising the reduction in value of goodwill that has a limited useful economic life. It is also a means of ensuring that where goodwill is not capable of continued measurement (so that annual impairment reviews would not be feasible), its depletion is recognised over a prudent but not unrealistically short period.

29 The FRED proposes that the useful economic life of goodwill is taken to be the period over which the value of the underlying business is expected to exceed the values of the identifiable net assets. This reflects the link between the carrying value of the goodwill and the continuing value of the goodwill in the acquired investment.

Useful economic lives in excess of 20 years

30 The economic benefits that goodwill and intangible assets represent are generally more nebulous than those of tangible assets. The useful economic lives of goodwill and intangible assets are correspondingly less certain than those of tangible assets and the Board believes that there should be a presumption that they do not exceed a specified maximum period, chosen to be 20 years. The Board recognises that there will be circumstances where there are valid grounds for rebutting the presumption. Such grounds will be based on the nature of the intangible asset or of the investment underlying a goodwill balance.

31 The choice of 20 years as the presumed maximum useful economic life of goodwill and intangible assets is based largely on judgement. This period was first proposed in the Working Paper. Few commentators questioned its reasonableness and accordingly the Board has not changed it in the FRED. Twenty years is not entirely consistent with IAS 22, the International Accounting Standard on goodwill: IAS 22 contains a presumption that the useful economic life of goodwill does not exceed five years and sets 20 years as the absolute maximum. Nevertheless, the alignment of the presumed maximum life in this FRED with the absolute maximum life specified by IAS 22 avoids the unnecessary complexities created by introducing a third arbitrary period.

32 The inconsistencies between IAS 22's presumed maximum life of five years and the 20 years proposed in the FRED reflect different underlying approaches. Whilst IAS 22 defines the useful economic life of goodwill as the period benefiting from the original purchased goodwill, the FRED defines it as the period over which the value of the underlying business continues to exceed the values of the identifiable net assets. The latter will normally be longer.

33 The longer the useful economic lives assigned to goodwill and intangible assets, the greater is the risk that the recoverable amount will fall below the carrying value in future. Where an amortisation period exceeds 20 years, the Board believes that the risk is sufficiently high to require amortisation to be supplemented by annual reviews for impairment. It follows therefore that goodwill and intangible assets may be assigned a useful economic life in excess of 20 years only if it will be possible to carry out such reviews – in other words, if their values are expected to be capable of continued measurement in future.

Indefinite useful economic lives

34 In exceptional circumstances, the nature of the goodwill or intangible asset will be such that its life is indefinite. In such circumstances, amortisation over an arbitrary period may not be an appropriate method of reflecting the depletion of the goodwill or intangible asset. This will be the case where the value of the goodwill or intangible asset is significant and is expected to be capable of continued measurement in future. In such circumstances, the Board believes that a true and fair view will be given only if the goodwill or intangible asset is not amortised, but is instead subject to annual reviews for impairment.

35 The Board has been advised that non-amortisation of goodwill constitutes a departure from the specific requirement of companies legislation to depreciate the value attributed to goodwill over a limited period that does not exceed its useful economic life. However, departure from

specific requirements such as this one is permitted by companies legislation in exceptional circumstances where it is necessary for the overriding purpose of providing a true and fair view.[11] Accordingly, the Board has limited the circumstances in which it proposes that goodwill is not amortised to those special circumstances where systematic amortisation would not provide a true and fair view. It has also incorporated within the proposed disclosure requirements, the disclosures that are required by companies legislation where advantage has been taken of the true and fair override provisions.

The requirement for impairment reviews for goodwill and intangible assets that are also amortised

36   It is accepted practice that an asset should not be carried at more than its recoverable amount, ie the higher of the amount for which it could be sold and the amount recoverable from its future use.[12]

37   Systematic amortisation ensures that the carrying value of an asset is reduced to reflect any gradual reduction in the asset's recoverable amount over its useful economic life. An asset that is amortised in an appropriate manner is unlikely to become materially impaired unless it is impaired on initial recognition or subsequent events or changes in circumstances cause a sudden reduction in the estimate of the recoverable amount. Thus, where goodwill and intangible assets are amortised, a requirement for an impairment review to be performed each period would be unnecessary and unduly onerous. The Board believes that, in such circumstances, impairment reviews are necessary only at the end of the first full financial year following initial recognition and, thereafter, if subsequent events or changes in circumstances indicate that the carrying value may not be recoverable.

38   The requirement to perform an impairment review at the end of the first full financial year following the initial recognition of goodwill and intangible assets ensures that any impairment arising on acquisition (ie any overpayment) is recognised as a loss at that time, rather than being amortised over the life of the asset.

Revaluations and restoration of past losses

39   As explained in paragraph 26 above, the Board believes that internally developed intangible assets should be capitalised only if they have a readily ascertainable market value. Similarly, it believes that internally generated goodwill should never be capitalised. Revaluation of goodwill and intangible assets has the effect of recognising amounts that have been internally developed. Hence, it is proposed to permit revaluation only of intangible assets that have readily ascertainable market values.

40   Following the recognition of an impairment loss, the value of the impaired goodwill or intangible asset may return towards its previous carrying value. Such an increase will usually be attributable to the internal generation of goodwill or intangible asset value, and as such should not be recognised as a restoration of a past loss.

41   Less frequently, the increase in value may be attributable to the unexpected reversal of an external event that caused the original impairment to be recognised. In these limited circumstances, the reversal of the impairment loss can be measured more reliably (by reference to the original impairment) and is required by companies legislation to be recognised in the financial statements.[13] Accordingly, the Board proposes to permit restoration of past losses in such circumstances.

---

[11] SEE PARAGRAPHS 6 AND 20 OF APPENDIX I 'NOTE ON LEGAL REQUIREMENTS'.

[12] EXPOSURE DRAFT 'STATEMENT OF PRINCIPLES FOR FINANCIAL REPORTING', PARAGRAPH 5.7.

[13] SEE PARAGRAPH 15 OF APPENDIX I 'NOTE ON LEGAL REQUIREMENTS'.

Negative goodwill

42   The Board's Working Paper did not include any proposals for the accounting for negative goodwill.

43   In developing the proposals in the FRED, the Board considered the benchmark approach adopted in International Accounting Standard (IAS) 22, whereby negative goodwill is eliminated by reducing the fair values assigned to the non-monetary assets of the acquired entity. However, it rejected this approach, which it believed to be inconsistent with the principle underlying FRS 7 'Fair Values in Acquisition Accounting', ie that on acquisition of a business, the assets should be valued at their fair values.

44   The Board wished to align the accounting for negative goodwill with that for positive goodwill. There are no legal requirements to 'amortise' negative goodwill and negative goodwill can normally be attributed to a known cause, the reversal of which can be monitored. Hence the Board believes that the treatment of negative goodwill should mirror the impairment review approach to positive goodwill: the FRED proposes that negative goodwill is written back as the difference between the value of the acquired business and the values of its identified net assets reduces.

45   Where the negative goodwill can be attributed to a bargain purchase, it is clear that it represents an unrealised gain and should be released to the statement of recognised gains and losses. Where the negative goodwill arises because of an expectation of future reorganisation costs or operating losses, it might be argued that the release of the negative goodwill should be reflected in the profit and loss account as the associated costs or losses materialise. However, such a treatment would have the practical effect of offsetting the reorganisation costs or operating losses against the release of the negative goodwill. This is inconsistent with the treatment of such costs and losses under FRS 7, which requires all post-acquisition expenditure to be charged in the profit and loss account. Hence, the reversal of negative goodwill is not matched against the post-acquisition expenses but is treated as a separate gain. Only if the gain has been realised (through realisation of the underlying investment) may negative goodwill be written back in the profit and loss account.

46   The [draft] FRS does not permit purchased goodwill to be divided into positive and negative components. Given that the individual components of goodwill are not separable and capable of being measured reliably, it would be inappropriate to subdivide a net balance into positive and negative components. Thus, the amounts that can be attributed to any factors identified as causing negative goodwill are limited to the total negative goodwill arising on the acquisition.

CHANGES MADE TO WORKING PAPER PROPOSALS

47   In the light of comments made by those responding to the Working Paper and those presenting their views at the public hearing, a number of minor changes have been made to the Working Paper proposals. This section explains the reasons for the changes.

48   The proposed requirement to limit the values assigned to purchased intangible assets to values that do not create or increase negative goodwill has been relaxed. The Board accepts that where an intangible asset has a readily ascertainable market value, such a requirement would be unreasonable and inconsistent with the principles of FRS 7 'Fair Values in Acquisition Accounting'.

49   The Working Paper proposed a rebuttable presumption that goodwill has a life that does not exceed 20 years. The FRED proposes that this presumption should also apply to intangible assets. This achieves greater consistency between the accounting for goodwill and the accounting for intangible assets. (The Board recognises that circumstances in which evidence exists to rebut the presumption may arise more frequently for intangible assets than for goodwill.)

50   The Working Paper proposal that the useful economic life of an intangible asset cannot exceed that of any legal right underpinning it has been relaxed. As certain respondents noted, if a

legal right can be renewed, and the renewal process is assured, then it would be inappropriate to base the useful economic life of the related intangible asset on the assumption that the legal right will not be renewed.

51 The proposed requirement to perform the initial impairment review at the end of the financial year in which the goodwill or intangible assets are acquired has been amended. The FRED proposes that the initial review should instead be performed at the end of the first full financial year following acquisition. The Board acknowledges the views of several respondents who noted that it may not be possible to perform a meaningful impairment review at the earlier date.

52 The Working Paper proposal to prohibit the restoration of past losses has been relaxed. The Board accepts that where an external event causing an impairment to be recognised in a prior period reverses, the impairment loss should be restored to the extent that it no longer applies. The FRED proposes to limit the circumstances permitting reversal of impairment losses to those where it is clear that the reversal is caused by the reversal of an external event rather than the creation of internally generated goodwill or intangible asset value.

THE ALTERNATIVE VIEW

53 As explained in Appendix IV, one Board member favours an alternative approach to that proposed in the FRED. Under this alternative approach, purchased goodwill would be deducted immediately from shareholders' equity, being debited to a separate goodwill reserve. If subsequent events or changes in circumstances were to indicate that the goodwill had become permanently impaired, the impairment would be quantified and charged in the profit and loss account. Intangible assets not amortised would be reviewed for impairment in the same manner as goodwill.

54 The other Board members reject this approach for several reasons. First, they do not believe that the approach would provide the accountability and stewardship that is suggested in Appendix IV. They argue that:

• Impairment reviews that are performed only when there is cause to believe that an asset is permanently impaired are not sufficient on their own to ensure that all impairment losses will be recognised as soon as they occur. Inevitably, in the absence of annual impairment reviews, impairment losses will tend to be overlooked until a major problem comes to light. The Board has concluded that, in the absence of amortisation, impairment reviews of goodwill have to be performed annually to be effective.

• Some companies have told the Board that they will not always be able to perform regular impairment reviews. In such circumstances, it would be inappropriate for the fall-back position to be one of doing nothing: amortisation may not be perfect, but it is a better surrogate for impairment reviews than nothing.

• Immediate deduction of goodwill from shareholders' equity fails to highlight goodwill as part of the cost of an investment on which a future return must be earned. This is the case, even if the deduction is shown in a separate reserve on the face of the balance sheet. The Board's proposed approach does not claim that goodwill is an asset as defined in its draft Statement of Principles. By showing goodwill amongst the assets of the reporting entity rather than as a deduction from shareholders' equity, it is simply being recognised that goodwill is part of a larger asset, the investment, for which management remains accountable.

55 Secondly, the Board believes that many items that are treated as intangible assets are very similar in nature to goodwill: a brand name, like goodwill, represents an expectation of enhanced future earnings. The Board members who reject the alternative approach believe that it is not meaningful for goodwill to be deducted from shareholders' equity when intangible assets that are similar in nature to goodwill are shown as assets on the balance sheet.

56 It is of note that, of the 40 respondents to the Working Paper who commented on the presentation of goodwill on the balance sheet, 85 per cent believed that it should be shown amongst

the assets and only 15 per cent that it should be deducted from shareholders' equity.

57   One of the arguments in Appendix IV is that the Board's approach, despite prohibiting recognition of internally generated goodwill, will allow internally generated goodwill to be included within the carrying value of purchased goodwill in the years following acquisition. This is because an impairment is identified and charged in the profit and loss account only if the carrying value of the purchased goodwill is not supported by the current value of goodwill in the acquired business. It is of note, however, that any method of accounting for purchased goodwill introduces inconsistencies with the accounting for internally generated goodwill. Further, the alternative approach does not eliminate the inconsistency: it seeks to measure impairment on exactly the same basis.

58   Finally, the approach being proposed in the FRED is attracting significant international interest. It is an approach that is seen by many as a meaningful alternative to the current international practice of capitalisation and automatic amortisation. In contrast, the alternative approach seems less likely to be favoured internationally. One reason for this is that it is based on deduction of goodwill from shareholders' equity, a treatment that does not receive widespread support in other countries. Another reason is that, in following the progress of the UK proposals, other standard-setters have been particularly interested in assessing whether the requirements for impairment reviews are sufficiently robust to prevent abuse. The less stringent requirements of the alternative approach would be more likely to be rejected as insufficient.

APPENDIX IV
ALTERNATIVE VIEW

One Board member favours an alternative approach, which is outlined in the Preface. The Board member's views are explained in this appendix.

1   The alternative approach is designed to place greater emphasis on the needs of users and the nature of goodwill, recognising that it is neither an asset nor an immediate loss in value and concludes that goodwill should not be presented as an asset or in any way amortised but should be deducted from shareholders' equity. This is the accounting presently followed by over 95 per cent of UK companies with goodwill in their financial statements.

2   Users have indicated that whilst they treat any amounts attributed to goodwill with considerable scepticism, they are concerned to hold management accountable for the amounts spent on goodwill. Immediate write-off with the amounts subsumed within reserves as practised by the majority of companies reporting goodwill has clouded such accountability. But the measure of such accountability is the relationship between the amounts spent and the likelihood and timing of improved earnings and cash flows. Users are thus concerned with stewardship and whether goodwill has been impaired, but not with arbitrary amortisation, which they eliminate.

3   Goodwill is not an asset as defined under the draft Statement of Principles for Financial Reporting and possesses unique characteristics which distinguish it from an asset. It may or may not have any relationship to the expenditures incurred to create it; there is no reliable or continuing relationship of value with any historical cost and such cost frequently and quickly loses any significance it may ever have possessed. Above all, goodwill differs from other costs, whether or not capitalised, in that it is not used or consumed in operations nor depleted as a matter of course. If goodwill is not an asset and is qualitatively different from assets as generally recognised, it is misleading to report it as such.

4   The notion that purchased goodwill remains as long as the value of the underlying business exceeds the values of the identifiable net assets means that what is being reported is some measure of the current value of the acquired business rather than the original purchased goodwill. In reality, purchased goodwill inevitably wanes, only to be replaced in whole or in part by new goodwill arising from current expenditures and events. In effect, internally generated goodwill is being revalued (which is already precluded by the [draft] FRS) and offset against declining purchased goodwill.

5   Amortisation is asserted to be necessary to recognise the reduction in the value of goodwill that has a limited useful life or as a surrogate for impairment reviews where such reviews are not feasible. Since the life of purchased goodwill is indeterminable and not regularly measurable, any period of amortisation is completely arbitrary. The requirement that immeasurable goodwill (already acknowledged not to be an asset) should be reported in the balance sheet for 20 years belies its nature.

6   A proper matching of costs and revenue does not call for amortisation of every asset: it calls only for amortisation of those assets that can be related to earnings on some realistic and systematic basis so that the charge reasonably reflects the cost of the economic benefits consumed during the period. Since goodwill is not consumed or depleted as a matter of course, amortisation is not relevant.

7   Irrespective of whether the consideration is cash, shares or debt, purchased goodwill reduces shareholders' current equity for the prospect of enhanced income in the future. Part of shareholders' funds (in terms of 'hard assets') has been disbursed: if cash is used, it has gone; if

shares, the company could have received cash for the share issue as opposed to goodwill. In both cases, something tangible has been exchanged for something intangible.

8   Goodwill should be deducted from shareholders' equity to reflect the fact that shareholders' funds have been used. This treatment would recognise that goodwill is neither an asset nor an immediate loss in value. However, in order to facilitate accountability and subsequent monitoring, the deduction should be by way of establishing a goodwill reserve within shareholders' equity. This presentation of goodwill as a separately identified balance (quasi-asset) would stress stewardship for the amounts spent but not in such a way as to suggest it is an asset, which it is not.

9   While the business continues to be held, the goodwill would be kept under review for permanent impairment. This would be achieved by using high-level impairment indicators to identify possible impairment and using the full impairment reviews outlined in the [draft] FRS only for that goodwill whose value is in doubt.

10   Intangible assets would be identified as set forth in the [draft] FRS. Only those intangible assets with a recognised market value or otherwise measurable on some recognised basis would be capitalised; the remainder would form part of goodwill. Only those intangible assets with a clear finite economic life and whose use could be related to earnings on a rational basis would be amortised. Intangible assets not amortised would be reviewed for impairment in the same manner as goodwill.

AUTHOR BIOGRAPHIES

Kylie Adcock   holds a B.Com. and a BLL from the University of Queensland, Australia. She qualified as a chartered accountant while working with Arthur Andersen as a consultant in their Taxation Division in Brisbane. Kylie was a business analyst with Andersen Consulting in Sydney before joining Interbrand. As a brand valuation consultant, Kylie has experience in the telecommunications industry and has worked on a range of brand evaluation projects during her time with Interbrand; her clients include Lion Nathan, BP and ICI.

Philip J. Adkins   received a BA in East Asian Studies from Columbia University in the city of New York in 1980. While based in Japan for Citicorp Investment Bank from 1981 to 1988 he invented several structures to allow the export of capital from Japan, outside the control of the Japanese Ministry of Finance. Philip was responsible for the successful execution of transactions totalling over US$30bn, involving most OECD Government borrowers, international airlines and blue-chip corporates. The most complex structures involved brand, royalty and 'intangible asset-based' financing. He founded Cadenza International in 1988 as a private investment-banking boutique. Cadenza has acted on behalf of The Walt Disney Company, Southland (7-Eleven), Alitalia and TGI Friday's Inc as an investment banking adviser. Philip currently acts as managing director and chief executive officer of J. Boag & Son in Australia, owned by Cadenza since 1991.

David Andrew   is founder managing director of Interbrand Pacific in Sydney. His eight years with the company coincide with the ascendancy of Interbrand as the leading exponent of brand valuation worldwide, and during this period he has had extensive experience in valuing brands in Australia and New Zealand. Prior to joining Interbrand he was associated for many years with McCann Erickson and Ogilvy & Mather, with assignments in New York, London, Tokyo, Milan, Southeast Asia and Australia. He is an American and a graduate of Cornell University.

John Björkman   studied International Marketing at the Swedish School of Economics and Business Administration in Helsinki and gained a Masters Degree in Economics. From 1991 to 1994 he worked as brand manager at Hartwall where he was responsible for various domestic beer brands as well as for international brands launched in Finland. These included Guinness, Sol, Fosters and Tuborg. His major task was to change the sales trend of the domestic beer brand Karjala which had been in decline for more than a decade. Since 1995 John has been brand manager at Fazer Chocolates where he is responsible for the Karl Fazer brand, regarded as number one in Finland. His task today is to transfer this success onto the international market-place, making the brand more valuable for its owners.

Tom Blackett   is deputy chairman of Interbrand Group Plc. He started his career in market research, joining Attwood Statistics in 1969. From there he joined Unilever's in-house market research agency, where he became intensively involved in new- product research and simulated market testing. After some six years at Unilever, in 1978 he moved to Inbucon Management Consultants (now part of the PE Group) where he specialised in new-product development across a wide range of consumer, business-to-business and industrial markets. Tom joined Interbrand in 1993 and has been a key figure in its recent growth. He has written and spoken widely on the subject of brands and is currently working on what he describes as a 'fool's guide to trade marks', which is due for publication in 1997.

Ed Brody	has a BS in Math & Philosophy from CCNY and a CDP (Certificate in Data Processing). He is Senior Vice President and Associate Director of Marketing Sciences at BBDO. Joining the agency in 1969, he managed the computer systems group and developed models for new products, consumer pharmaceutical advertising, advertising awareness and multi-national resource allocation. He has taught at Columbia University and New York University and is currently President-Elect of the INFORMS College on Marketing.
Charles E. Brymer	chief executive officer, Interbrand Group. Charles Brymer is acknowledged internationally as a leading authority on branding. He has written and lectured extensively on the subject of branding, corporate identity, naming and brand valuation and has been featured in such publications as *Newsweek*, *New York Times*, *Chicago*, and *Fortune Magazine*, among others. Charles realized the importance and enormous potential of brands while working for BBDO. In 1982 he opened, and ran BBDO's Houston office. During his tenure at Interbrand, Charles has personally supervised projects for several of Interbrand's major clients including AT&T, Glaxo, IBM, Procter & Gamble, Merrill Lynch, Philip Morris, Control Data, Johnson & Johnson, Time Inc. Magazines, General Motors and MCI.
Edward Buchan	is managing director of the Corporate Finance division of Close Brothers Group Ltd where his work involves him in financial structuring, business valuations, mergers and acquisitions for a wide range of companies. He was previously managing director of corporate finance at Hill-Samuel Bank.
Gerald Corbett	has been group finance director of Grand Metropolitan since 1994, having held the same post at Redland since 1987. He began his career as a consultant at Boston Consulting Group, and subsequently moved to Dixons Group where he held the positions of group financial controller and corporate finance director.
Steve Cuthbert	is the director general of the Chartered Institute of Marketing. Previously, as chief executive for 13 years, he helped Brent International Plc grow into a speciality chemical business with an annual turnover of £120m. After attending university Steve joined Price Waterhouse, London, where he became a senior manager before moving to Brent, originally as finance director. He is a member of the CBI's Council and sits on the Education and Training Affairs Committee, is a former member of its President's Committee and an ex-chairman of the CBI's Southern Region. His background is in applied technology, finance and industrial marketing. Steve is also on the Advisory Boards of the International Corporate Identity Group and the Loughborough Business School.
Caroline Davies	is trade mark manager of Imperial Chemical Industries Plc and has been in this position since 1993. Prior to joining ICI, Caroline had been at Glaxo Holdings Plc for 8½ years, also in the Trade Marks Department. Caroline began her career in trade marks with Glaxo after graduating in law from the University of Warwick. Caroline is a member of the International Trade Mark Association, of the Institute of Trade Mark Agents, European Community Trademark Association and represents ICI on the Trade Mark, Patents and Designs Federation.
Nicholas Davies	holds a degree in Economics from Cambridge University and a Masters Degree from the London School of Economics. He is now a research executive in the corporate finance division at Close Brothers Group Ltd.

Howard Finkelberg	holds a BEE (Electrical Engineering) from Cornell University and an MS (Operations Research) from New York University. He is Senior Vice President and Associate Director of Marketing Sciences at BBDO. In 15 years at BBDO he has developed techniques for evaluating advertising effectiveness, brand equity and marketing resource allocation. Prior to joining BBDO, Mr. Finkelberg held marketing and management science positions at American Airlines. He is currently Vice President of the INFORMS College on the Practice of Management Science and Chairman of the Franz Edelman Award Competition.
Janet Fogg	is chairman of Markforce (as well as being managing director of Interbrand UK Limited), having been with the latter company since 1985. She is a qualified (by examination) Trade Mark Attorney, a Fellow of the Institute of Trade Mark Agents and a Registered Trade Mark Agent. She has a wide range of experience within private practice, and has represented a large number of clients with varied activities. Janet is also a member (and former chairman) of the Joint Examination Board, the body which administers the examination for entry onto the Registers of Trade Mark and Patent Agents.
Christopher Glover	is a chartered accountant and holds a Masters degree in International Banking and Financial Studies. He is a member of the Institute of Investment Management and Research. He has practised as an independent share-valuation specialist for the past 14 years. Prior to becoming an independent specialist Christopher obtained over ten years' experience in the field of company valuation, first as an investment analyst with a major firm of City stockbrokers and the final eight years specialising exclusively in the valuation of unquoted shares with one of the 'big six' accounting firms. He has written *Valuation of Unquoted Companies*, a book published by Gee & Co, and now in its second edition. He is also the author of *Accountants Digest 299 'The Valuation of Unquoted Shares'* published by the Institute of Chartered Accountants in England and Wales in 1993.
Karen Hack	joined Interbrand from Price Waterhouse where she qualified as a chartered accountant. Her clients at Price Waterhouse included many branded-goods companies, among them UBS and Eastern Electricity. She studied Economics at Reading University and also worked for a year in East Africa. Karen has worked on a wide range of brand valuation and strategy clients while at Interbrand. Work for these clients has included co-ordinating a world-wide internal licensing programme across all business units of a major international oil company, balance sheet valuations, and brand portfolio assessments.
David Haigh	is managing director of Brand Finance Limited, a consultancy specialising in marketing accountability. David read English at Bristol University before qualifying as a chartered accountant with Price Waterhouse in London in 1980. He worked in international financial management and was financial director of The Creative Business, WCRS & Partners and a director of Publicis. He was a director in the global brand valuation practice of Interbrand, responsible for technical accounting issues, producing submissions to the UK Accounting Standards Board and the International Accounting Standards Committee. He has conducted brand valuations in a wide range of sectors; for litigation, tax, royalty rate setting, management control and balance sheet reporting purposes. He is the author of 'Rewarding the Advertising Profession', 'Strategic Control of Marketing Finance' and the IPA guide to Brand Valuation. He has written extensively for the financial and marketing press. David is a Fellow of the UK Chartered Institute of Marketing.

Terry Harding

trained as a chartered accountant in the UK and, after a short spell as a financial accountant in the aerospace industry, returned to public practice with a 'big six' accounting firm in Auckland, New Zealand in 1989. He established and managed the firm's New Zealand national professional practice department. In 1993 he returned to the UK to take up the position of senior research manager with the International Accounting Standards Committee (IASC). In that position, he was responsible for a number of projects including foreign currency translation, retirement benefit costs, intangible assets and the presentation of financial statements. In 1996 he joined the Technical Services Department of Ernst & Young in London as senior manager, advising UK and overseas clients and audit teams on accounting and auditing issues. He remains responsible, on a part-time basis, for IASC's project on the presentation of financial statements.

Raymond Perrier

has recently been given responsibility for Interbrand's brand-valuation activities in the UK and farther afield. He joined Interbrand after graduating from New College, Oxford, with a Masters Degree in Philosophy and Theology. He has some seven years' experience of brand evaluation and his clients include British Airways, Chanel, National Geographic, B.A.T., Danone, United Biscuits, Lion Nathan, Inchcape and Grand Metropolitan. He speaks French, German, Italian and Spanish and has worked extensively abroad. Valuations conducted by Raymond have been used in submissions to the UK Government's Monopolies and Mergers Commission, the UK Inland Revenue, the US IRS and the Australian Tax Office. Recent work has included the development of a unique new on-line measurement system for monitoring brand performance which is now being introduced by major brand-goods businesses in the USA and Europe.

Jeremy Phillips

studied law at Cambridge, Kent and UCLA before taking up academic posts in Dublin, Durham and London. A former editor of *Trademark World* he is currently consultant editor of *Managing Intellectual Property*. He is an intellectual property consultant with city law firm Slaughter and May and is the author of numerous books, the most recent being *The Trade Mark Companion for 1995*. He has recently been appointed editor of Sweet & Maxwell's new *European Trade Mark Reports*.

Ken Runkel

executive vice president, Interbrand US. Mr. Runkel brings to Interbrand over seventeen years of extensive strategic marketing, branding and advertising experience. His career began at BBDO in New York where he worked with such client businesses and brands as Pepsi-Cola, Lever Brothers, Avis and Chrysler. He then joined Tracy-Locke in Dallas as senior vice president responsible for the Dial and Marion Labs accounts. From there Mr. Runkel founded his own consulting firm specializing in the development of a wide range of strategic marketing and communications programs. Mr. Runkel is an honors graduate of Arizona State University.

Jeremy Sampson

has a BA(Hons) in visual communication from Canterbury College of Art, England. He qualified 30 years ago and has worked between London and Johannesburg, carrying out projects for a wide range of top companies primarily on corporate branding. His first contact with Interbrand was in 1985, and since returning to Johannesburg in 1992, he has represented Interbrand in Southern Africa. He is a Fellow of the Chartered Society of Designers (UK), Fellow of the Royal Society of Arts (UK) and a former president of the Society of Designers in South Africa.

Martin Scicluna

is chairman of Deloitte & Touche. He joined the firm in 1973 and qualified as a chartered accountant in 1976. Martin was admitted to the Partnership in 1982, and was Head of London Audit from 1990–5. At the Institute of Chartered Accountants in England and Wales he was chairman of the London Society in 1989–90, and a member of Council. He is a Freeman of the City of London.

Jane Simms	edits *Marketing Business*, the monthly marketing title published by Premier Magazines for The Chartered Institute of Marketing. Before that she edited *Financial Director*, the monthly magazine for finance directors published by VNU Business Publications. Jane has also worked on *Management Consultancy* and *Accountancy Age*, as well as contributing freelance articles to *The Independent, The Times* and *The Financial Times*.
Lucinda Spicer	is a partner in Price Waterhouse, in the Mergers & Acquisitions Tax Services Group. She also leads the UK firm's tax valuations team and has worked with many UK and international clients on mergers, acquisitions, disposals and reorganisations, advising on tax, financial structuring and valuation issues. Lucinda spent a short period in commerce with 3i, the UK venture capital organisation, as assistant to the technical director, dealing with financial, tax and other technical aspects of venture capital investments.
Susan Symons	is an internal corporate tax partner in Price Waterhouse and head of International Tax Services in the UK. She works with major UK and international groups and has extensive experience of advising on structuring and financing, managing the tax charge, international tax planning and how to handle tax authorities. Specialist areas include intellectual property and transfer pricing. Susan's extensive domestic and international experience includes 16 years working for the Inland Revenue. Her Revenue background gives her a particular insight into a tax inspector's approach to a review of a company's affairs.
Ken Wild	qualified as a chartered accountant with one of the major firms in their York office. After qualifying, he moved to London and worked for the Institute of Chartered Accountants in England and Wales, where he was part of the Secretariat to the Accounting Standards Committee. Having joined Touche Ross in 1980 he was made a partner in 1984. He is currently National Accounting Technical Partner at Deloitte and Touche. Ken is a member of the Council of the ICA in England and Wales. He is a member of the Accounting Standards Board, and chairman of its Public Sector and Not-for-profit Committee. Ken is also a member of the CBI Companies Committee and its financial reporting and law panels. He is the author or joint author of a number of books on accounting subjects including *Financial Reporting and Accounting Manual* and *The Financial Reporting and Accounting Service* published by Butterworths. He is also a well-known speaker on accountancy.

INDEX